SEASONAL ARTS AND CRAFTS ACTIVITIES FOR EARLY CHILDHOOD

Lorraine Clancy

PARKER PUBLISHING COMPANY
West Nyack, New York 10995

10 9 8 7 6 5 4 3 2 1

To Love, Joy—and Children
especially
Lauren and Douglas

ART DIRECTOR: Penina M. Wissner

COVER DESIGN: William H. Osbun

COVER ILLUSTRATIONS: Katherine Anne Conrad, *AGE 6 (SNOWFLAKE, FLOWER, SUN)*
Karinna Beth Sjo-Gaber, *AGE 4 (LEAF)*

COVER ILLUSTRATION COORDINATOR: Judy Sjo-Gaber

Library of Congress Cataloging-in-Publication Data

Clancy, Lorraine.
Seasonal arts and crafts activities for early childhood.

1. Creative activities and seatwork. 2. Education, Preschool—United States—Activity programs.
3. Kindergarten—United States—Activity programs.
I. Title.
LB1140.35.C74C57 1988 372.5 88-5991

ISBN 0-13-796806-X

PARKER PUBLISHING COMPANY
BUSINESS & PROFESSIONAL DIVISION
A division of Simon & Schuster
West Nyack, New York 10995

Printed in the United States of America

ABOUT THIS BOOK

Seasonal Arts and Crafts Activities for Early Childhood makes learning as natural as the seasons! It is a year-round treasury of over 80 projects that will expand your students' minds, increase their manual dexterity, and foster many other readiness skills through your children's arts and crafts participation in the exciting world that surrounds us. In this book, the love of learning and the desire to create that are typical of young children are directed to produce exciting, enjoyable arts and crafts projects. These activities are all related to concepts you teach throughout the school year, thereby reinforcing your lessons in a creative manner.

Some projects focus on the "art" in arts and crafts; others, on the "craft." Either way, these activities are child-centered, providing fun while building readiness skills and peaking interest in the change of seasons and the abundance of holidays. This integrating of arts and crafts into your curriculum can be a broadening experience. If you encourage your children to discuss their special project at home, you can foster positive child/parent/school relationships while enhancing the learning experience.

All these projects support your readiness objectives and help develop essential early childhood skills. The activities in this book contribute to:

- Conceptual development
- Eye-hand coordination
- Small muscle control
- Shape recognition
- Sequencing
- Spatial relationships
- Body awareness
- Creative dramatics
- Color recognition
- Detail awareness
- Perceptual discrimination
- Patterning

Each project in the book includes at least one ready-to-use pattern that can be traced and creatively finished with a variety of art media, or else it can be used to give children a visual head-start in creating their own unique project. Tracing a pattern is a viable means to reinforce eye-hand coordination, making it a valid part of an arts and crafts lesson for young children. Many of the pattern pages are suitable to be traced onto dittos or photocopied. The materials needed for these projects are readily available in most schools or are inexpensive and easy to buy. The projects are geared to success for children of varying early childhood skill levels.

Because patterns are provided, along with step-by-step instructions, you need no artistic talent to guide your students through these projects. The ideas, patterns, and easy-to-follow directions take the hassle out of classroom art projects. You are then free to put your energies into productively interacting with your students rather than into lengthy preparation. The projects are easy to make, requiring a minimal amount of adult supervision. The results, however, are uniquely exciting to the children, sparking their natural curiosity and love of creating and learning. The projects become concrete teaching tools for the classroom, as well as vehicles for creative expression and learning for the child.

The book is chronologically arranged based on the school year, including summer and special projects that can be used throughout the year. For example:

- In the Fall section, the children will use a variety of media to involve themselves in the wonder and color of the season and its contrast to summer. The excitement of Halloween is heightened and the cornucopias of Sukkot and Thanksgiving become real to the children.
- The environmental changes of winter and their effect on nature and animals greet the children in the Winter section. The projects for the wondrous holidays of Christmas and Hanukkah capitalize on the children's enthusiasm at this time of year. Also included are projects for New Year's Eve, Valentine's Day, St. Patrick's Day, and the Chinese New Year.
- Nature's renewal in the spring is a fascinating science to discover through creative arts. The projects in the Spring section can be used to tell of the wonderful changes that the earth and nature go through. From the dramatic push-paint butterfly to the caterpillar finger puppet, these projects peak spring fever. April showers, rainbows, flowers, Easter, and Passover arouse the children's interest in this wonderful season.
- The Summer section offers projects that help children learn about their environment and heritage. Included are activities for the Fourth of July, as well as special projects for space flight and animals that can be used throughout the year.

A special feature of the book is the Skills Index that will help you quickly locate all the activities for reinforcing a particular skill, such as body awareness or shape discrimination.

By using *Seasonal Arts and Crafts Activities for Early Childhood* , you will add excitement to your lessons while building skills, aiding cognitive growth, and providing varied art experiences.

Lorraine Clancy

ABOUT THE AUTHOR

Lorraine Clancy received her B.S. in Early Childhood Education from the State University at Old Westbury, New York. She is presently teaching pre-K at St. Joseph's School in Garden City, New York, a program she began in 1980.

Mrs. Clancy has taught arts and crafts workshops for elementary teachers, as well as summer classes for children. She is a charter member of the Early Childhood Circle of the Diocese of Rockville Centre.

My thanks to my good friend Barbara
and my husband Jerome

Illustrated by
Lauren and Douglas Clancy

CONTENTS

Theme: Christmas

Theme: Hanukkah

Theme: New Year's Eve

Theme: Valentine's Day

Theme: St. Patrick's Day

Theme: Chinese New Year

Theme: Space Flight

Theme: Animals

SKILLS INDEX

ACTIVITIES	Body Awareness	Color Awareness/Mixing	Conceptual Development	Concrete Counting	Creative Dramatics	Detail Awareness	Eye-Hand Coordination	Following Directions	Manual Dexterity	Measuring	Patterning	Sequencing	Shape Discrimination	Small-Muscle Control	Spatial Relationships
FALL															
1-1 Sun-Glow Fall Leaves		X	X				X							X	
1-2 Leafy Me	X		X											X	X
1-3 Sponge Painting—Fall Tree (with Roots)			X				X				X				X
1-4 "Stretch" the Scarecrow	X		X			X	X							X	
1-5 Tree Rings			X	X			X				X				
HALLOWEEN															
2-1 Magic Alakasam			X				X	X					X		X
2-2 Push-Paint Jack-o'-Lantern			X				X			X				X	
2-3 Witch "Greenie"	X		X				X						X	X	X
2-4 "Batty" the Flying Bat			X				X	X						X	
2-5 "Spunky" the Spider			X	X	X		X						X	X	
2-6 Boootiful Card			X				X							X	
2-7 "Gus" the Ghost			X				X				X				X
SUKKOT															
3-1 Cornucopia		X	X				X								X
3-2 Sukkah			X						X					X	
THANKSGIVING															
4-1 Mayflower			X				X							X	
4-2 Pilgrim, King, Indian Stick Puppets			X		X	X	X							X	
4-3 Indian Man in Canoe	X		X				X		X						X
4-4 "Gobbles" the Turkey		X	X				X							X	
WINTER															
5-1 "Rolly" the Snowman			X				X						X	X	
5-2 "Tired" the Turtle			X		X						X			X	
5-3 Sponge-Painted Frosty			X				X								X

SKILLS INDEX

ACTIVITIES	Body Awareness	Color Awareness/Mixing	Conceptual Development	Concrete Counting	Creative Dramatics	Detail Awareness	Eye-Hand Coordination	Following Directions	Manual Dexterity	Measuring	Patterning	Sequencing	Shape Discrimination	Small-Muscle Control	Spatial Relationships
CHRISTMAS															
6-1 "Angela" the Angel			X				X							X	
6-2 Push-Paint Christmas Tree			X							X	X			X	
6-3 Stuffed Stocking			X				X	X						X	
6-4 Sponge-Painted Santa			X		X	X								X	X
6-5 Baby Jesus in Crib			X				X	X				X			X
6-6 Santa's Train			X		X		X						X	X	
6-7 Snip-Snip Tree			X				X						X		X
6-8 The Holy Family			X		X		X							X	
6-9 Poinsettia			X	X							X			X	X
6-10 Dip-Dot Tree			X				X				X				X
6-11 "Wags" the Christmas Puppy			X		X		X							X	
HANUKKAH															
7-1 Menorah			X				X							X	X
7-2 Pop-Up Hanukkah Card			X				X							X	
NEW YEAR'S EVE															
8-1 New Year's Hat			X				X							X	
VALENTINE'S DAY															
9-1 Sun-Glow Heart		X	X				X				X			X	X
9-2 "I Love You" Pull Card			X									X		X	X
9-3 "This Much" Pop-Up Card	X		X			X	X							X	
9-4 Mossaic Heart			X				X				X			X	
9-5 Valentine Place Card			X				X							X	
ST. PATRICK'S DAY															
10-1 "Leapin'" the Leprechaun	X		X		X		X								
10-2 "Leapin's" Pot of Gold			X				X	X	X						
10-3 Sun-Glow Shamrock			X				X				X			X	X
10-4 Saint Patrick			X			X	X							X	X
CHINESE NEW YEAR															
11-1 Dragon			X		X		X							X	

SKILLS INDEX

ACTIVITIES	Body Awareness	Color Awareness/Mixing	Conceptual Development	Concrete Counting	Creative Dramatics	Detail Awareness	Eye-Hand Coordination	Following Directions	Manual Dexterity	Measuring	Patterning	Sequencing	Shape Discrimination	Small-Muscle Control	Spatial Relationships
SPRING															
12-1 The Incredible Seed			X				X							X	
12-2 April Showers Umbrella			X				X							X	X
12-3 Sponge-Painted Rainbow		X	X				X								
12-4 "Catherine" the Caterpillar			X		X					X			X		
12-5 Marvelous Monarch		X	X				X			X	X				
12-6 Mosaic Flower			X				X				X				
12-7 Momma Robin			X		X		X							X	
EASTER															
13-1 Bunny Blue			X		X		X							X	
13-2 Sponge-Painted Egg			X				X				X				
13-3 "Quacky"			X		X		X							X	
13-4 Bunny Mask			X		X		X				X			X	X
13-5 Wet Chalk Egg			X				X				X			X	X
13-6 Bunny Pop-Up Card			X			X	X							X	
PASSOVER															
14-1 Sun-Glow Elijah's Cup			X				X				X			X	
14-2 Seder Place Card			X				X							X	
14-3 Passover Candle			X				X				X			X	
SUMMER															
15-1 The Grand Seal			X				X							X	
15-2 "Al E. Gator"			X		X		X							X	
15-3 "Gilly" the Fish			X		X		X							X	
15-4 "Crabby"			X	X	X		X							X	X
FOURTH OF JULY															
16-1 Uncle Sam			X			X	X				X		X		
16-2 Statue of Liberty's Crown			X		X		X								X
16-3 Fourth of July Card			X				X				X			X	

SKILLS INDEX

ACTIVITIES	Body Awareness	Color Awareness/Mixing	Conceptual Development	Concrete Counting	Creative Dramatics	Detail Awareness	Eye-Hand Coordination	Following Directions	Manual Dexterity	Measuring	Patterning	Sequencing	Shape Discrimination	Small-Muscle Control	Spatial Relationships
SPACE FLIGHT															
17-1 Space Shuttle Columbia			X		X		X							X	
17-2 Kathryn Sullivan			X		X	X	X							X	
ANIMALS															
18-1 “Bessy”			X		X	X	X							X	
18-2 “Pokey” the Pig			X				X						X	X	
18-3 “Barney” the Basset Hound			X			X	X						X		
18-4 “Sneaky” the Snake			X		X		X						X	X	
18-5 Circus Bear			X		X		X							X	
18-6 “Jumbo”			X		X		X							X	

FALL

Fall, the third season of the year, begins September 23, on the Autumnal Equinox (equal day and night hours). It lasts for 89 days and 19 hours, and ends December 21. In the fall, the nights grow longer and the days grow shorter. The growing season comes to a close, and the harvesting of many foods begins. Plants and animals get ready for winter. Leaves on trees turn from green to shades of brown, red, and gold. Squirrels gather acorns and nuts for the long winter.

1-1 SUN-GLOW FALL LEAVES

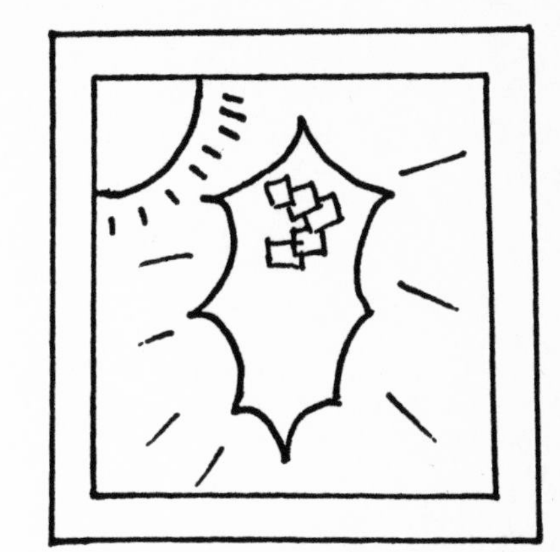

Theme Fall

Skills Conceptual development—nature
Color mixing
Eye-hand coordination
Small-muscle control

Ages 3–8

Leaf Facts

Every green leaf on a tree is a tiny food factory. The leaf factory runs without workers! Its machines are small, oval green bodies, which are stuffed full of green matter called chlorophyll. All summer long the factory is busy making the leaves grow. In the fall great changes appear. The leaf stops making chlorophyll. As the green chlorophyll disappears, beautiful reds, yellows, browns, and oranges appear. These colors are always present in the green leaves, but you cannot see them in the summer because there is so much more green (chlorophyll) than these other colors.

Materials for Each Child

- 9″ x 12″ piece of tracing paper
- Newspaper
- White glue, water, mixed half and half in a small bowl or cup (can be shared by 2 or 3 children)
- Paintbrush
- Yellow, red, and brown tissue paper, cut into approximately 1½″ squares
- Scissors
- Tape

Teacher Directions

Children should be able to do this craft independently after you explain the terms "light coat" (a once-over brush stroke) and "small area" (about 2″ x 2″). This project can also be done on white construction paper if you don't have tracing paper. The results are still very nice; however, you lose translucency.

Steps for Students

1. Trace the maple leaf pattern onto your tracing paper. (Or, look at a large maple leaf and try to copy it onto your paper.)
2. Tape the edges of tracing paper to newspaper.
3. Paint a light coat of glue mix onto a small area of the tracing paper. Apply tissue squares, one at a time. Repeat to cover leaf. Overlap edges to achieve color blending. (A yellow-red overlap will make a beautiful fall orange!)
4. Paint a light coat of glue over entire surface.
5. Let the leaf dry.
6. Take the tape off the edges of tracing paper; cut out the leaf on lines you traced.
7. Tape them onto windows, or string and hang them around a doorway.

Follow-ups

1. Go on a nature walk and collect maple leaves. Match them to tissue art leaves by color.
2. Try to find leaves that still have some green (chlorophyll) in them.
3. Leaves come in all shapes and sizes. Try drawing some leaves. Then, color them, cut them out, and glue them onto construction paper.

1-2 LEAFY ME

Theme Fall

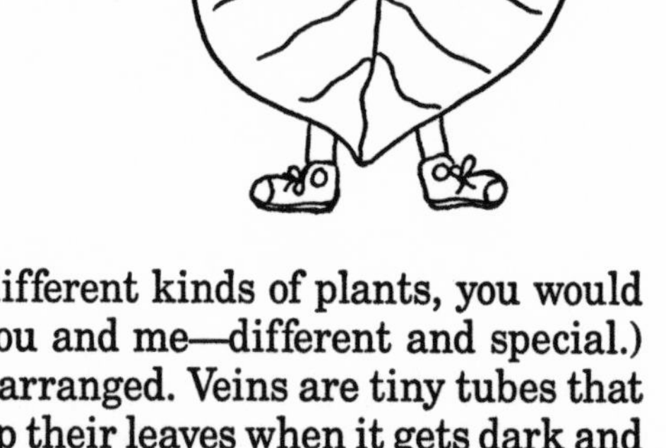

Skills Conceptual development—nature
Spatial relationships
Small-muscle control
Body awareness

Ages 4–6

Leaf Facts

If you examined thousands of leaves from many different kinds of plants, you would not find two that were exactly alike! (Just like you and me—different and special.) The shape of a leaf depends on how its "veins" are arranged. Veins are tiny tubes that carry food and water to the leaf. Some plants fold up their leaves when it gets dark and open them in the sunlight. Many plants turn their leaves toward the sun. The leaf needs the sun to power its food-making process (photosynthesis).

Materials for Each Child

- 9″ x 12″ piece of light-colored construction paper
- Felt-tipped pens or crayons
- Glue
- Scissors

Teacher Directions

Discuss with the children the concept of veins as lifelines. Have them look at the veins in their arms. From real leaves have them feel the veins, and note the different vein patterns.

Steps for Students

1. Select type of leaf for your "body."
2. Place the leaf pattern in the middle of your construction paper and trace around it. (Or, try to draw a leaf of your own.)
3. Draw the center vein.
4. Draw smaller veins from the center vein to the outside edge of the leaf.

5. Color each section of the leaf a different fall color.
6. The leaf will be your body in this "Leafy Me" project. Now add a neck, head, arms, legs, and any other details you have on your body. How about a sun, and some grass?

Variations

1. Press the fall leaves in an old magazine and place it under some books. Glue the pressed leaves onto construction paper and paint with a half-and-half glue/water mixture to ensure permanence and shine. The leaf will be the child's body. Add arms, legs, head, and so on.
2. Have the children collect a variety of leaves. Ask them to carefully strip away the leaf matter, leaving the veins. They can do this by carefully peeling away the leaf matter with their fingers, or by using a short-bristled brush in an up-and-down motion on the shiny side of the leaf. Discuss the varying vein patterns. Children can glue veins in interesting patterns on construction paper for a vein collage.

1-3 SPONGE PAINTING—FALL TREE (WITH ROOTS)

Theme Fall

Skills Conceptual development—nature
Patterning
Spatial relationships
Eye-hand coordination

Ages 4–6

Tree Roots Facts

The roots of a tree bring water and minerals from the soil to the tree; they are the tree's anchor and can be close to half of its weight. No matter how thick the roots are near the tree, or how far they travel, they end in a very fine tip covered with tiny hairs. Since a fully grown tree is very top-heavy, its underground anchor must spread wide and deep. Sometimes roots reach 900 feet down into the earth.

Materials for Each Child

- 9″ x 12″ blue construction paper
- Styrofoam meat tray—2 or 3 children can share tray (for throw-away ease, cover the tray with aluminum foil)
- 4 pieces of sponge (approximately 1″ square)
- Tempera paint: brown, yellow, orange, red
- Scissors

Teacher Directions

Spoon about three tablespoons of brown paint onto the tray. After the children have finished sponge painting the tree, add the three leaf colors to the same tray. It's fine if the colors run together, as most fall leaves are not one solid color. Explain "sliding" the sponge—gliding along the paper (for the tree); "dabbing"—up and down motion on paper (for leaves); and using the edge of the sponge for a finer line.

Steps for Students

1. Trace the tree trunk about 3″ from the bottom of your construction paper, or draw one yourself.
2. Dip a sponge into brown paint and slide it on the tree trunk to paint the trunk brown. Add branches by sliding the sponge up from the top of the trunk. You can use the edge of the sponge to make a thin line.
3. Make roots coming from the bottom of the trunk, using the edge of the sponge.
4. With the sponge for yellow paint, dab on leaves; repeat with red and orange.

Variations

1. Make a fall color sponge design by dabbing your fall-color sponges in an original pattern on construction paper.
2. Make a frame for a special picture or written work by dabbing around the edge of a 9″ x 12″ piece of construction paper.

Follow-up

When winter arrives, make a "Tree in the Winter." Make the tree in the same manner as the fall tree; instead of leaves, use white paint and a sponge to make snow fall on and around the tree.

1-4 "STRETCH" THE SCARECROW

Theme Fall

Skills Conceptual development—nature
Eye-hand coordination
Small-muscle control
Body awareness
Detail awareness

Ages 5–8

Scarecrow Facts

Crows are large, shiny, black birds whose favorite food is corn. This makes them an enemy of farmers. In order to scare the crows away from his corn fields, farmers put up scarecrows. The farmer makes his scarecrow by stuffing his old clothes with straw to make a "man" that will look something like himself. Then the farmer puts the scarecrow on a broomstick and sets it out in his corn field. Because crows are very clever birds they usually learn quickly that the scarecrow can not harm them, so they go back to stealing the corn.

Materials for Each Child

- 9″ x 12″ white construction paper or oaktag
- Craft stick
- Felt-tipped pens or crayons
- Scissors

Teacher Directions

Demonstrate how to place the patterns so that they both fit on the paper. The slits in the scarecrow's body are easy to make if you put the pattern on top of a newspaper and use a ruler and a straight-edge razor to make them.

Steps for Students

1. Trace the two patterns on your paper.
2. With your felt-tipped pens or crayons, give Stretch a face. Color his hat and clothes. Don't forget the small details: eyes, eyelashes, belt—how about some patches?

3. Make two slits in his body as indicated on the pattern.
4. Glue Stretch's head to the craft stick. Let it dry.

5. Insert the stick in and out of the slits, starting from the back.

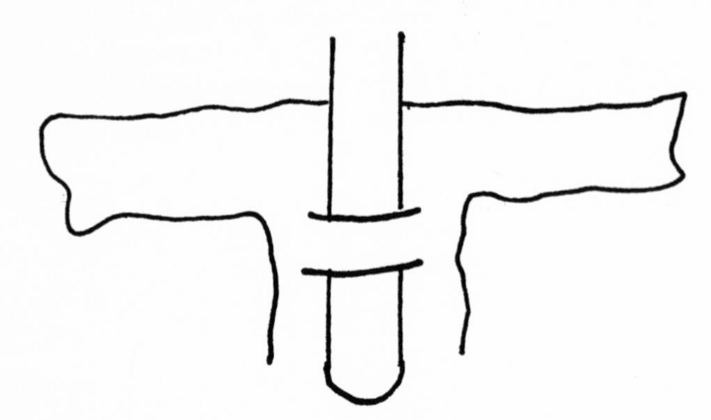

6. To make Stretch stretch, move the stick up and down.

Variation

If you have some straw or dried grass, glue it at the ends of Stretch's arms, legs, and around his head for hair. You may also cut up some yellow construction paper and glue it in these places.

1-5 TREE RINGS

Theme Fall

Skills Conceptual development—nature
Patterning
Eye-hand coordination
Concrete counting

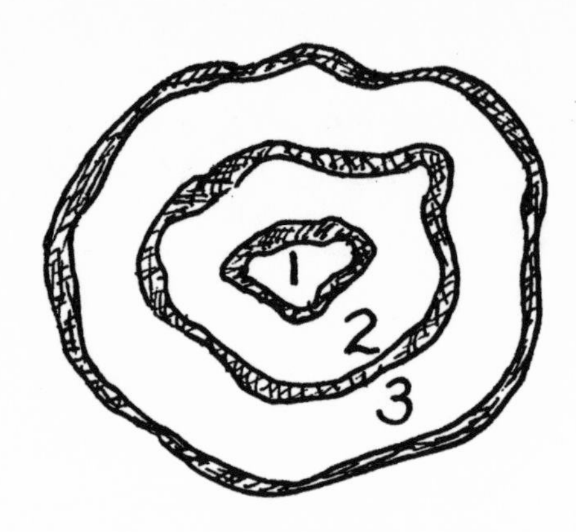

Ages 4–8

Tree Ring Facts

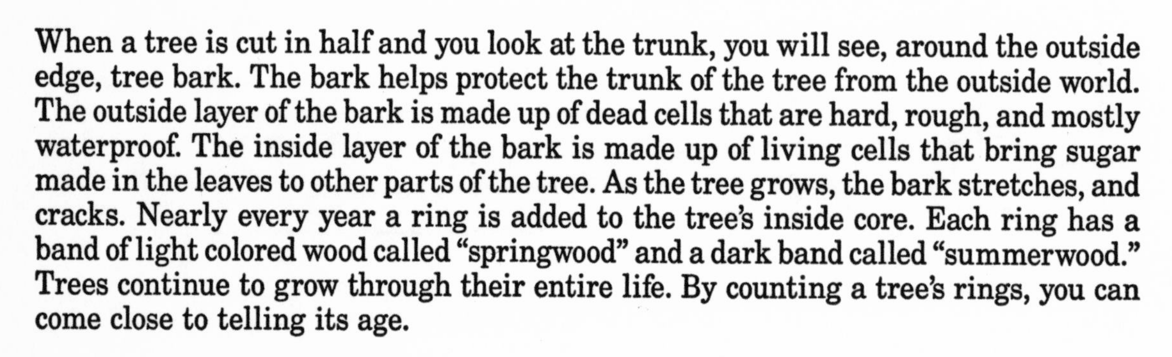

When a tree is cut in half and you look at the trunk, you will see, around the outside edge, tree bark. The bark helps protect the trunk of the tree from the outside world. The outside layer of the bark is made up of dead cells that are hard, rough, and mostly waterproof. The inside layer of the bark is made up of living cells that bring sugar made in the leaves to other parts of the tree. As the tree grows, the bark stretches, and cracks. Nearly every year a ring is added to the tree's inside core. Each ring has a band of light colored wood called "springwood" and a dark band called "summerwood." Trees continue to grow through their entire life. By counting a tree's rings, you can come close to telling its age.

Materials for Each Child

- 9″ x 12″ white construction paper
- Yellow and brown felt-tipped pens or crayons
- Scissors

Teacher Directions

Have the children look at a cross-section of a tree trunk, or a picture of one. This project may be photocopied or traced over onto a ditto master. Depending on the time you have allocated for this project, children may trace the pattern, color the whole pattern yellow, then add bark and rings, or, after tracing the pattern, children could color in the bark, then a ring of yellow, then a ring of brown, and so on until they reach the center.

Steps for Students

1. Trace pattern on white construction paper.
2. With your brown marker or crayon, color in the outside layer of bark.
3. Next to the ring of bark, color in a ring of yellow; continue with a ring of brown, then a ring of yellow, until you reach the center.
4. Count your yellow rings to tell how old your tree is.

2-1 MAGIC ALAKASAM

Theme Halloween

Skills Conceptual development—nature/history
Shape discrimination
Eye-hand coordination
Following directions
Spatial relationships

Ages 4–7

Cat Facts

Cats are members of the *felidea* (from the Latin *felis*, a cat) family, which also includes lions, tigers, jaguars, and leopards. Cats have long, stiff, sensitive whiskers, which act as feelers to help their eyesight at night. Their eyes have pupils that close to slits in bright light, and become large and round in the dark. The eyes of cats are made so that they can see well when there is very little light. This is important, for nearly all cats are most active at night. Cats have very keen hearing. They can hear the footsteps of a mouse twenty feet away. Cats have been pets to man for more than 4,000 years! The Egyptians made their dead cats into mummies. The penalty for killing a cat in Egypt was death. Some people believe black cats are bad luck.

Materials for Each Child

- 4½″ x 12″ (½ of a 9″ x 12″) oaktag or white construction paper
- Felt-tipped pens or crayons
- Paper fastener (brad)
- Yarn (any bright color)—six 1½″ pieces of broom straws (or pine needles)
- Glue
- Scissors

Teacher Directions

Discuss the shapes in Alakasam. Show the children how to place patterns so they both fit on the paper. Depending on the skill level of the child, the teacher may wish to insert the paper fastener.

Steps for Students

1. Trace one cat and one circle on oaktag or white construction paper. (Be sure to place the patterns so that they both fit on your paper.)
2. Color the cat black.
3. Draw a "Y" in the circle to separate it into thirds. Use three bright colors to color sections of the circle.

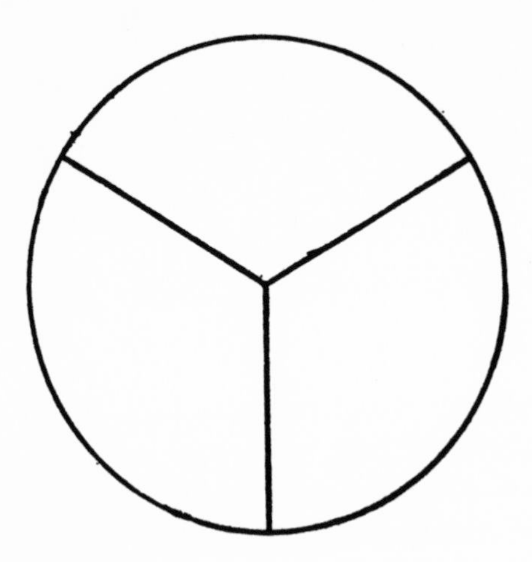

4. Cut out Alakasam and the circle. Carefully cut out the cat's eyes.
5. Insert paper fastener in the center of the cat and through center of the colored circle.
6. Glue the whiskers on the cat (three on each side).
7. Make a handle for turning the circle using the method shown here:

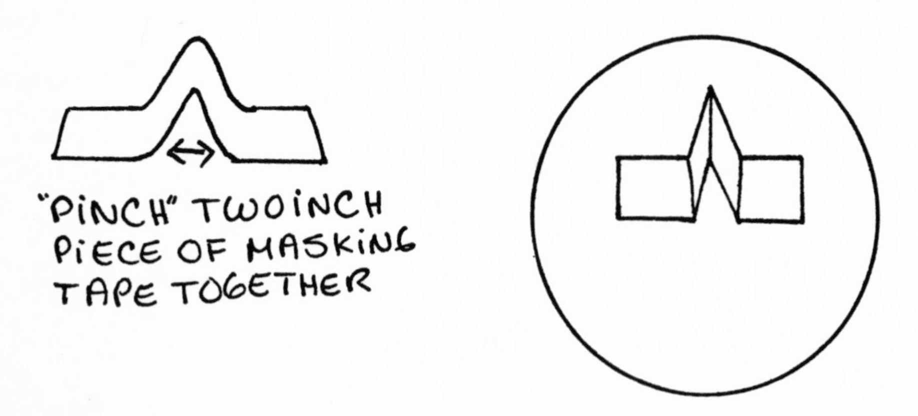

8. Turn the handle around to make Alakasam's eyes change color.

Variation

Draw your own cat head (be sure it's large enough to cover the circle behind it). You can color your cat with stripes like a tabby, or with a different color face and ears like a Siamese; or, color your Alakasam in your own special design!

Follow-ups

1. Learn this little poem, and say it as you change Alakasam's eyes: "Alakasam, Alakazoo, watch, I'll change my eyes for you!"
2. Use Alakasam as a puppet, and tell a story using some of the "Cat Facts."
3. If you were Magic Alakasam on Halloween night, tell what you would do to have fun!

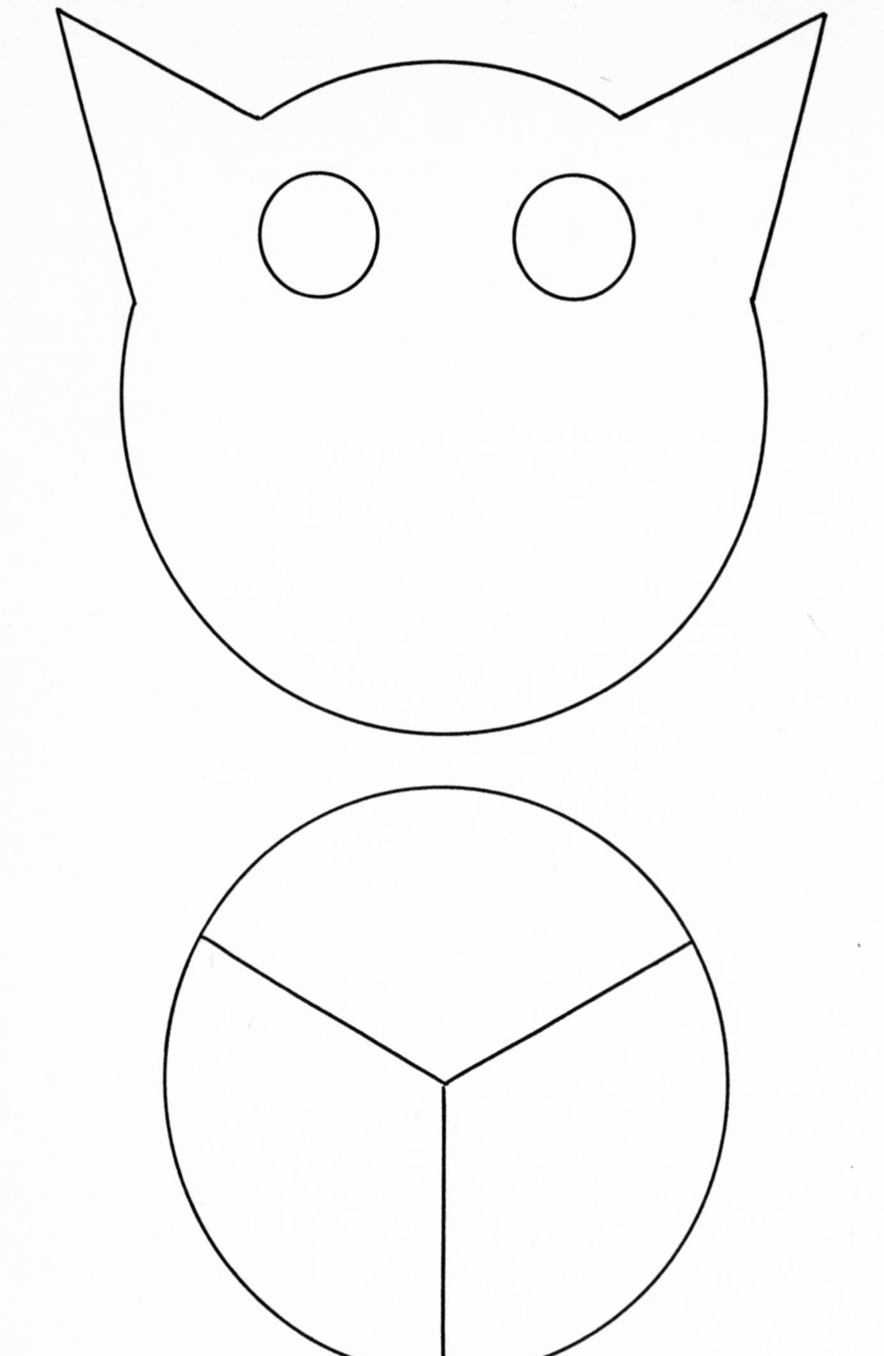

2-2 PUSH-PAINT JACK-O'-LANTERN

Theme Halloween

Skills Conceptual development—legends
Measuring
Small-muscle control
Eye-hand coordination

Ages 3–8

Jack-O'-Lantern Facts

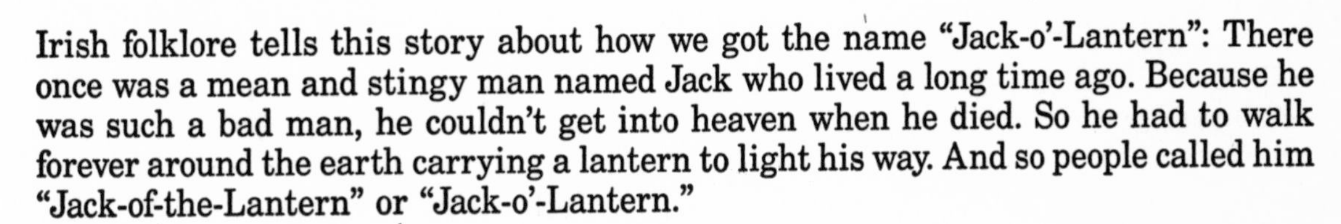

Irish folklore tells this story about how we got the name "Jack-o'-Lantern": There once was a mean and stingy man named Jack who lived a long time ago. Because he was such a bad man, he couldn't get into heaven when he died. So he had to walk forever around the earth carrying a lantern to light his way. And so people called him "Jack-of-the-Lantern" or "Jack-o'-Lantern."

Materials for Each Child

- One cup each of yellow and orange tempera paint (children may share cups)
- Plastic spoons—one for each cup
- 9″ x 12″ white construction paper
- Black felt-tipped pen or crayon
- Scissors

Teacher Directions

Children love to watch each other do this project, so you can assemble and set up supplies in order for the children to take turns at watching and doing. Spread newspaper on the project table. Demonstrate for the children how to make small drops of paint on the paper by taking a spoon of paint and touching it to the paper in various spots, allowing a drop to drip off. Remind them not to shake the paint off the spoon as it will splatter on them.

Steps for Students

1. Trace the pumpkin on white construction paper and fold the paper in half with the pumpkin on the outside. Open the paper.

2. Spoon drops of yellow and orange paint on to the paper.
3. Close the paper on the fold and gently push the drop of paint with your fingers to spread, and mix the colors.
4. Carefully rub a craft stick or ruler from top to bottom of the paper to squeeze out any excess paint.
5. Open the paper and let it dry.
6. Cut out the pumpkin from the reverse (pattern-lined) side.
7. With your black felt-tipped pen or crayon, color in the eyes, nose, and mouth.

Variations

1. Use red and yellow paint. Let children determine proportions of each color. Colors will blend when paper is folded. The results will be varied shades of orange.
2. Have the children cut out eyes, nose, and mouth from black construction paper. Glue them in place on their push-paint pumpkin.

Follow-ups

1. These Jack-o'-Lanterns make a very effective lobby or hall display. You could make signs "Scary," "Funny," "Friendly," and so on and have children categorize their pumpkin.
2. Make a large push-paint pumpkin for your door. Children can get together in groups and design eyes, nose, mouth—hat, bowtie!

2-3 WITCH "GREENIE"

Theme Halloween

Skills Conceptual development—make-believe
Body awareness
Shape discrimination
Eye-hand coordination
Spatial relationships
Small-muscle control

Ages 4–6

Witch Facts

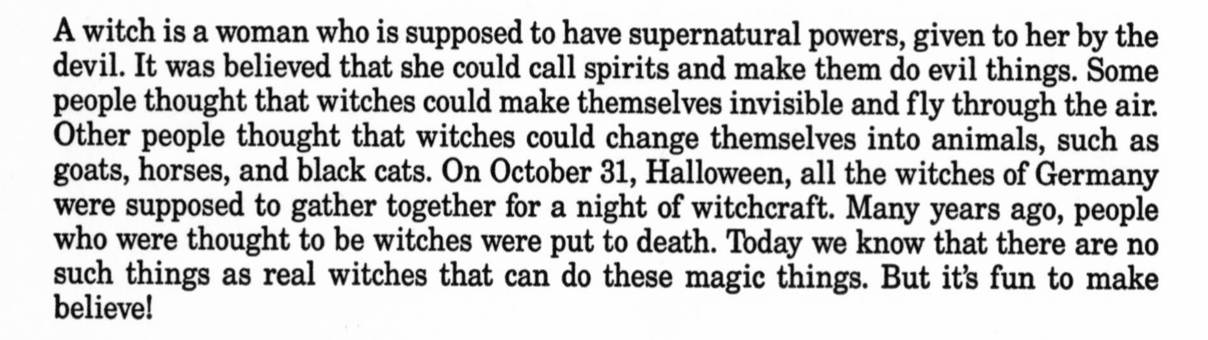

A witch is a woman who is supposed to have supernatural powers, given to her by the devil. It was believed that she could call spirits and make them do evil things. Some people thought that witches could make themselves invisible and fly through the air. Other people thought that witches could change themselves into animals, such as goats, horses, and black cats. On October 31, Halloween, all the witches of Germany were supposed to gather together for a night of witchcraft. Many years ago, people who were thought to be witches were put to death. Today we know that there are no such things as real witches that can do these magic things. But it's fun to make believe!

Materials for Each Child

- 9″ x 12″ blue construction paper
- 4½″ x 6″ (¼ of a 9″ x 12″) light green construction paper
- 4½″ x 6″ (¼ of a 9″ x 12″) black construction paper
- Felt-tipped pens or crayons
- ½-sheet of green tissue paper
- Glue
- Scissors

Teacher Directions

Ask the children to name the shapes that make up Greenie. Explain the positioning of the circle and triangle. Talk about the different parts that make a whole person.

Steps for Students

1. Trace the circle on the light green paper.
2. Trace the triangle on the black paper. (You can use chalk to trace on black paper.)
3. Cut the green tissue paper into strips for Greenie's hair.
4. Cut out the circle and the triangle.
5. Glue the circle near the top part of the blue construction paper. Glue the tissue paper hair on the sides of the circle. Glue the triangle (hat) on top of the circle, slightly overlapping the circle. Add the rectangle brim:

6. Draw Greenie a scary or funny face using a lot of different colors.
7. Draw a witchy body, arms, legs, and so on.

Variations

1. What other kind of pictures can you make with the triangle and the circle? Add other shapes and see what you can make.
2. Add a moon and stars to your picture with glue and sparkles. How about a magic broom and a black cat?
3. Take three or four small circles and triangles and make a picture of witches having a party on Halloween night.

Follow-ups

1. Have children sit in a circle, and take turns thinking up "spells"; for example, "I'm going to change my desk into a dragon and ride him home!"
2. Instruct children to add all the parts of the body they can think of on Greenie. Then ask them to point to Greenie's ears, ankles, and so on.

2-4 "BATTY" THE FLYING BAT

Theme Halloween

Skills Conceptual development—nature
Small-muscle control
Eye-hand coordination
Following directions

Ages 4–6

Bat Facts

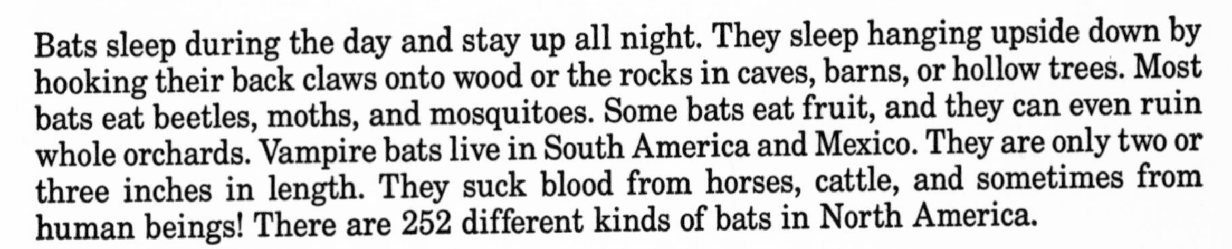

Bats sleep during the day and stay up all night. They sleep hanging upside down by hooking their back claws onto wood or the rocks in caves, barns, or hollow trees. Most bats eat beetles, moths, and mosquitoes. Some bats eat fruit, and they can even ruin whole orchards. Vampire bats live in South America and Mexico. They are only two or three inches in length. They suck blood from horses, cattle, and sometimes from human beings! There are 252 different kinds of bats in North America.

Materials for Each Child

- 4½″ x 12″ (½ of a 9″ x 12″) yellow construction paper
- Felt-tipped pens or crayons
- Craft stick
- Glue
- Scissors

Teacher Directions

Note to the children the points on the bat's wings, which they are to connect with a line to separate the wings into sections. Depending on the skill level of the child, the teacher may wish to cut out "Batty." If you feel that the amount of coloring is too much for your children, have them do dots, stripes, or circles in the wing sections.

Steps for Students

1. Trace the bat on yellow construction paper.
2. Draw a line to separate the bat's head from its body. Make lines to separate Batty's wings into sections.

3. Using Halloween colors (black, purple, green, orange) color in the wings and the body.
4. Draw a scary or a funny face.
5. Cut out the bat.
6. Glue on the craft stick halfway up the bat's back.
7. Fold bat wings at joints.
8. Wave "Batty" back and forth to make it "fly."

Variations

1. Look at encyclopedia pictures of different kinds of bats. Try to color your bat to look like the one you like best, or least!
2. Use glue and sparklers to make Batty's eyes glow.
3. Add clawed feet by pushing a pipe cleaner through the bottom part of Batty's body, twisting on small pieces of pipe cleaner as shown:

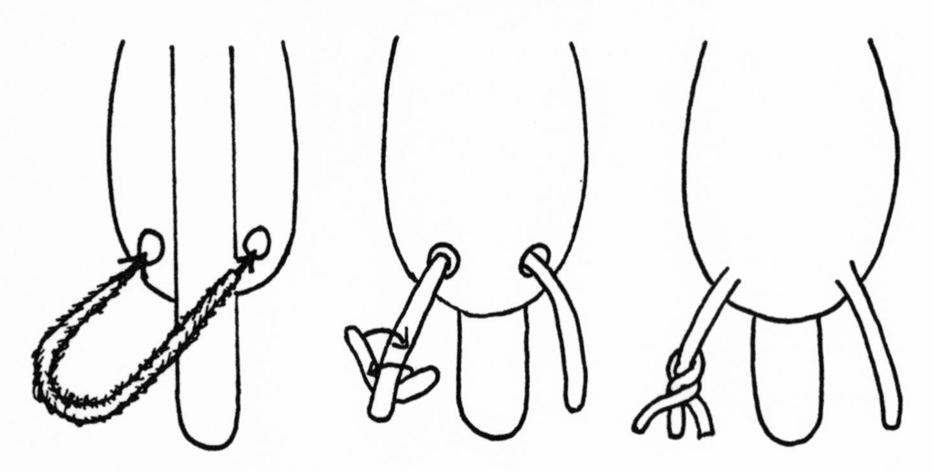

Now you can hang Batty upside down to sleep!

Follow-ups

1. Punch a hole in Batty's head and tie on a 3" piece of string. Go into the yard and have a bat flying contest.
2. Think about what it would be like to sleep all day and stay up all night. Would you like to do that? Why? What would you be missing?
3. Do a follow-the-leader bat dance, gliding high and swooping down.
4. With your teacher's help, hang upside down on the monkey-bars to feel how a bat sleeps.

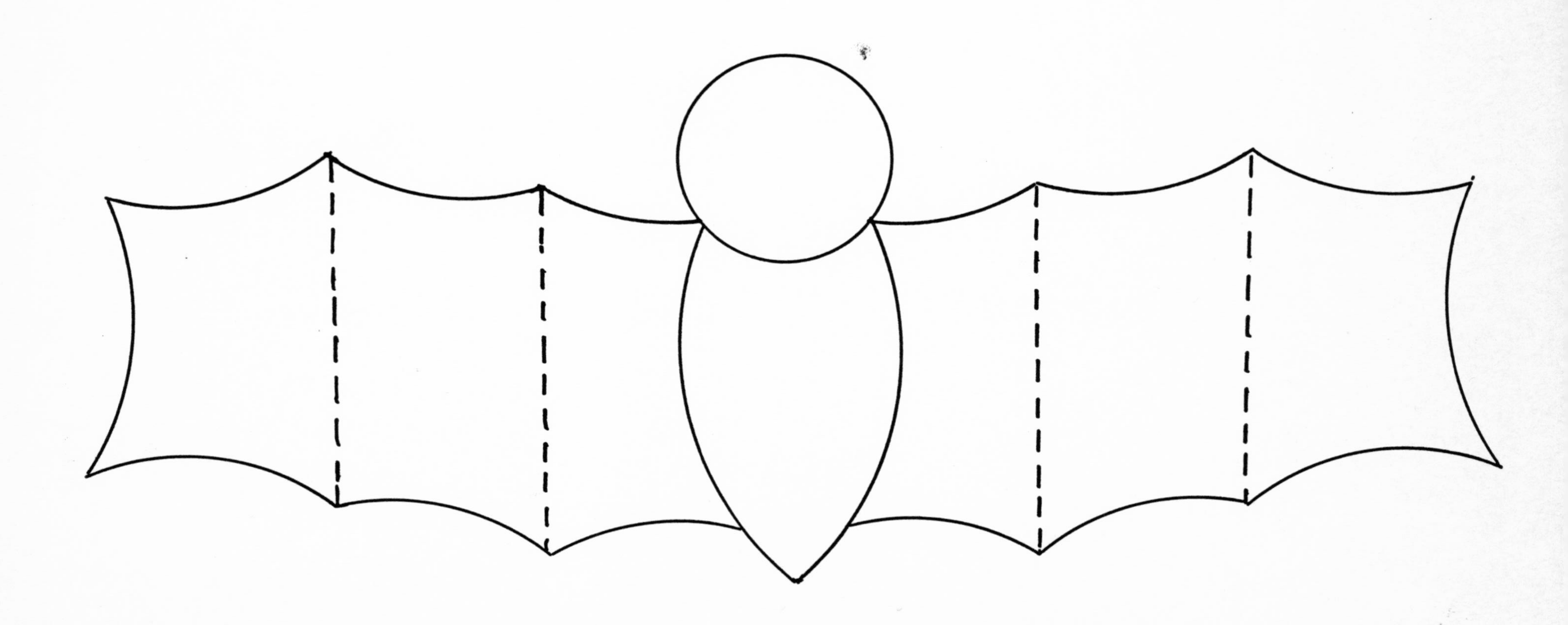

2-5 "SPUNKY" THE SPIDER

Theme Halloween

Skills Conceptual development—arachnids
Creative dramatics
Concrete counting
Eye-hand coordination
Small-muscle control
Shape discrimination

Ages 4–7

Spider Facts

Spiders are really manufacturing plants! This means they make or manufacture silk and use it to make houses, cocoons to hold their eggs, traps, and lifelines to travel on. The spider makes the silk in a part of his stomach and then pushes it out through a tiny hole at the tip of its stomach. It comes out as a liquid and turns solid when it hits the air. Spiders are "arachnids," animals that have a two-part body and four pairs of walking legs. Spiders are not insects. All spiders have eight legs, insects have six legs. Spiders vary in size from twelve inches to those that you can hardly see. Tarantulas in Colombia, South America, actually capture birds! Most spiders live only one year. They come in a variety of brilliant colors: red, orange, green, yellow; some, however, are jet black, white, or dull brown. If a spider's leg is broken off, he can grow a new one!

Materials for Each Child

- 6″ x 9″ (½ of a 9″ x 12″) oaktag or white construction paper
- 4½″ x 6″ (¼ of a 9″ x 12″) black construction paper
- Felt-tipped pens or crayons
- 6″ pipe cleaner
- Scissors

Teacher Directions

A good opener is to use "Spunky" (a finger puppet) to tell children about spiders and elicit discussion. Have Spunky ask the children if they want to make a friend for him. Discuss the shape of Spunky. Depending on the skill level of the children, the teacher may wish to do Step 7 for them.

Steps for Students

1. Trace spider body on oaktag or white construction paper and draw a line to separate the head from the body.
2. Color the spider's body in your own design of stripes, zigzags, dots, and so on.
3. Fold the black construction paper in half three times the long way.
4. Open the paper and cut on the fold lines; you will have eight legs.
5. Accordion-pleat the legs, or just fold them in half three or four times.
6. Glue the legs on underside of spider's body, four on each side.
7. Insert the pipe cleaner in the head, leaving a finger loop on the underside of the spider, and twist it on top as shown here:

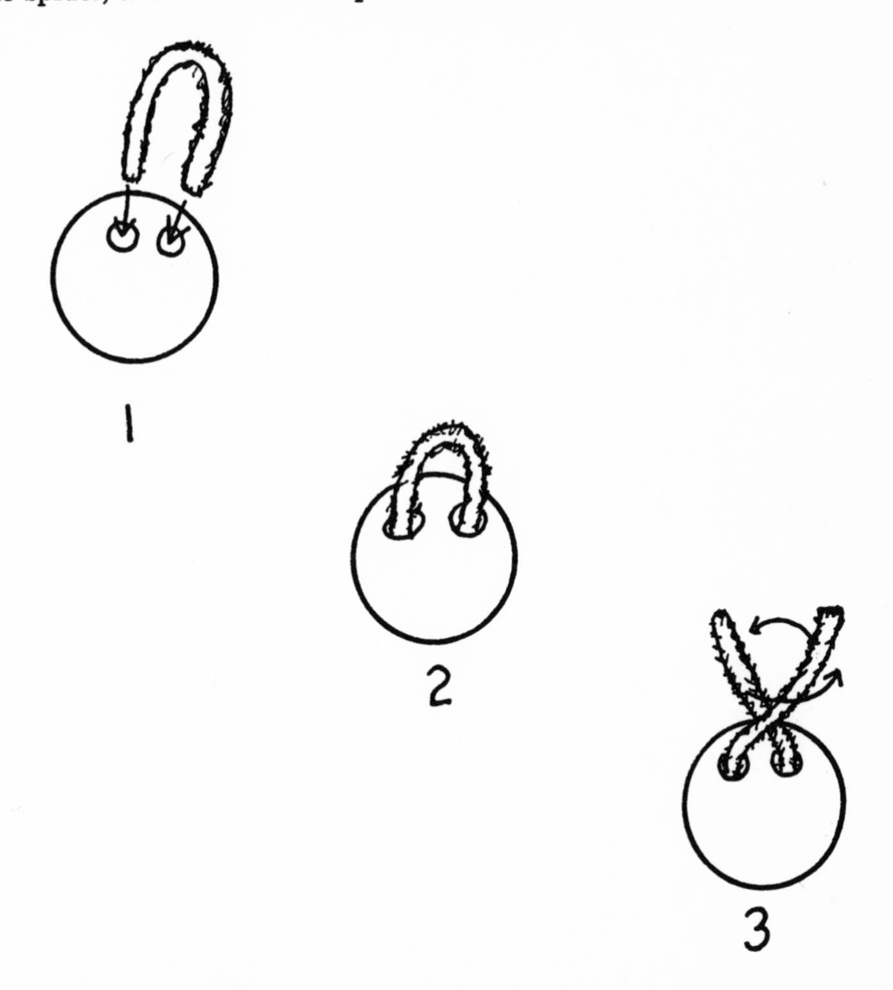

8. To make Spunky's eyes, cut small circles from the scraps, then glue them on the ends of the pipe cleaner.
9. Insert your index finger in pipe cleaner loop and move it up and down to make Spunky dance.

Variations

1. Instead of coloring Spunky, dip-dot him! Put small amounts of different colors of tempera paint in the recesses of a styrofoam egg carton. Dip the end of a 3″ piece of a straw into paint, and "dot" onto Spunky. Repeat to dip-dot his whole body. Let dry. Proceed with the legs and the finger loop in the instructions.
2. After coloring Spunky and attaching his eight legs, glue three pieces of string, 8″ long, to spunky's body:

When the glue dries, tie the ends of the string together and make Spunky move like a marionette.

2-6 BOOOTIFUL CARD

Theme Halloween

Skills Conceptual development—make-believe
Eye-hand coordination
Small-muscle control

Ages 5–8

Ghost Facts

It is said that ghosts are the spirits of people who have died. Ghosts are not supposed to have any great power and can only "appear" and try to haunt (or scare) people. A ghost is portrayed to look like steam—you can partly see through it. It is said that the ghosts of murdered people haunt the place where they were killed—especially on Halloween night!

Materials for Each Child

- 9″ x 12″ white construction paper
- Felt-tipped pens or crayons
- Glue
- Scissors

Teacher Directions

You may wish to write on the board some of the children's suggested Halloween greetings for them to pick from and copy onto their cards. Don't forget (on the front), "Have a booo...(inside)...tiful Halloween!" (*Alternative:* This project may be photocopied or traced onto a ditto master.)

Steps for Students

1. Cut the construction paper in half on the 12″ side.
2. On one half trace the ghost pattern.
3. Cut it out.
4. Give your ghost two big eyes and a smiley mouth.

5. Fold the other piece of your paper in half, then open it.
6. Fold your ghost as shown, then glue it into your card:

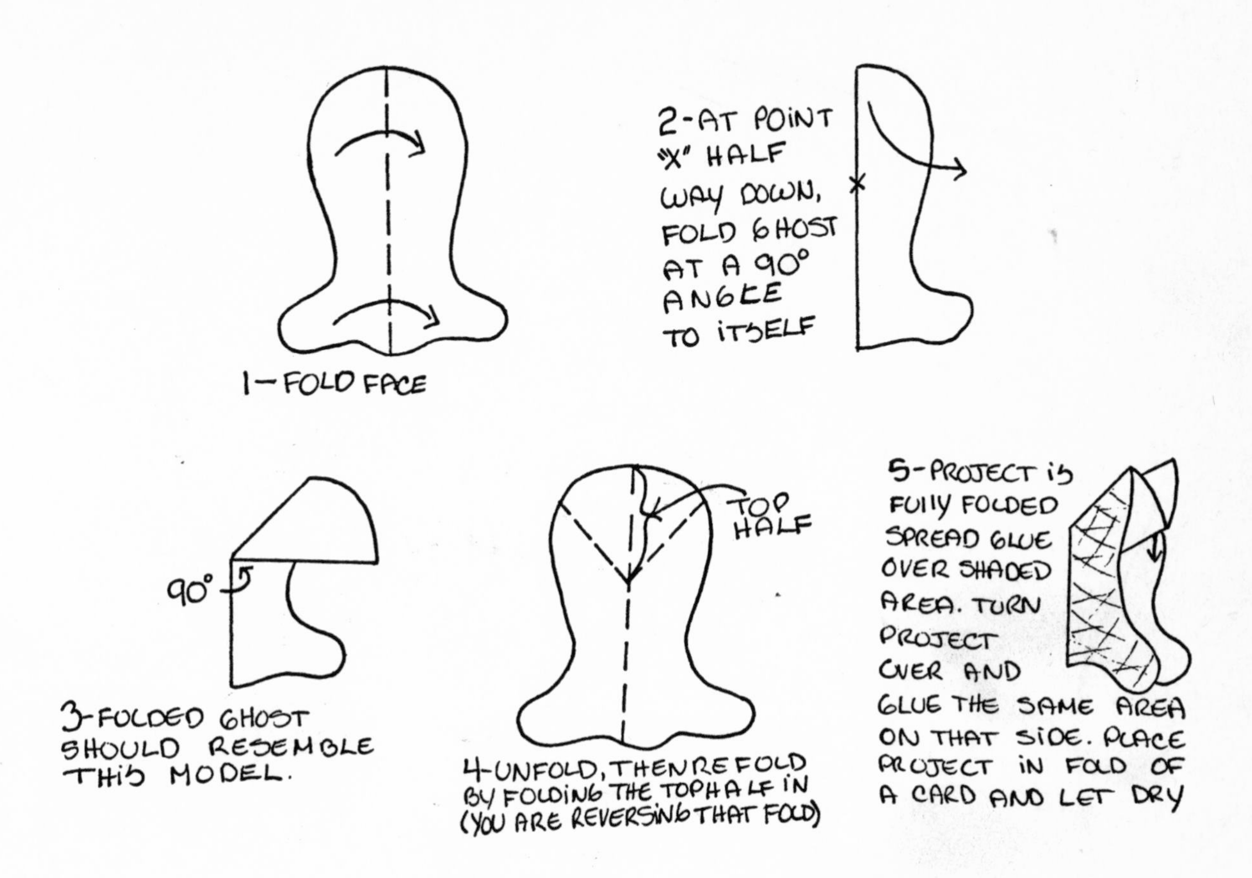

7. Decorate the front of your card and write a Halloween greeting.

2-7 "GUS" THE GHOST

Theme Halloween

Skills Conceptual development—make-believe
Eye-hand coordination
Patterning
Spatial relationships

Ages 3–8

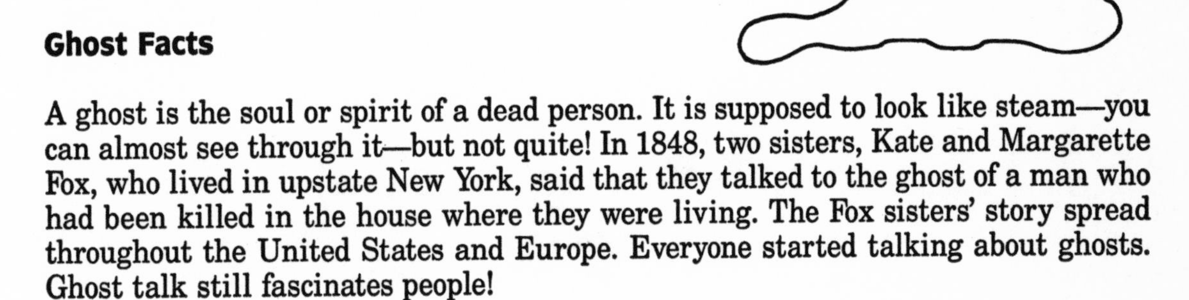

Ghost Facts

A ghost is the soul or spirit of a dead person. It is supposed to look like steam—you can almost see through it—but not quite! In 1848, two sisters, Kate and Margarette Fox, who lived in upstate New York, said that they talked to the ghost of a man who had been killed in the house where they were living. The Fox sisters' story spread throughout the United States and Europe. Everyone started talking about ghosts. Ghost talk still fascinates people!

Materials for Each Child

- 9″ x 12″ tracing paper
- 1½″ white tissue squares
- Black crayon or felt-tipped pen
- White glue, water, mixed half-and-half in small bowl or cup (can be shared by two or three children)
- Paintbrush
- Scissors
- Hole puncher

Teacher Directions

Demonstrate brushing a small amount of glue mix on paper and laying a square of tissue on it. Overlapping the tissue square is desirable. Make sure children cover drawn line of the ghost.

Steps for Students

1. Trace the ghost on tracing paper.
2. Brush a small amount of glue mix onto paper. Cover this area with tissue square. Repeat to cover the entire ghost.
3. Brush on a light coat of glue mix over the surface of the tissue squares.
4. Let Gus dry; then cut him out.
5. With your black crayon or marker, give Gus some big eyes, a mouth, and so on (depending on how your ghost is feeling today).

6. Punch a hole in Gus's head and tie a piece of yarn in the hole to hang Gus up, or staple to a piece of black construction paper, with a slight bulge in the middle of Gus.

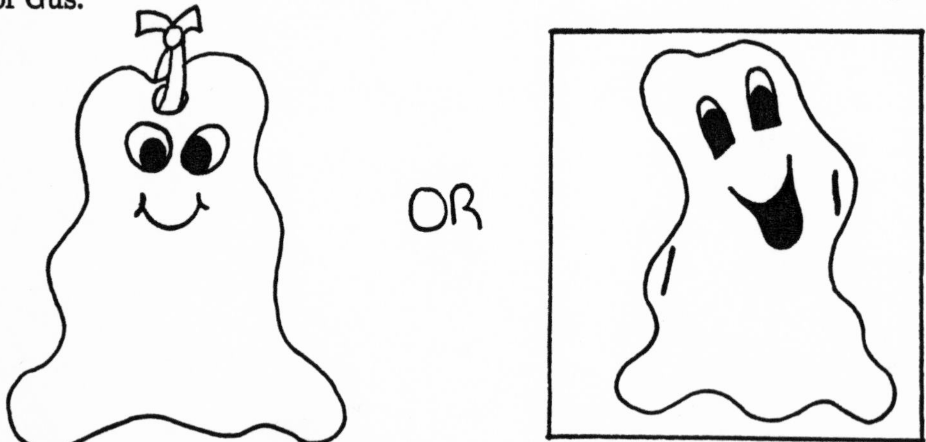

Follow-up

Ghosts love the dark. On white paper, with a white crayon, draw and color in a white ghost. Of course, he's hard to see now! Make a black wash (½-cup water and ½-teaspoon black tempera paint) and brush it over Gus. Watch him appear!

3-1 CORNUCOPIA

Theme Sukkot

Skills Conceptual development—religion
Color recognition
Eye-hand coordination
Spatial relationships

Ages 5–8

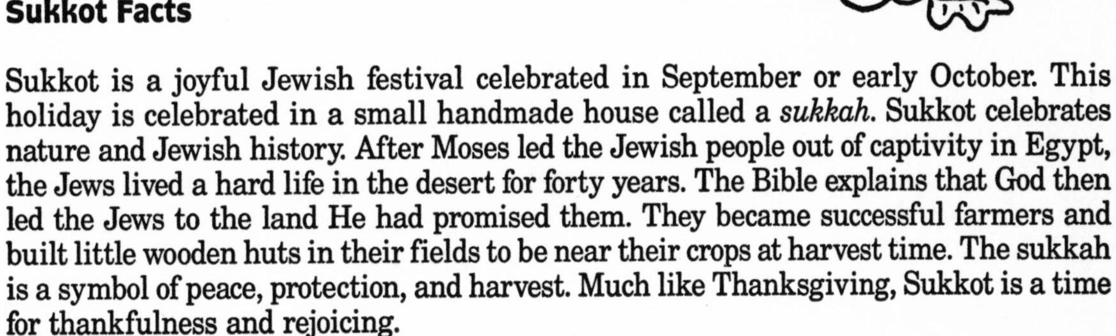

Sukkot Facts

Sukkot is a joyful Jewish festival celebrated in September or early October. This holiday is celebrated in a small handmade house called a *sukkah*. Sukkot celebrates nature and Jewish history. After Moses led the Jewish people out of captivity in Egypt, the Jews lived a hard life in the desert for forty years. The Bible explains that God then led the Jews to the land He had promised them. They became successful farmers and built little wooden huts in their fields to be near their crops at harvest time. The sukkah is a symbol of peace, protection, and harvest. Much like Thanksgiving, Sukkot is a time for thankfulness and rejoicing.

Materials for Each Child

- 9″ x 12″ white construction paper
- 9″ x 12″ green construction paper
- Assorted felt-tipped pens or crayons
- Glue
- Scissors

Teacher Directions

Explain that a cornucopia is a symbol of an abundant harvest. Therefore, it is an appropriate decoration for Sukkot, as the Jewish people are remembering the good crops that were harvested after forty years of living in the desert.

Steps for Students

1. Trace the cornucopia, fruits, and vegetables on white construction paper.
2. Color the fruits and vegetables with felt-tipped pens or crayons the "real" color of each item. Cut them out.

3. Color the cornucopia yellow or make it look like a basket by making crossed lines on it with your brown crayon or marker:

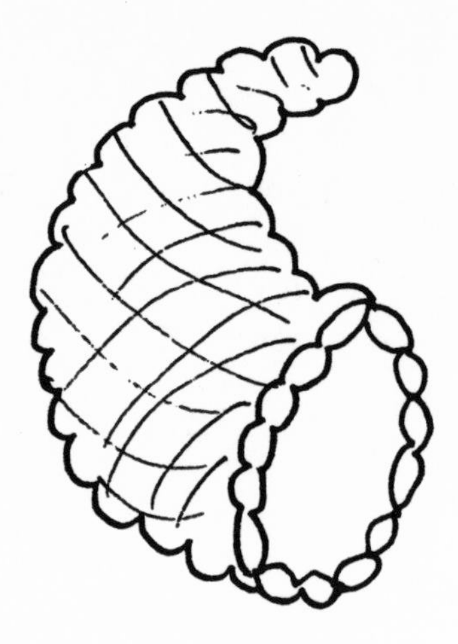

4. Cut it out.
5. Cut a slit in the cornucopia as dash-line indicates:

6. Glue the cornucopia onto the green construction paper. Glue on the fruits and vegetables, sticking some of them halfway into the slit:

Follow-up

The children can cut out pictures of fruits and vegetables from magazines or supermarket ads and glue them on a large poster or bulletin board entitled: "Fruits and Vegetables We Love," "We're Thankful for Fruits and Vegetables," and so on.

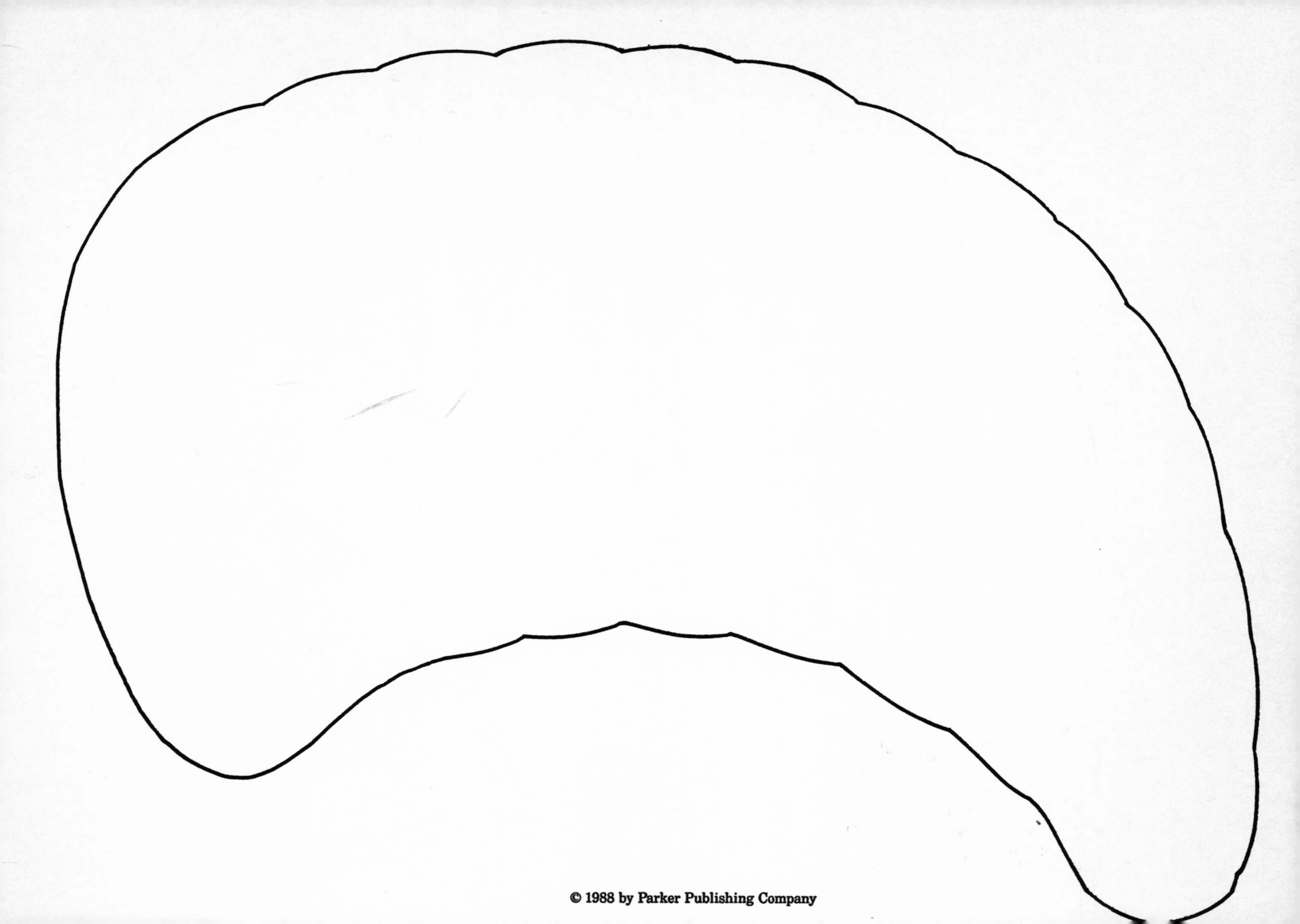

3-2 SUKKAH

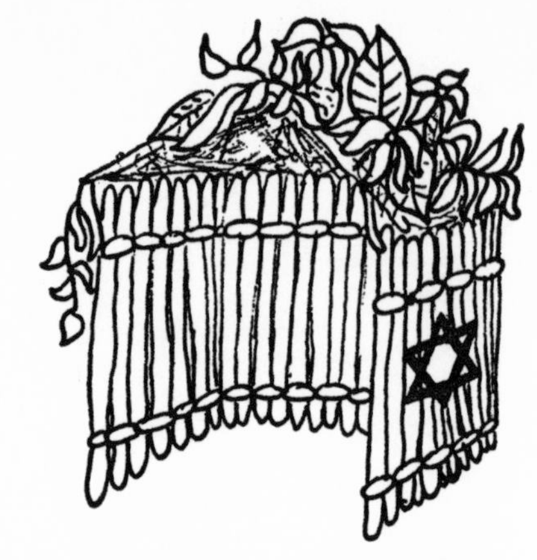

Theme Sukkot

Skills Conceptual development—religion
Manual dexterity
Small-muscle control

Ages 5–8

Sukkah Facts

When Jewish people yearly celebrate sukkot, the family gets together and builds a *sukkah*—a small, portable hut. It has been built in many different ways by Jews all over the world. The sukkah must be built under the open sky, with no tree or second story above it. The roof covering must be made from plants or branches. The sukkah is often decorated with fruits and vegetables of autumn. An Israeli sukkah might have hangings of pomegranates, quinces, persimmons, figs, and grapes. The sukkah reminds the Jewish people of their togetherness and of God's continuous protection.

Materials for Each Child

- 9″ x 12″ yellow construction paper
- 9″ x 12″ green construction paper
- 9″ x 12″ blue construction paper
- Glue
- Scissors

Teacher Directions

Fold yellow construction paper in thirds; then unfold it half way and stand it up:

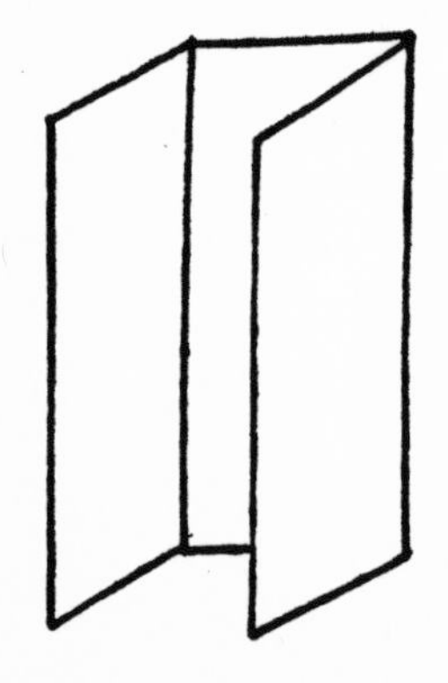

These are the three walls of the sukkah.

Steps for Students

1. Trace the leaf pattern five times on the green construction paper.
2. Cut out each leaf and snip the edges:

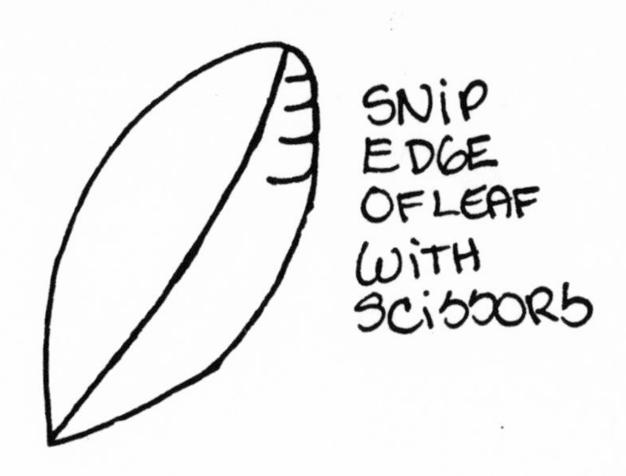

3. Trace the Torah and the Star of David twice on the blue construction paper. Cut them out and glue them on the outside walls of the sukkah (folded yellow construction paper).
4. Carefully put a small amount of glue on the top edge of the sukkah and lay on your leaves.

Follow-up

As a class project, cut away one side of an appliance carton, and paint and decorate it like a sukkah.

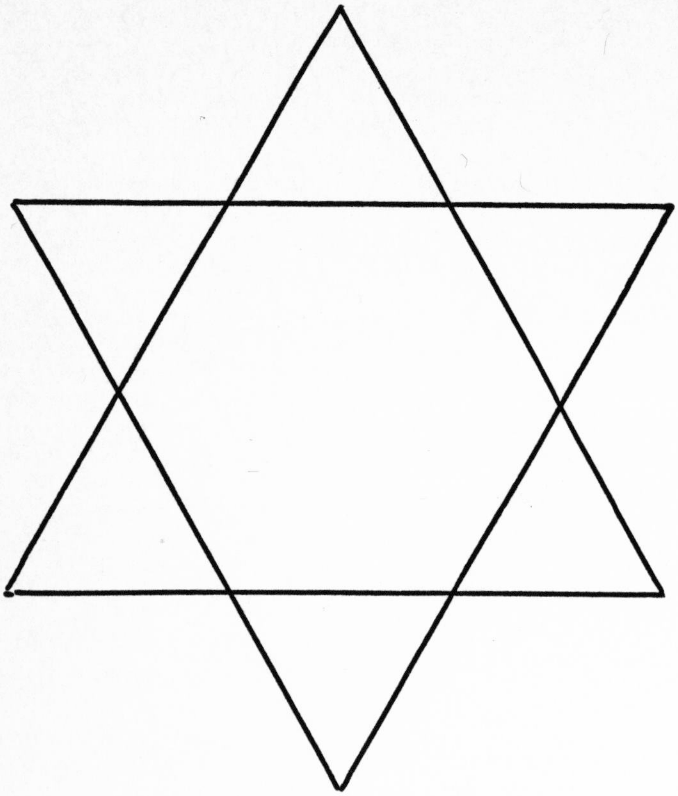

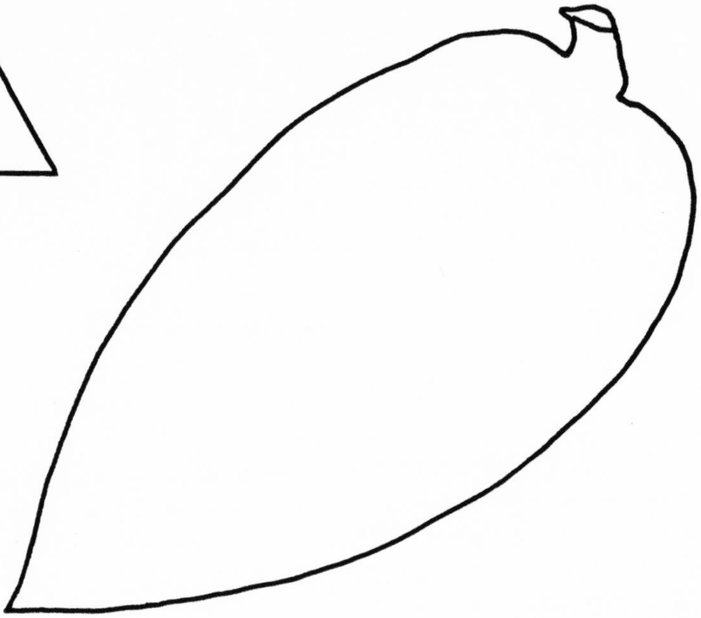

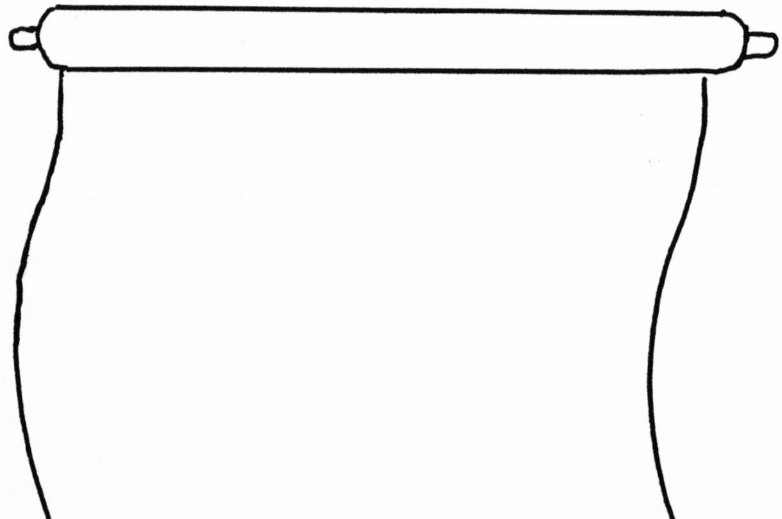

4-1 MAYFLOWER

Theme Thanksgiving

Skills Conceptual development—history
Eye-hand coordination
Small-muscle control

Ages 4–7

Mayflower Facts

The Mayflower is probably the most famous American sailing ship. At the time the Pilgrims used the Mayflower for their famous trip, the boat was about twenty years old. The Mayflower was a three-masted wooden ship, driven by sails. It was about ninety feet long, and twenty-five feet wide. Christopher Jones, captain of the Mayflower, was an expert sailor. It took him sixty-three days (more than two months) to cross the Atlantic Ocean. The Mayflower arrived at Cape Cod on November 21, 1620. It sailed again and anchored in Plymouth Harbor on December 21. During the first winter, the Mayflower served as the headquarters for the Pilgrims while they were building their homes on land. In the spring, the Mayflower sailed back to England.

Materials for Each Child

- 4½″ and 12″ (½ of a 9″ x 12″) brown construction paper
- 3 wooden coffee stirrers or craft sticks
- 4½″ x 12″ (½ of 9″ x 12″) white construction paper
- 9″ x 12″ blue construction paper
- Scissors

Teacher Directions

Explain that the blue construction paper is the Atlantic Ocean, the coffee stirrers, or sticks, are the masts that hold the white sails. Remind the children to place the Mayflower toward the lower part of their "ocean" to allow room for the masts and sails.

Steps for Students

1. Trace the Mayflower on the brown construction paper and cut it out.
2. Glue it on the lower half of the blue construction paper.
3. Make lines of glue where the masts will go. Lay the sticks in place.

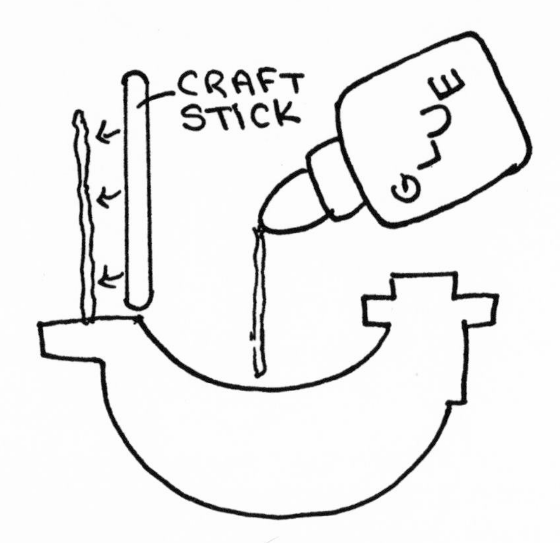

4. Trace the sails on the white construction paper and cut them out. Glue them onto masts.

Variations

1. From an old white sheet you can tear strips to cut into sails. (One sheet will last for many Thanksgivings!)
2. Using a black, felt-tipped marker or crayon, the children can draw "plank" lines on their Mayflower:

3. With a white crayon or chalk, they can draw wave lines on their ocean.

Follow-ups

1. Count with the children sixty-three days back from November 21 and mark it on the calendar to show the children how long the Pilgrims were on the Mayflower.
2. Measure ninety feet (the length of the Mayflower) in the hall and label the measurement as the length of the Mayflower that carried one hundred two passengers.

4-2 PILGRIM, KING, INDIAN STICK PUPPETS

Theme Thanksgiving

Skills Conceptual development—history
Eye-hand coordination
Detail awareness
Small-muscle control
Creative dramatics
Spatial relationships

Ages 4–7

Thanksgiving Facts

In the 1600s, the Pilgrims were a group of English people who did not want to worship in the Church of England or follow the Church's rules. Since it was against the King of England's laws to worship in any other way, many of the Pilgrims were jailed for holding their own religious services. In 1620, a group of one hundred two men, women, and children decided to find a new homeland, where they could worship as they wanted. In 1620, they boarded the Mayflower and sailed for America. The trip was very hard, the ship was crowded, the food scarce, and the sea rough. One sailor died. A baby was born during the voyage. He was named Oceanus, because he was born while crossing the ocean. When the Pilgrims finally landed in Plymouth, Massachusetts, they were happy to meet friendly and helpful Indians. Squanto, a member of the Pawtuxet tribe, showed the Pilgrims how to fish, plant corn, dig for clams, and hunt. Other Indians also helped the Pilgrims. Because of the Indians' help, the Pilgrims' crops grew very well. To celebrate, the Pilgrims had a three-day feast to thank God and their Indian friends—that was the first Thanksgiving.

Materials for Each Child

- 9″ x 12″ white construction paper
- 4 craft sticks, or 1″ x 4″ strips of cardboard
- Felt-tipped pens or crayons
- Scissors

Teacher Directions

Explain the individual puppet's role in the Thanksgiving story. Discuss how the outlined shapes of the puppets reveal which character they play in the story. (*Alternative:* This project may be photocopied or traced onto a ditto.)

Steps for Students

1. Trace Thanksgiving puppets on white paper.
2. Draw facial features on each head and color their hats.
3. Glue a craft stick to back of each puppet.
4. When dry, use the puppets to tell the story of Thanksgiving.

Follow-up

How about a simple Thanksgiving play? Select a narrator, then divide the class in thirds: the King of England and his bishops, Pilgrims, Indians.

Narrator: This is how it was in England in 1620.

King and Bishops: You must go to our church."

Pilgrims: "No, No. We want to go to our own church."

Kings and Bishops: "You must."

Pilgrims: "No. No."

King and Bishops: "Then off to jail."

Narrator: The Pilgrims escaped from jail and rented the Mayflower to take them to a new land.

Pilgrims: (In line with hands on each others' shoulders, rocking back and forth) "This is an awful trip, but we can't turn back."

Narrator: After sixty-three days, the Pilgrims landed in America.

Indians: "Hi, Pilgrims. We will help you learn how to live in our beautiful country."

Pilgrims: "Thanks, Indians."

Narrator: The Indians taught the Pilgrims many things.
Four Indians (one at a time): "How to fish."
"How to clam."
"How to hunt."
"How to grow vegetables."

Pilgrims: "Please join us for dinner. We are thankful to you and God."
Indians: "Sounds good! We'll be there!"

4-3 INDIAN MAN IN CANOE

Theme Thanksgiving

Skills Conceptual development—history
Spatial relationships
Manual dexterity
Eye-hand coordination
Body awareness

Ages 5–8

Indian Facts

At Thanksgiving, we often see pictures of Indians in headdresses or feathered bonnets. The Indians that lived around the Pilgrim's colony at Plymouth wore their hair in a line running from front to back with one eagle feather stuck in it. In the mild weather, the Indian men wore only a deerskin apron. The Pilgrims did not see any Indians at their settlement in Plymouth until February. From stories they had heard, the Pilgrims thought the Indians would be unfriendly. In March, an Indian called Samoset walked into the Pilgrim colony. He was friendly and spoke some English. He soon brought his friend Squanto. Since all of Squanto's tribe had died of "Indian sickness" (mumps or measles carried to the Indians by white traders and fishermen), he decided to live with the Pilgrims. Squanto taught the Pilgrims how to grow corn. He also taught the Pilgrims how to fish and how to tell which berries and herbs were safe to eat.

Materials for Each Child

- 9″ x 12″ white construction paper or oaktag
- Felt-tipped pens or crayons
- Stapler
- Scissors

Teacher Directions

Demonstrate tracing the canoe on the fold, emphasizing that you do not cut on the fold line. You may wish to staple the sides of the canoe for the children. When doing so, bow one half of the canoe at each side before stapling to create an opening for the Indian.

Steps for Students

1. Fold your paper up 3″ on the 9″ side.

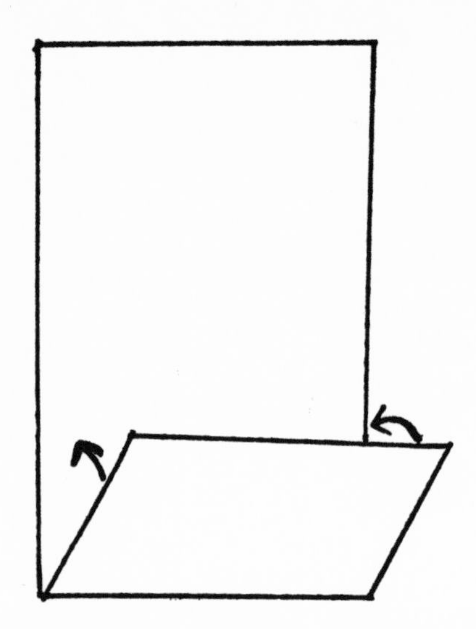

2. Trace the canoe on this part of the paper, with bottom of the canoe on the fold:

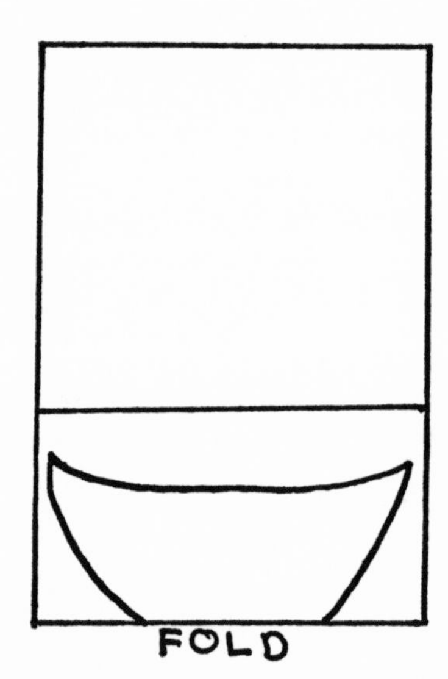

3. Trace the Indian on remaining part of the paper or draw your own Indian.
4. Wth crayons or markers, give your Indian a face, feathers, and a deerskin apron. Cut him out.

5. Cut out your canoe. Do not cut on the fold line. Decorate your canoe with some Indian symbols:

6. Bow the canoe a little and staple the sides together.

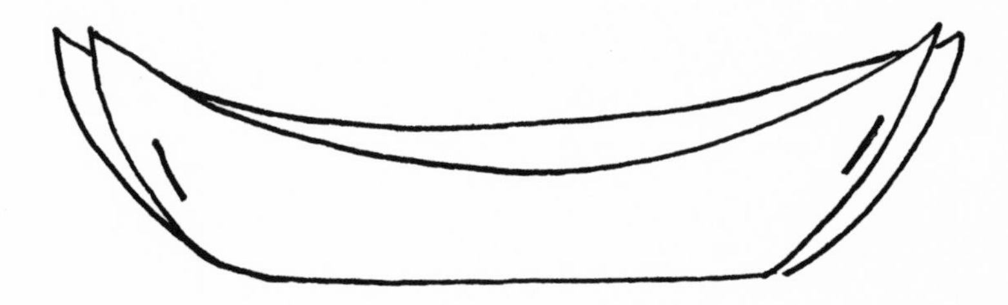

7. Put your Indian in his canoe and send him off on an adventure.

Follow-up

Make a clay canoe. It's easy! Roll a ball of clay into the shape of a log. With a plastic knife, small spoon, or pencil, dig the clay out of the middle of the log. Squeeze the bottom and each end into a "v" shape. Try to make an Indian for your canoe.

4-4 "GOBBLES" THE TURKEY

Theme Thanksgiving

Skills Conceptual development—animals
Color recognition
Eye-hand coordination
Small-muscle control

Ages 4–7

Turkey Facts

The turkey is the most popular symbol of Thanksgiving. The male turkey is much larger than the female and has beautiful, bright feathers. A full-grown male turkey, called a "gobbler," is about three feet high and weighs about twenty to twenty-five lbs. Turkeys are found only in North and Central America.

Material for Each Child

- 9″ x 12″ yellow construction paper
- Four 2¼″ x 12″ (¼ of 9″ x 12″) orange, brown, red, green construction paper (one of each)
- Glue
- Felt-tipped pens or crayons
- Scissors

Teacher Directions

Children will be "snipping" edges of the turkey feathers. It is good to demonstrate this step to show approximately how long a snip should be. With a yardstick, show the children what "three feet high" looks like. Discuss the turkey's height compared to that of other birds.

Steps for Students

1. Trace turkey on yellow construction paper then cut it out.
2. Give the turkey an interesting face.
3. Trace the feather on each of your four colored strips of paper.

4. Carefully snip edges of each feather.

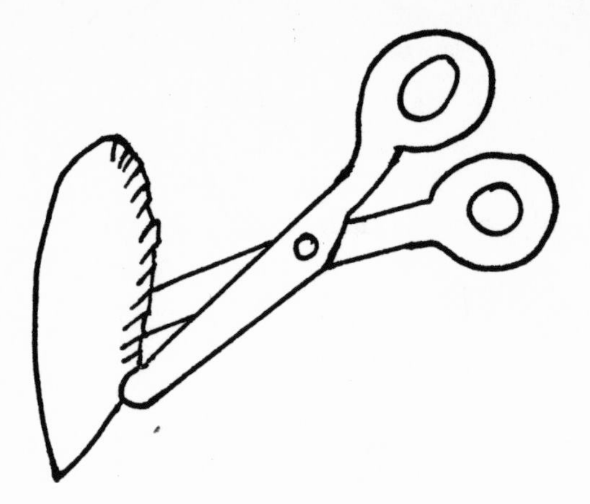

5. Glue the feathers in back of your turkey's body.

6. With your brown crayon or marker, draw on feet.

Follow-up

Make a bulletin board entitled: "We Are Thankful for..." Have the children cut out feathers and tell you (if they can't write) things they are thankful for. Write them on the feathers and arrange them on the bulletin board.

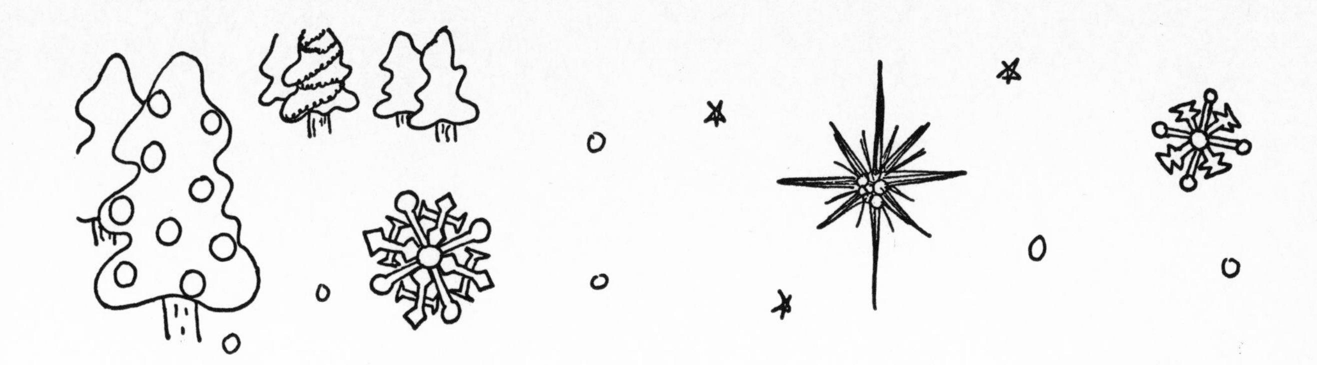

WINTER

Winter begins December 21, and lasts eighty-nine days and one hour. It ends March 21. Winter is the time when night hours are the longest and day hours are the shortest. Winter is a harsh time for creatures in cold places. Each kind of animal prepares for winter in its own way. Some birds travel south (this is called migration). In the south the weather is usually warm and birds can find food much more easily than in the cold north. Fish swim deep into ponds to be safe from the frost that sets on the top of the water. Many small and large animals sleep through the winter in a numb, unmoving state (hibernation). These animals include turtles, bears, snails, frogs, groundhogs, horseshoe crabs, and spiders. Many trees shed their leaves. This helps them to save water, because a tree loses water through its leaves.

5-1 "ROLLY" THE SNOWMAN

Theme Winter

Skills Conceptual development—nature
Eye-hand coordination
Small-muscle control
Shape discrimination

Ages 4–6

Snow Facts

Snow is frozen moisture (tiny specks of water) that falls to earth. Each snowflake has six arms and six sides, forming a crystal. (The word *crystal* comes from the Greek word meaning "ice.") No one knows just why snowflakes form this way, but they always do. People who have studied snowflakes say that they have never seen two snowflakes exactly alike. A snowflake is white because the snow crystal combines the colors of the light that strike it. When you put together all colors, you get white!

Materials for Each Child

- 9″ x 12″ white construction paper or oaktag
- 9″ x 6″ (½ of 9″ x 12″) black construction paper
- Paper fastener (brad)
- Black felt-tipped pen or crayon
- Scissors

Teacher Directions

Demonstrate for children the placement of the patterns so that they both fit on the paper. For inspiration, show the children pictures of snowmen/women.

Steps for Students

1. Trace the snowman and the circle on the white construction paper. Cut them out.

2. With your felt-tipped pen or crayon, give your snowman a face. Try making his face look as if it were made with coal or stones. Start with an "x," then keep adding cross lines:

Draw on stick arms.

3. Trace the snowman's hat on the black construction paper. Cut it out.
4. Glue the hat onto the snowman.
5. Attach the circle to the back of your snowman with the paper fastener, allowing the circle to stick out a little lower than the snowman:

6. Turn the fastener around a few times to loosen it.
7. Gently roll your snowman up your arm or on the carpet.

Variation

Make a wet chalk snowman. On a dark-colored piece of construction paper draw a snowman with white chalk dipped first into water.

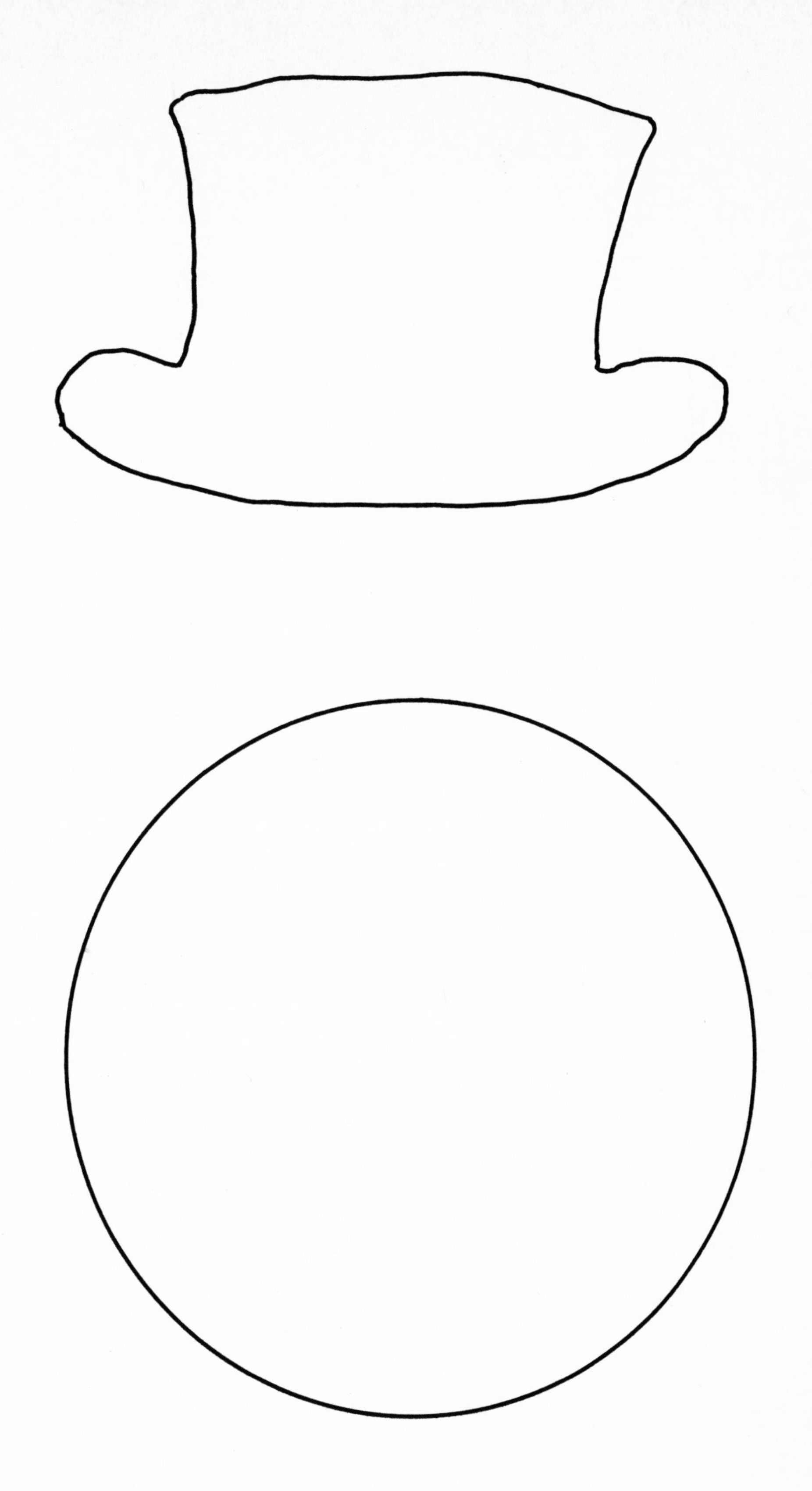

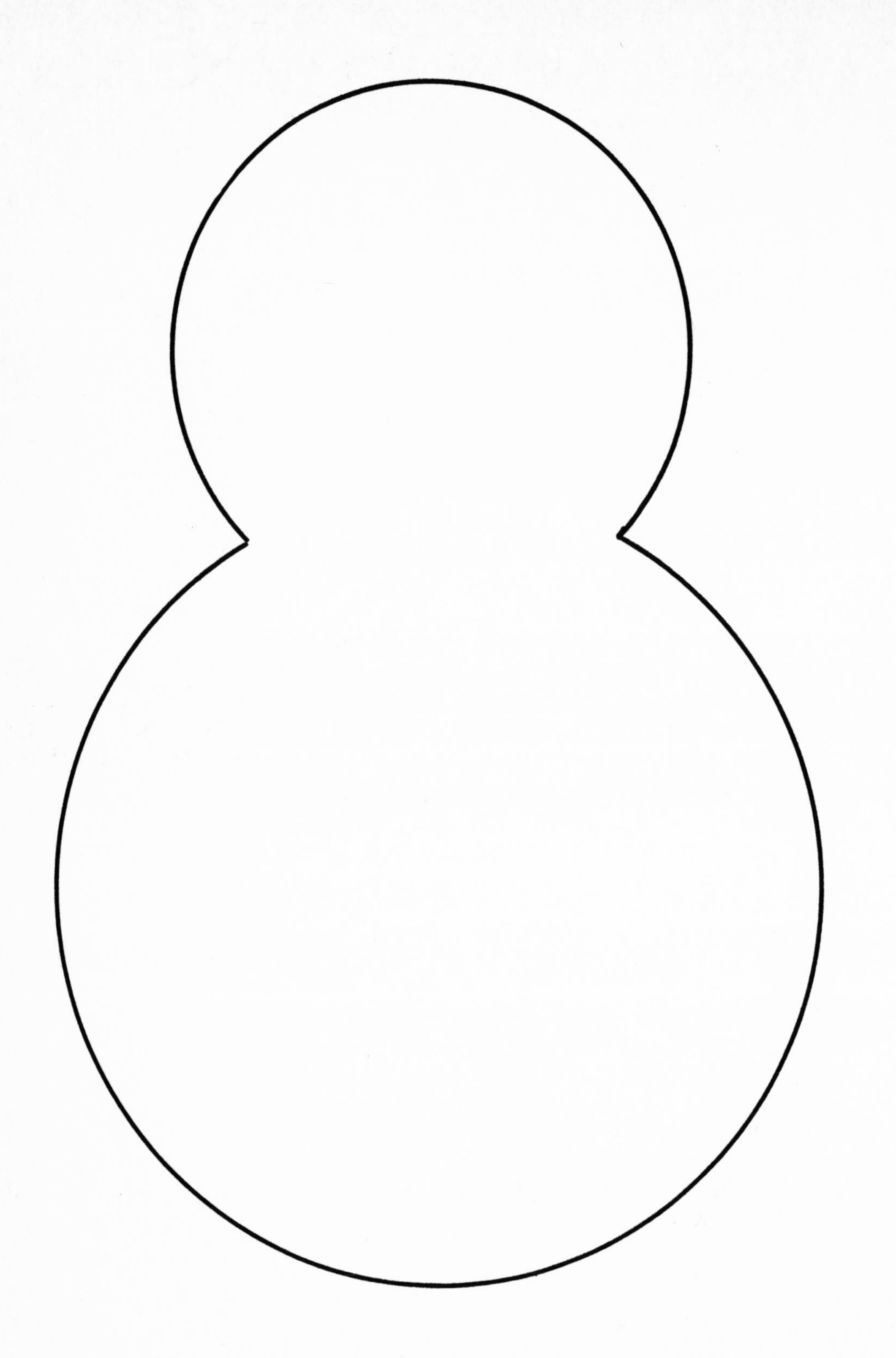

5-2 "TIRED" THE TURTLE

Theme Winter

Skills Conceptual development—nature
Small-muscle control
Creative dramatics
Patterning

Ages 4–7

Turtle-Hibernating Facts

The box turtle is a reptile that hibernates in the winter by digging down into the earth. The further north the turtle lives, the further down he must dig to get below the frost line. To prepare for hibernation the box turtle eats more than usual. Sometimes he overdoes it, and he can't fit all his legs, tail, and head back in his shell! The turtle must stop eating and rest for a while so he can close himself up. The box turtle pulls its top and bottom shells tightly together to completely enclose its body. By the sixth year of life, the box turtle's shell is so hard that its enemies cannot harm it. A box turtle can live twenty to forty years.

Materials for Each Child

- 9″ x 12″ white construction paper or oaktag
- 2 paper fasteners (brads)
- Felt-tipped pens or crayons
- Scissors

Teacher Directions

Depending on the skill level of your children, you may wish to insert the paper fasteners and make the tape handle.

Steps for Students

1. Trace the turtle shell, head, and tail on your paper.

2. Make box lines on your turtle shell:

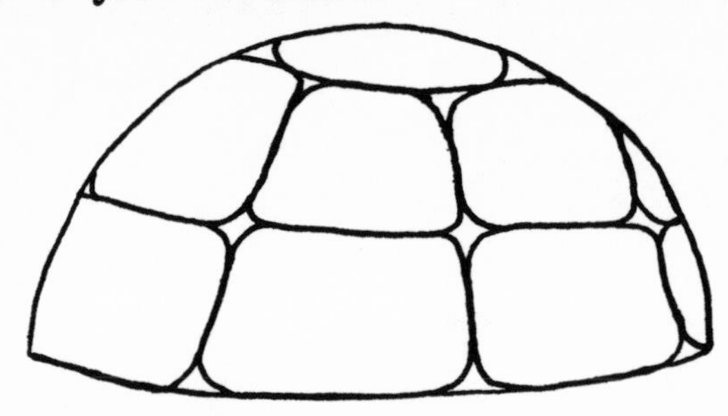

Color the boxes with your favorite colors, or, if you want him to look like a box turtle, use brown and yellow.

3. Give the turtle's head a face, and color his tail.
4. Attach the head and tail behind the shell with the two paper fasteners.

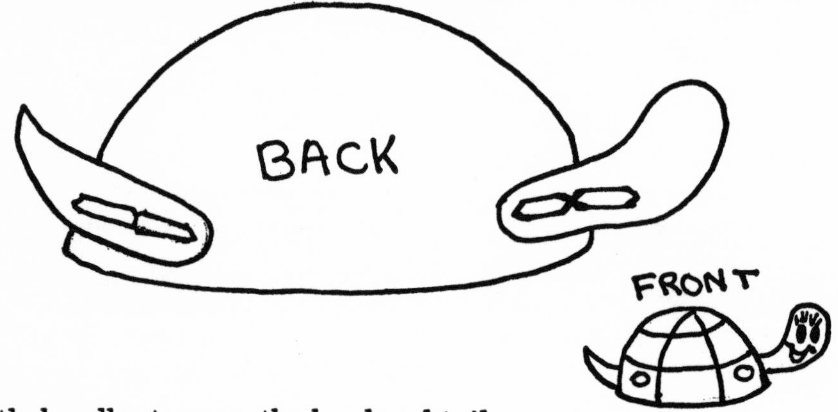

5. Make little handles to move the head and tail:

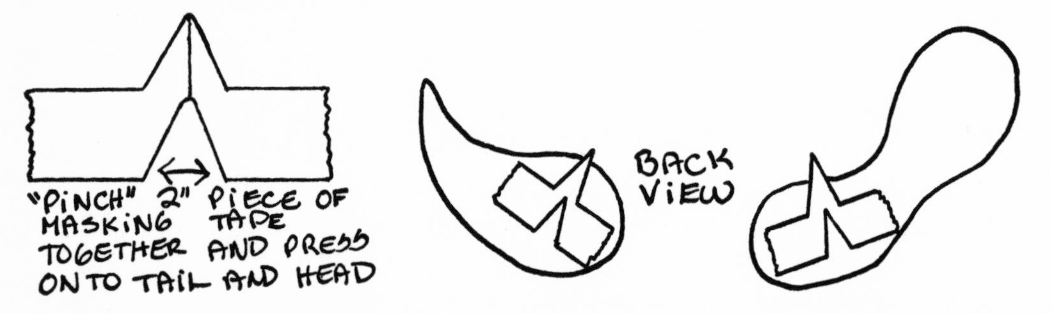

6. Move the head and tail back into shell when you want "Tired" to hibernate.

Follow-up

Learn this little poem and say it using Tired as a puppet:

This is my turtle
He lives in a shell
He likes his home very well
He pokes his head out
When he wants to eat
He pulls his head back
When he wants to sleep.

—traditional

5-3 SPONGE-PAINTED FROSTY

Theme Winter

Skills Conceptual development—history
Eye-hand coordination
Spatial relationships

Ages 4–7

Snowman Facts

No one knows who the first sculptor of snow was. It wasn't until the early 1920s that anyone thought about the beauty and fun of making snow people and buildings. The Dartmouth College students in 1923 were the ones who really made snow sculpture popular. They turned a winter pastime into an art form.

Materials for Each Child

- 9″ x 12″ blue construction paper
- 9″ x 12″ white construction paper
- Black felt-tipped pen or crayon
- Small piece of sponge
- White tempera paint
- Plastic lids or styrofoam meat tray (can be shared by 2 or 3 children)
- Scissors

Teacher Directions

Demonstrate the up-and-down motion of sponge painting. This motion, instead of "sliding" the sponge, will produce a snowy look. Instruct children in cutting out the *inside* of the snowman, leaving a negative snowman:

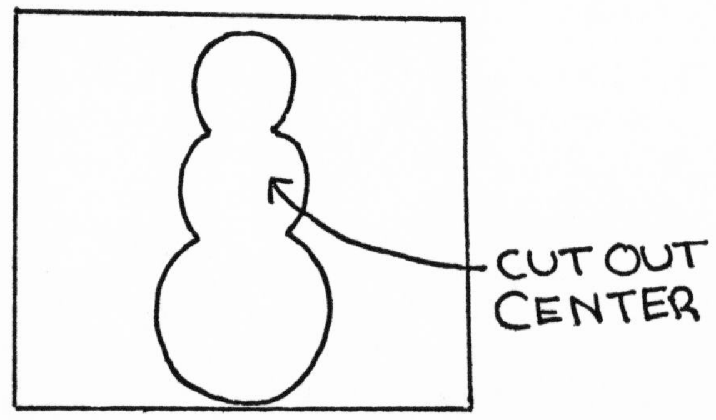

Tape silhouette onto blue paper. Put a small amount of white paint on plastic lid or tray.

Steps for Students

1. With an up-and-down motion, dab white paint over the surface of your snowman. Be sure to dab right over stencil lines:

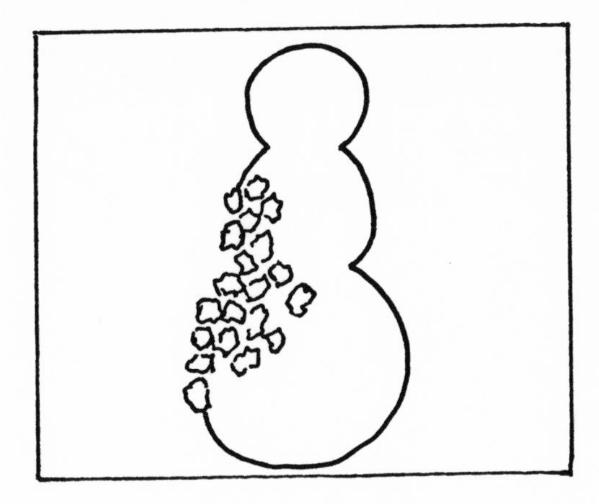

2. Let your snowman dry. Remove the stencil.
3. With black crayon or felt-tipped marker, give Frosty a face, arms, and a hat.

Variations

1. With your sponge and white paint make your own Frosty. How about adding some friends for Frosty? Decorate them with special hats, faces, and so on.
2. Add "snow" to any of your other winter projects by just dabbing with your sponge.

6-1 "ANGELA" THE ANGEL

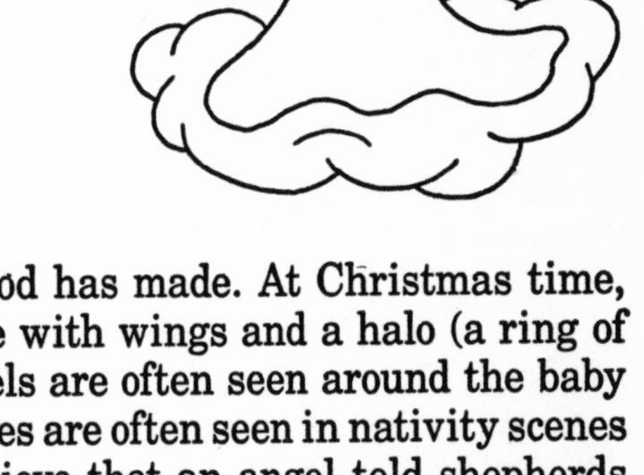

Theme Christmas

Skills Conceptual development—religion
Small-muscle control
Eye-hand coordination

Ages 5–7

Angel Facts

According to the Bible, angels are spirits that God has made. At Christmas time, angels are usually pictured as white-robed people with wings and a halo (a ring of light around the head). On Christmas cards, angels are often seen around the baby Jesus in the stable where he was born. Angel statues are often seen in nativity scenes in Christian homes and churches. Christians believe that an angel told shepherds that Jesus was born. The angel then told the shepherds to go to a stable in Bethlehem where the baby Jesus lay.

Materials for Each Child

- 9″ x 12″ white ditto or construction paper
- 9″ x 12″ colored construction paper
- Felt-tipped pens or crayons
- Scissors

Teacher Directions

Angela is an easy coloring and cutting project that looks great when puffed out and stapled to contrasting construction paper. (You may wish to do the stapling.) (*Alternative*: This project may be photocopied or traced onto a ditto.)

Steps for Students

1. Trace Angela onto white construction paper. (Or, try drawing your own angel. Make it big enough to fill your piece of paper.)
2. Draw in lines separating her halo from her head, and her head from her body.
3. Color her halo yellow and the rest of Angela in your favorite colors and patterns.

4. Cut out Angela. Staple to colored construction paper with a puff in the middle:

Variation

After you color and cut out Angela, punch a hole near the top of her head and tie on a 6″ to 8″ piece of string. Tie all the angels on a piece of string strung across a corner of your room. The angels will "fly" in the breeze.

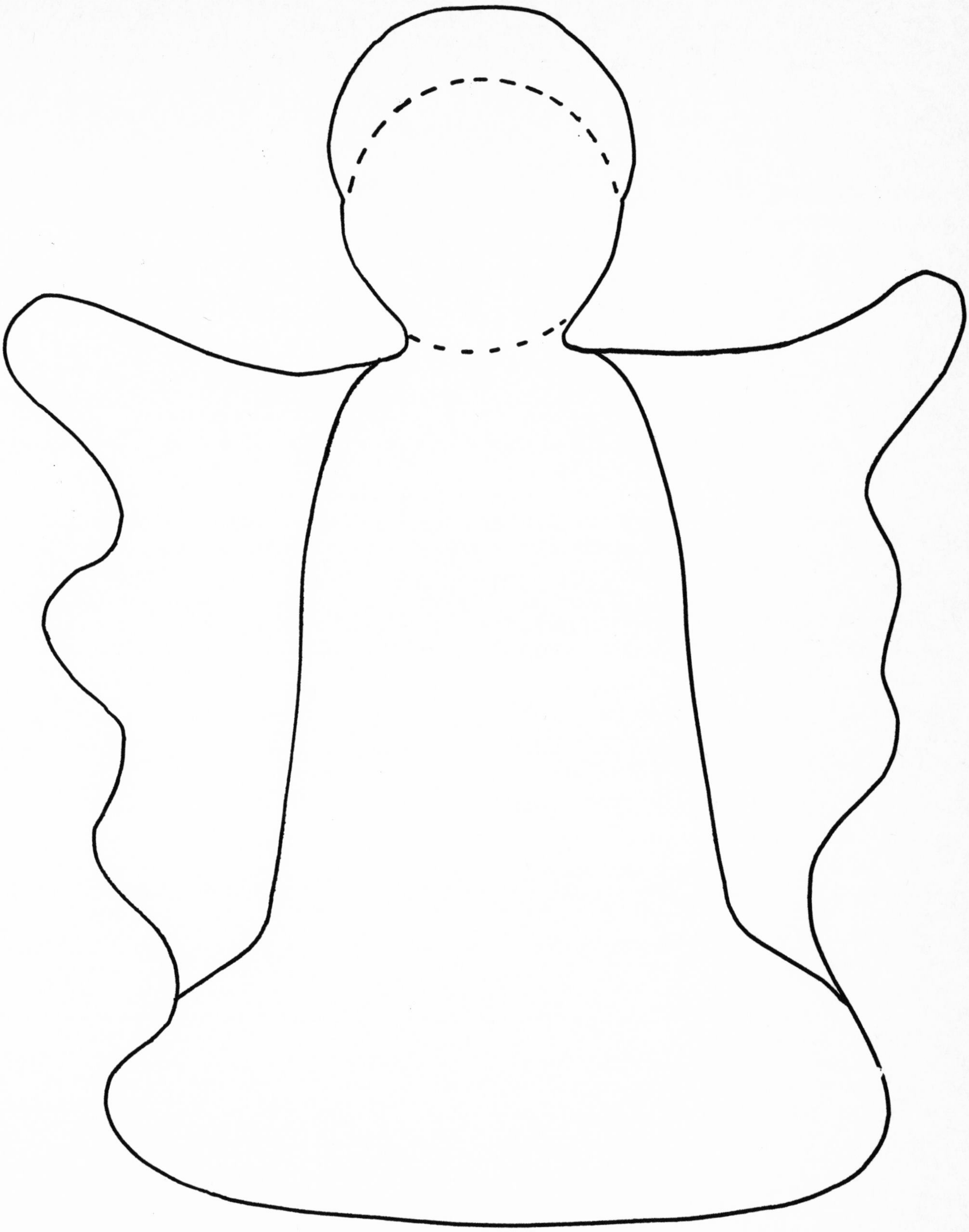

6-2 PUSH-PAINT CHRISTMAS TREE

Theme Christmas

Skills Conceptual development—history/religion
Quantity measuring
Small-muscle control
Patterning

Ages 3–7

Christmas Tree Facts

An old German story about the Christmas tree tells of a man who noticed the stars twinkling through the branches of a pine tree as he walked home on Christmas Eve. It was so beautiful that he wanted his wife to see it. So he cut down a small pine tree and brought it home. He put small lighted candles on it to look like twinkling stars. Other people saw the beautiful tree and did the same in their homes.

German people coming to America in 1830, brought the idea of the Christmas tree to our country.

Materials for Each Child

- 9″ x 12″ white construction paper
- 9″ x 12″ red construction paper
- Green and white tempera paint
- 2 small margarine cups or bowls
- 2 plastic spoons
- Scissors

Teacher Directions

Spread newspaper on the project table. Demonstrate for the children how to make small drops of paint on the paper by taking a spoon of paint and touching it to the paper in various spots, allowing a drop to drip off the spoon. Remind them not to shake the paint off the spoon, as it will splatter on them.

Steps for Students

1. Trace the tree pattern on the white construction paper (or, draw a big pine tree by yourself).
2. Fold the paper in half with the tree pattern on the outside.
3. Open the paper. Carefully take a spoon of green paint and make dots of paint on your paper.
4. Repeat using the white paint.
5. Close the paper back to its folded position, and gently "push" the paint to mix and flatten the colors.
6. Carefully rub a craft stick or ruler from top to bottom of paper squeezing out any excess paint onto the newspaper.
7. Open your paper and let dry.
8. From unpainted (pattern lined) side, cut out your tree.
9. Staple edges to red construction paper.

Variation

In connection with a lesson on the primary colors and color mixing, instead of using green and white paint, use blue and yellow. The blending of these two primaries produces a beautiful blend of colors from blue-green to light yellow-green.

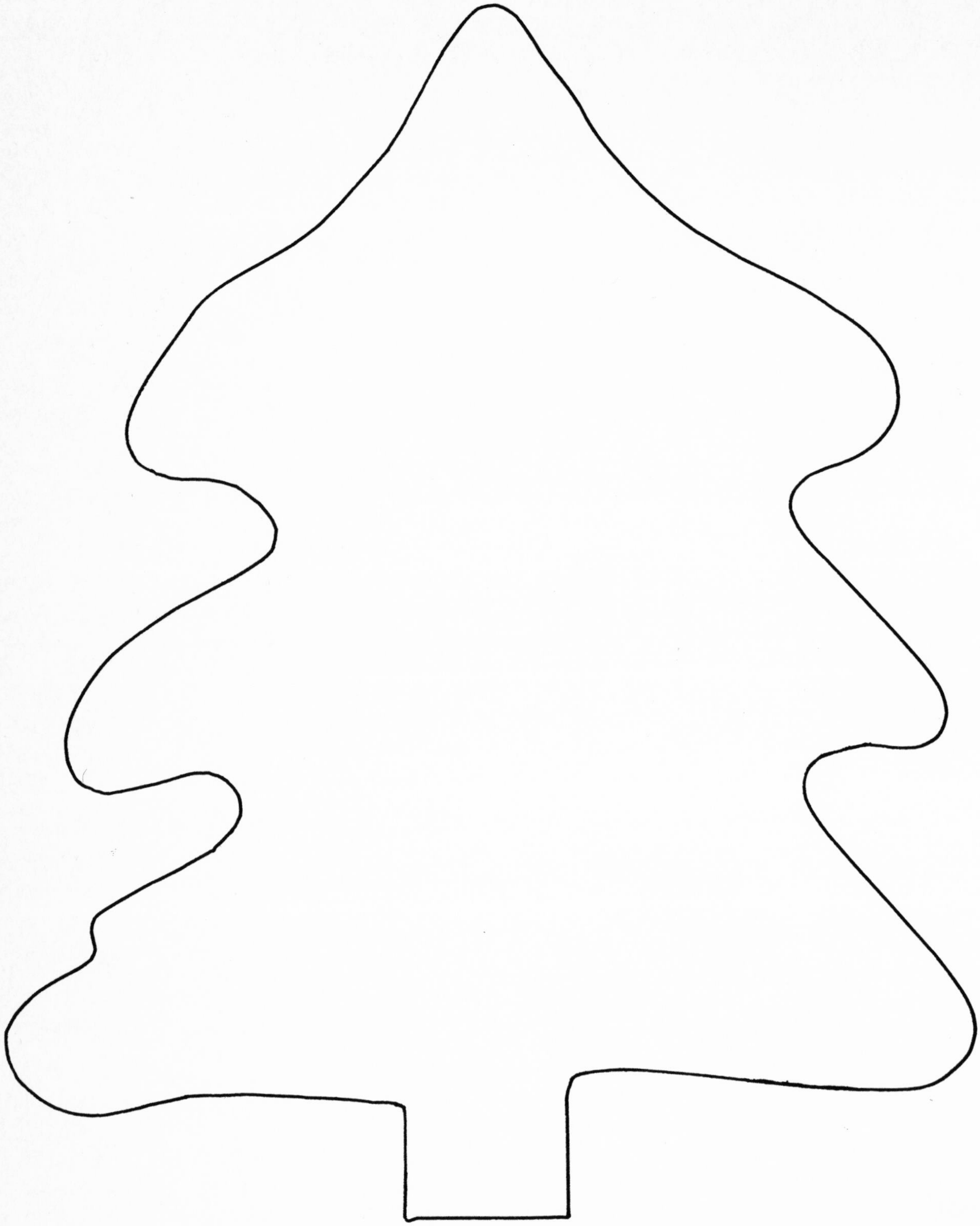

6-3 STUFFED STOCKING

Theme Christmas

Skills Conceptual development—legends
Following directions
Eye-hand coordination
Small-muscle control

Ages 3–7

Christmas Stocking Facts

An old story tells us that the kindly and generous St. Nicholas often helped out poor people wherever he went. When he came upon a man who did not have any money to give to his three daughters as wedding presents, St. Nicholas slipped a bag of gold in the man's window. It is said that some gold fell into a stocking that was drying by the fire. This is how the hanging of stockings on the fireplace at Christmas time started.

Materials for Each Child

- Two 9″ x 12″ white or yellow construction paper
- Felt-tipped pens or crayons
- Piece of newspaper
- 8″ piece of yarn
- Scissors
- Hole puncher

Teacher Directions

Show children how to fold the paper in half on the 12″ side and place the pattern on the fold for tracing:

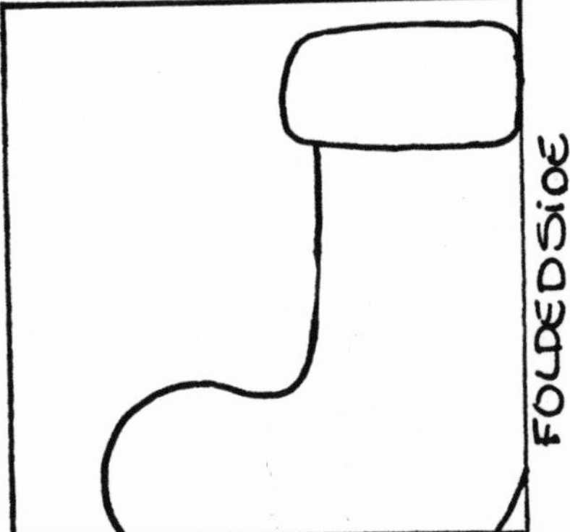

Steps for Students

1. Fold one piece of construction paper in half on the long side.
2. Place the back of the stocking pattern on the fold line and trace.
3. Decorate your stocking with felt-tipped markers or crayons.
4. Cut out the stocking. Do not cut on fold line.
5. Puff stocking slightly and staple:

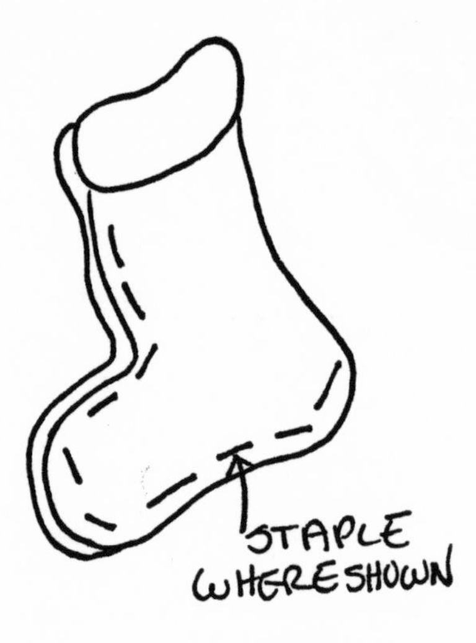

6. Rip newspaper into small pieces and stuff stocking half way up.
7. Trace the "stocking stuffers" on the other piece of construction paper.
8. Decorate them. Cut them out and place them in stocking.
9. Punch a hole in the top corner of the stocking and string it with yarn.

Variation

Cut out pictures of toys you like from magazines or toy catalogs and put them in your stocking.

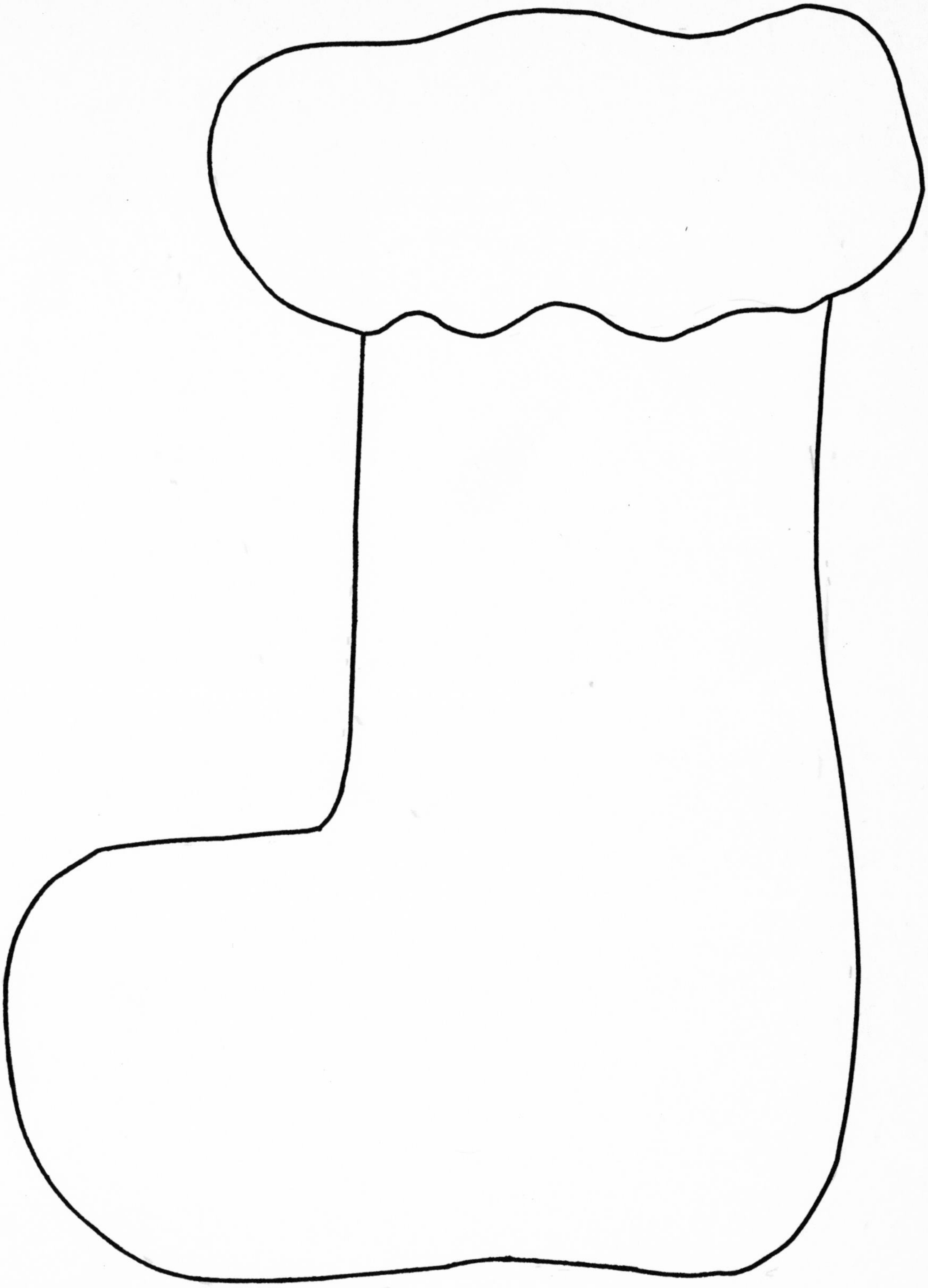

6-4 SPONGE-PAINTED SANTA

Theme Christmas

Skills Conceptual development—legends
Small-muscle control
Spatial relationships
Creative dramatics
Detail awareness

Ages 3–7

Santa Claus Facts

Stories about Santa Claus have been around for 1600 years! One old story tells us about a bishop named Nicholas. He was a very kindly man who helped many people. Because he did so many good deeds, the Church made Nicholas a saint. The German people called him "San Nikolaus," or "San Klaus" for short. Santa Claus is the American and English way of saying Saint Nicholas. Later, in Germany, Saint Nicholas became connected with Christmas and the idea of giving gifts.

Materials for Each Child

- 9″ x 12″ pink construction paper
- White tempera paint
- Small piece of sponge
- Styrofoam tray or piece of aluminum foil
- Felt-tipped pens or crayons
- Scissors

Teacher Directions

Discuss the parts of the face and their placement. Show the children some pictures of different looking Santas or men with beards to give them a sense of the variety of ways Santa can look. Then talk about the details of the face: eyelashes, eyebrows, cheeks, nostrils. Put a small amount of paint on the tray or foil (with edges folded up).

Steps for Students

1. Trace Santa onto pink construction paper.
2. Draw lines to separate Santa's hat and beard.

3. With your felt-tipped markers or crayons, give Santa a happy face. (Don't forget his rosy cheeks!)
4. Color Santa's hat red.
5. With the small piece of sponge dab on white paint to make Santa's beard, moustache, fur on hat, and pompon.

Variation

1. Make a Santa mask using oaktag instead of construction paper. Proceed as above. Cut out eyes.
2. Glue a craft stick halfway up on Santa's beard. Let it dry. Practice "Ho, ho, ho's"!

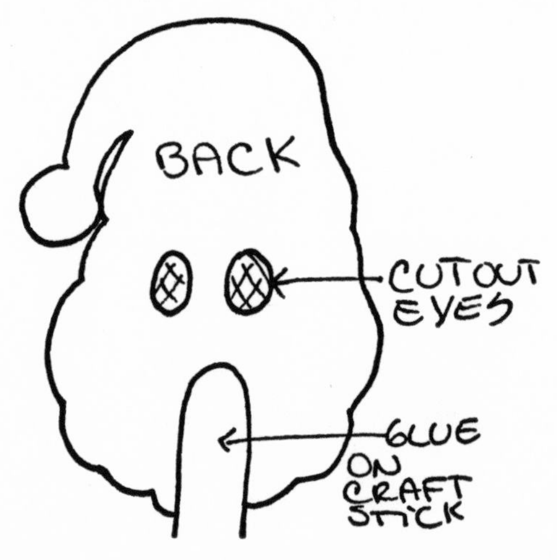

6-5 BABY JESUS IN CRIB

Theme Christmas

Skills Conceptual development—religion
Following directions
Spatial relationships
Sequencing
Eye-hand coordination

Ages 4–7

Christmas Facts

The Old Testament of the Bible promised a Messiah, or Savior, who would come to earth to save the people. Christians have believed that Jesus is the Messiah for nearly two thousand years. Jewish people and many others think that the Messiah has not yet come. Jesus was born in a stable in Bethlehem, Palestine. His mother is called the Virgin Mary, and his father, St. Joseph.

Materials for Each Child

- 6″ x 9″ (½ of 9″ x 12″) light tan or beige construction paper
- 9″ x 12″ blue construction paper
- Twigs, dried grass, dried pine needles, or small piece of yellow tissue paper
- Felt-tipped pens or crayons
- Scissors

Teacher Directions

Explain the sequence of placing the three parts of this project: crib first, hay second, baby Jesus last. If small twigs are used to make the crib, have children place the twigs, in formation, on their construction paper, and squeeze on drops of glue at the points where the twigs hit the paper.

Steps for Students

1. Trace, or draw, baby Jesus on your construction paper.
2. Draw lines for his halo and head:

3. Color Jesus' halo yellow. Give him a face. You can make him sleeping or awake. Color his blanket. Make it very pretty.

4. Cut baby Jesus out.
5. Glue craft sticks, stirrers, or twigs in an "x" on paper to make the crib.

6. Squirt some glue on the top part of your crib. Press some dried grass or hay, etc. onto glue.
7. Put glue on the back of your baby Jesus and gently place him on top of the hay.

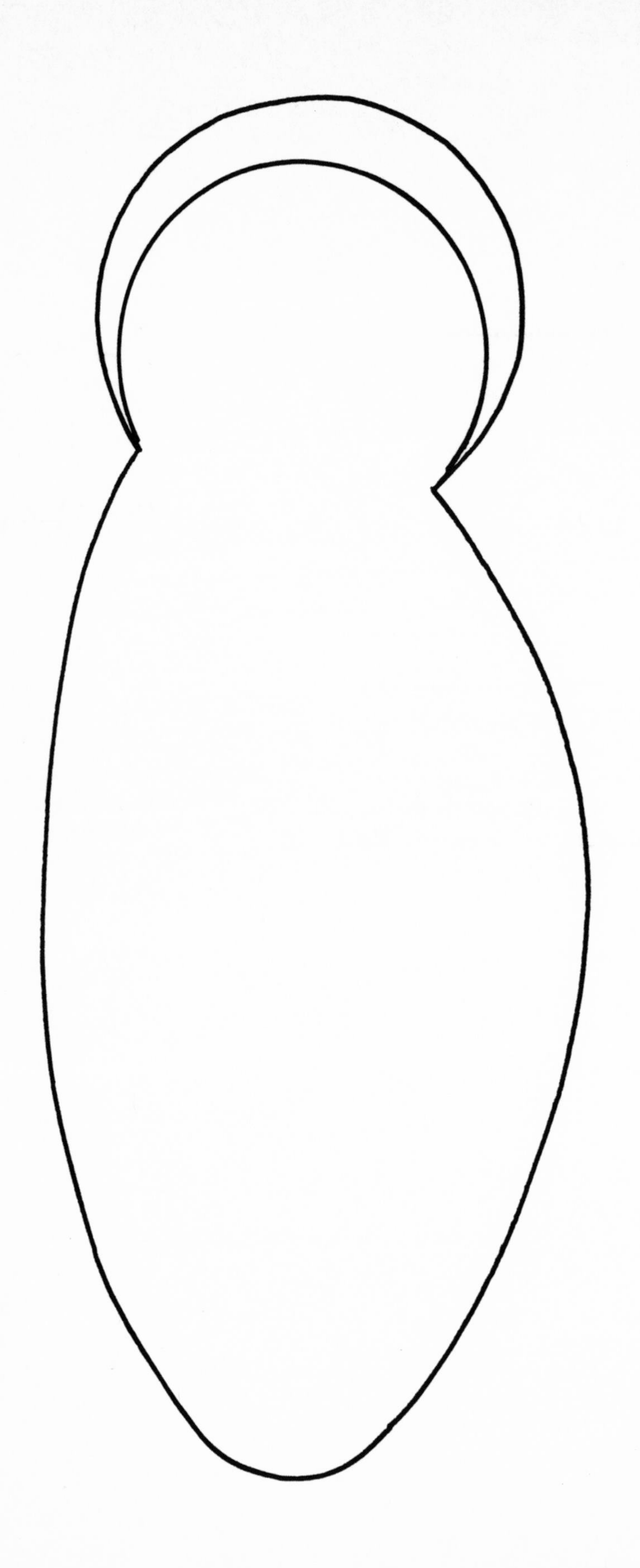

6-6 SANTA'S TRAIN

Theme Christmas

Skills Conceptual development—history
Shape discrimination
Small muscle control
Creative dramatics

Ages 5–8

Train Facts

The railroad was first seen in the United States in 1800. Before the steam engine, railroad cars were pulled along the tracks by horses and mules. The first steam engines burned wood, and later coal, to make their steam power. A speed of 30 miles per hour was considered fast for those trains. The cars were made of wood and they would shake and rattle as they rolled along. Passengers often got dirty and were choked by the smoke and soot from the coal fires. Today diesel engines smoothly pull trains along at average speeds of sixty to eighty miles per hour.

Materials for Each Child

- 9″ x 12″ white construction paper or oaktag
- 2 paper fasteners (brads)
- Felt-tipped pens or crayons
- Cellophane tape
- Scissors

Teacher Directions

Show children how to place patterns so that they all fit on their paper. Discuss with the children the shapes they can see in Santa's train. You may wish to attach the wheels with the paper fasteners. (After inserting each paper fastener turn it around a few times to make sure it is loose enough to allow the wheels to turn.) You may also want to attach the pocket in Step 5.

Steps for Students

1. Trace the train, wheels, and Santa patterns on your paper.
2. With your crayons or felt-tipped markers color the train—use bright, Christmas colors. Give Santa a red suit and hat. Black boots, belt, and buttons would be nice.
3. Cut everything out.
4. Attach the wheels with the paper fasteners, from front to back.

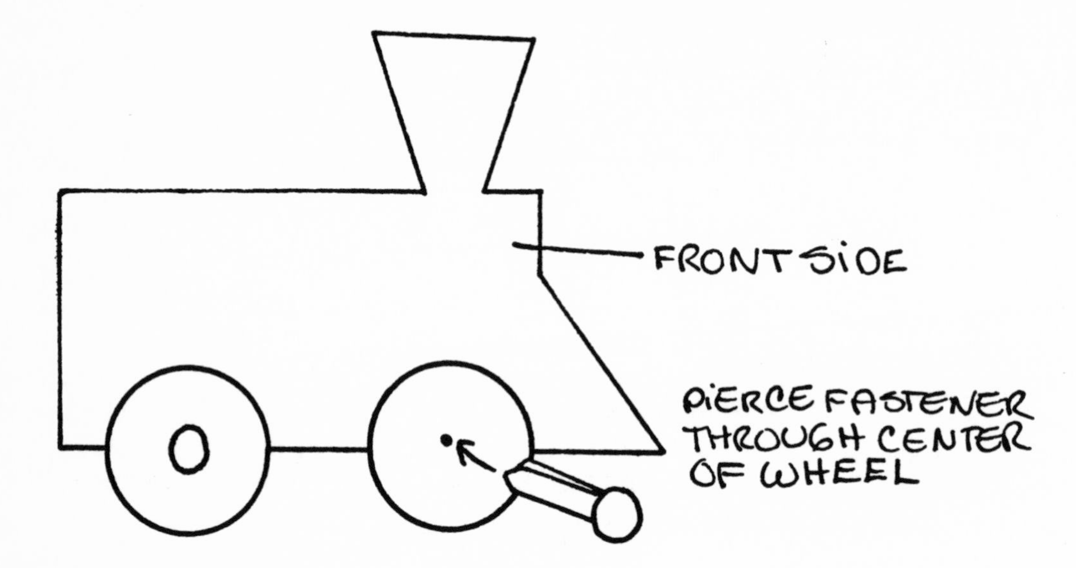

5. Make a little pocket for Santa to stand in by taping the square piece of paper to the back of the train:

6. Put Santa in his train and roll along the carpet or up your arm. Use your Santa to talk to your friends about what they want for Christmas.

Follow-ups

1. Now draw (or paint) a Santa and his train of your own.
2. You can add cars to Santa's train to hold his toys. Use 3″ x 6″ construction paper for the cars. Decorate the cars and add wheels and a pocket on the back of the car. Make some simple toy shapes and insert in pocket.

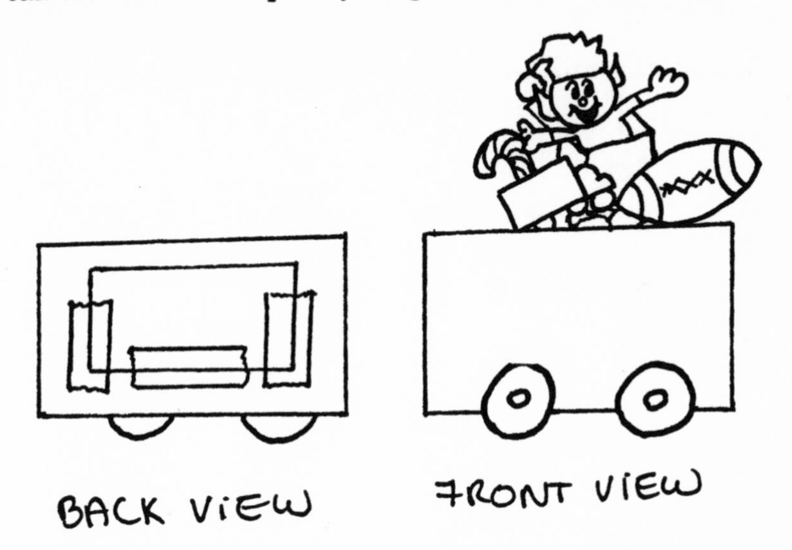

Attach to the engine with a peel-and-stick label or glue on a strip of construction paper.

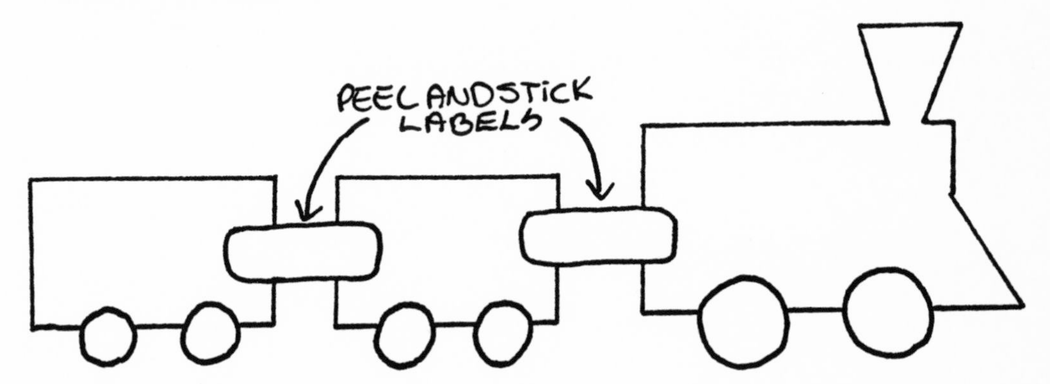

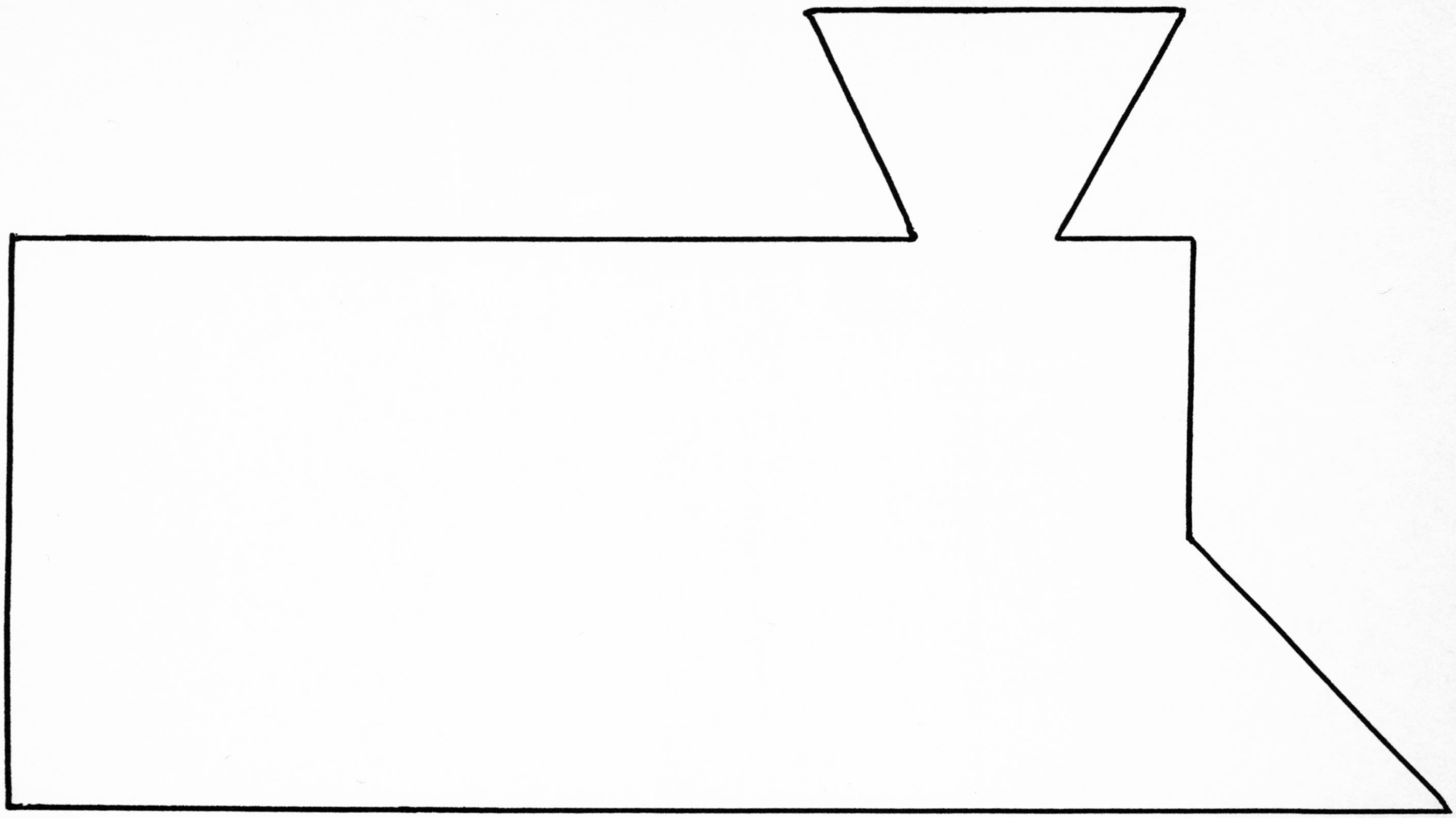

6-7 SNIP-SNIP TREE

Theme Christmas

Skills Conceptual development—nature
Eye-hand coordination
Size/shape discrimination
Spatial relationships

Ages 3–6

Evergreen Facts

The traditional Christmas tree is an evergreen. An evergreen is any plant that keeps its leaves or needles all year 'round. A popular evergreen is the fir tree. The white fir grows as high as 300 feet. It takes 150 to 250 years to finish growing. The wood of the Balsam fir is often used to make musical instruments and the masts of ships.

Materials for Each Child

- 9″ x 12″ green construction paper
- Scissors
- Stapler

Teacher Directions

This is a very easy project, with good results! Discuss the placing of the three circle patterns so that they all fit on the paper. (*Alternative*: This project may be photocopied or traced over onto a ditto.)

Steps for Students

1. Trace the three circle patterns on your paper.
2. Cut them out.
3. Snip the edges of all three circles:

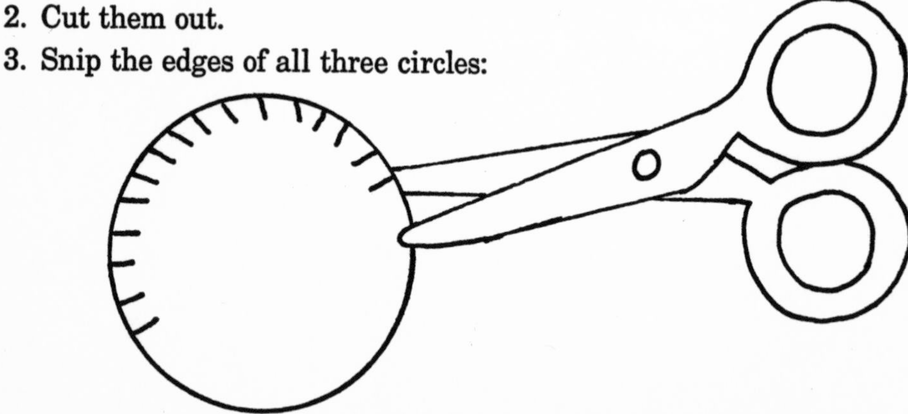

4. Gently bend the edges upward.
5. Cut each circle to the middle:

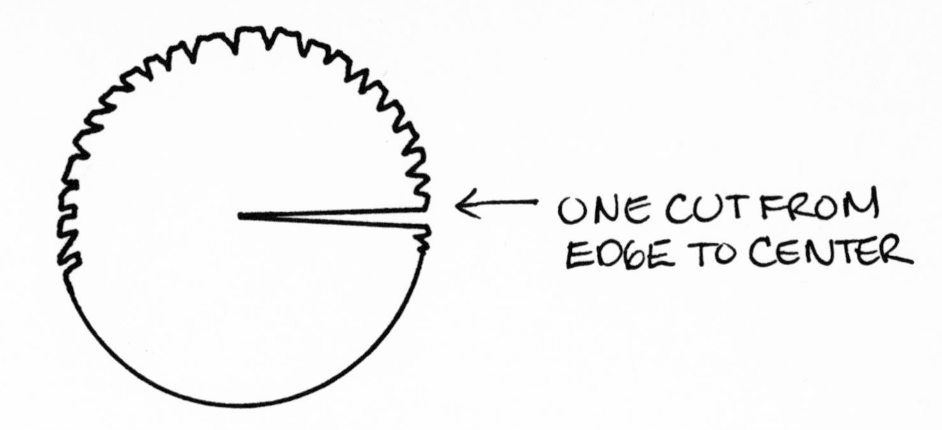

6. Form into a cone shape and staple:

7. Put the second largest cone on top of the largest, and the smallest on top of them.

Variations

1. Decorate your circles by making Christmas balls with your felt-tipped pens or crayons before you form them into cones.
2. Put drops of glue, then glitter your circles.

6-8 THE HOLY FAMILY

Theme Christmas

Skills Conceptual development—religion
Small-muscle control
Eye-hand coordination
Creative dramatics

Ages 4–7

Holy Family Facts

The story of Mary and Joseph starts in Nazareth, Palestine, the homeland of the Jews. Mary was engaged to Joseph, a carpenter. The Bible says God chose Joseph to be Mary's husband. Joseph was a kind and good man. Before their marriage, an angel came to Mary and told her that she would have a son, and that he would grow up to save his people. Several months later, Mary had to go with Joseph on business to the city of Bethlehem. There was no room for them to stay at the inn in Bethlehem, so they spent the night in a stable. There Jesus was born. His parents laid Jesus in a cattle-feeding trough, filled with soft straw.

Materials for Each Child

- 9″ x 12″ oaktag or white construction paper
- Felt-tipped pens or crayons
- Scissors

Teacher Directions

Show children how to place the patterns on their paper so that they all fit. Start with the two large patterns. Depending on the age of your children, you may wish to make the slits for the arms yourself. They are made easily by poking the point of a scissor through at the marked spot, or laying the pattern on newspaper and making the slit with a single-edge razor blade. (*Alternative*: This project may be photocopied or traced over onto a ditto.)

Steps for Students

1. Trace the patterns on your paper or oaktag, starting with the largest pattern.
2. With your felt-tipped pens or crayons, give Mary, Joseph, and Jesus happy faces. Color their clothes and arms.

3. Carefully cut out all the patterns.
4. Make slits in the Mary and Joseph patterns as shown:

5. Bend back the lower edges of Mary's and Joseph's robes and staple:

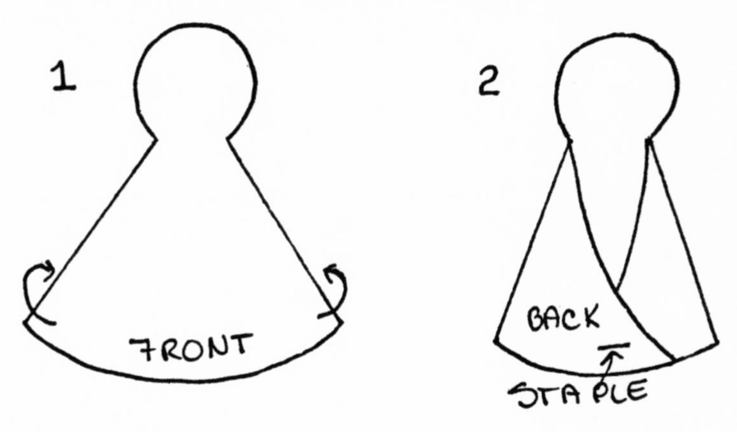

6. Insert the arms:

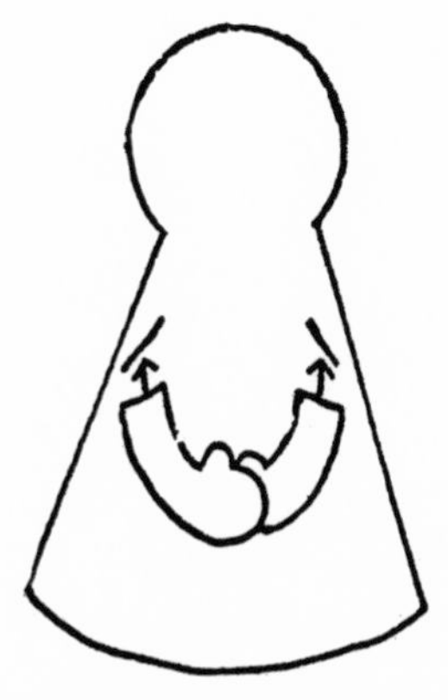

7. Place Baby Jesus in the arms of one of his parents.
8. Use the figures to tell the Christmas story.

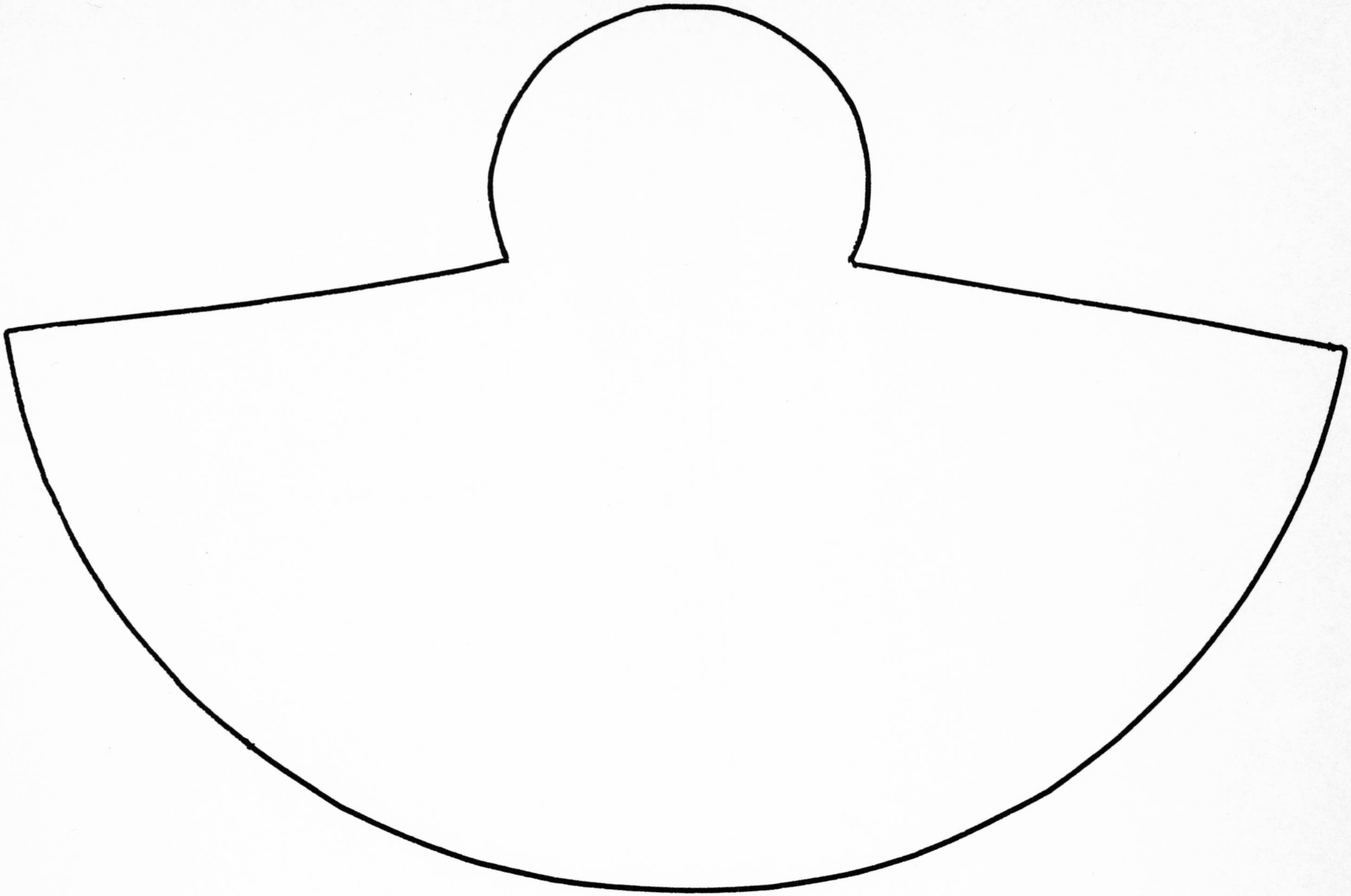

6-9 POINSETTIA

Theme Christmas

Skills Conceptual development—nature, legends
Spatial relationships
Small-muscle control
Concrete counting
Patterning

Ages 4–7

Poinsettia Facts

The poinsettia is the Christmas flower of North America. The poinsettia plant is actually a shrub that flowers in the winter. In Hawaii and in some parts of the southern United States they are grown outside as a hedge. One old story about the poinsettia plant is a tale about a poor Mexican girl who was heartbroken because she had nothing valuable or pretty to offer the Virgin Mary at Christmas. So, she picked some flowering weeds and placed them at the feet of a special statue of Mary. The weeds were immediately changed into brilliant poinsettias.

Materials for Each Child

- 9″ x 12″ red construction paper
- 9″ x 12″ green construction paper
- 9″ x 12″ white construction paper
- 2″ x 2″ yellow construction paper
- Glue
- Scissors

Teacher Directions

Demonstrate the placing of the patterns so that you can get six red leaves and six green. The green leaf has the pointed sides, and the red leaf has smooth sides.

Steps for Students

1. Trace the pattern for the red leaves on the red construction paper.
2. Trace the pattern for the green leaves on the green paper.
3. Cut out all your leaves.
4. Fold each leaf in the center, lengthwise. Then open it up halfway:

5. On the outside fold of the green leaves, put some glue.
6. Lay the green leaves in a circle on the white paper leaving about a 2″ circle in the center:

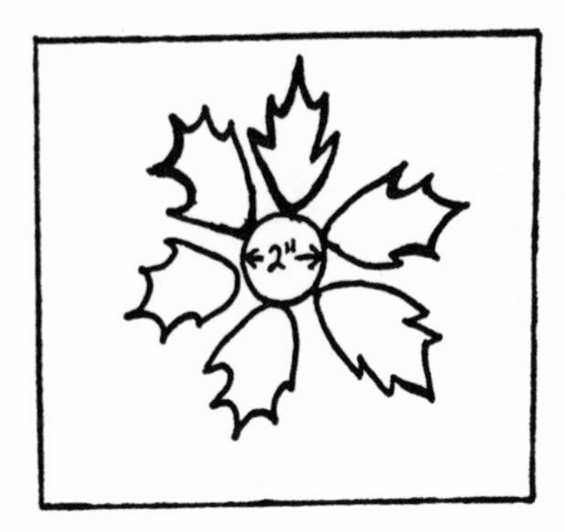

7. Glue the ends of the red leaves into the center of the circle.
8. Cut tiny circles, or just tiny pieces, out of your yellow construction paper. Glue them into the center of your flower.

Follow-up

Make several poinsettias. Glue them into a circle to make a poinsettia wreath. It makes a beautiful front door decoration.

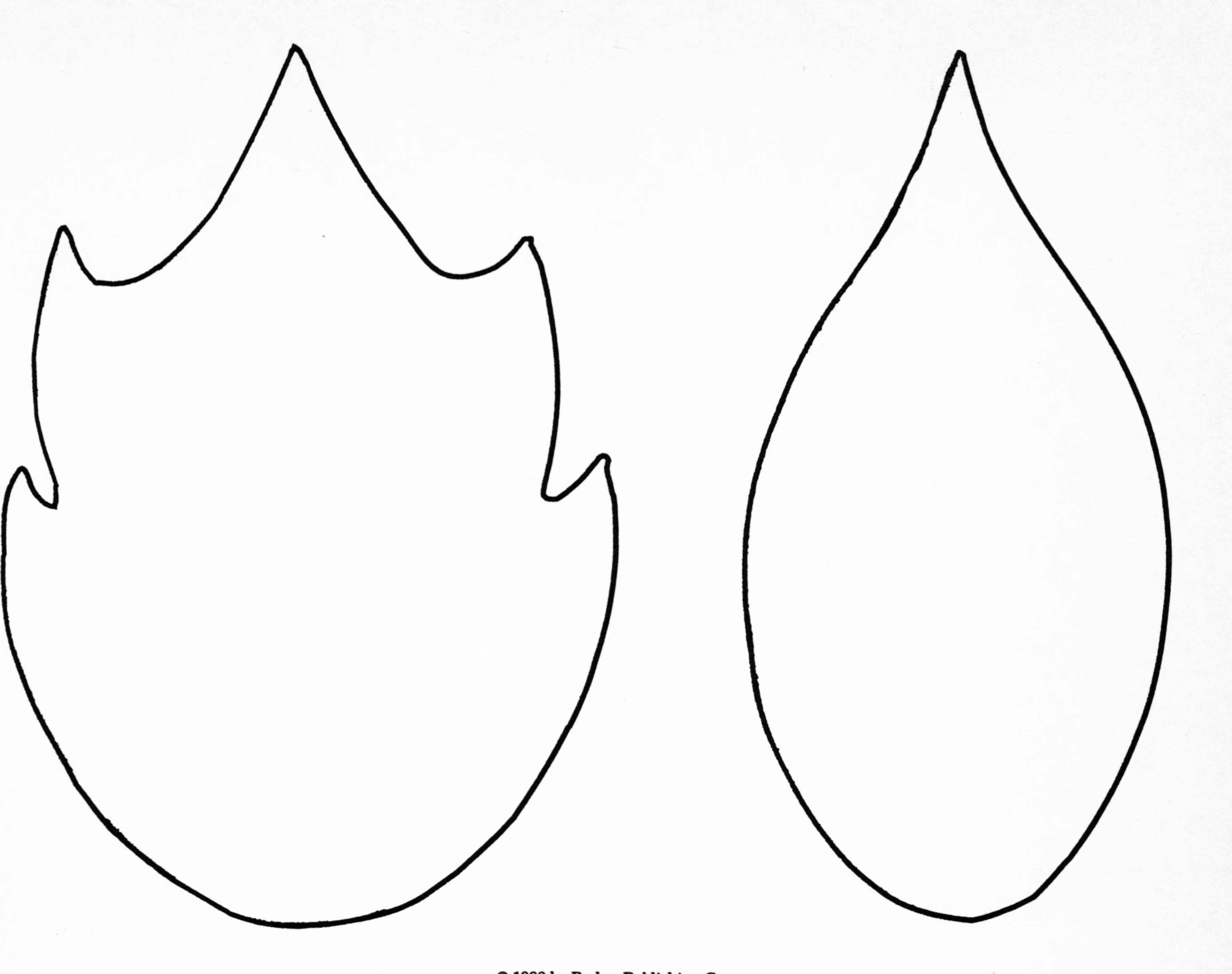

6-10 DIP-DOT TREE

Theme Christmas

Skills Conceptual development—legends
Eye-hand coordination
Spatial relationships
Patterning

Ages 3–7

Christmas Tree Facts

One of the legends about the origin of the Christmas tree says that the custom began even before Christmas began! People called Druids, who lived long ago in Europe, noticed that the evergreen tree was always green—even in winter. That made them think it must be a sign of long life. They began to honor the evergreen tree on their winter holidays. Later, when these people started to celebrate Christmas, they kept on using evergreen trees.

Materials for Each Child

- 9″ x 12″ green construction paper
- Styrofoam egg carton or small styrofoam or aluminum tray
- Yellow, red, blue tempera paint
- Three 3″ pieces of plastic straws

Teacher Directions

Put a small amount of each color paint in recesses of an egg carton or on a tray. Demonstrate dipping the end of the straw into the paint and dotting it onto paper. Discuss patterning (the tree on the left) or random spacing of dots (the tree on the right).

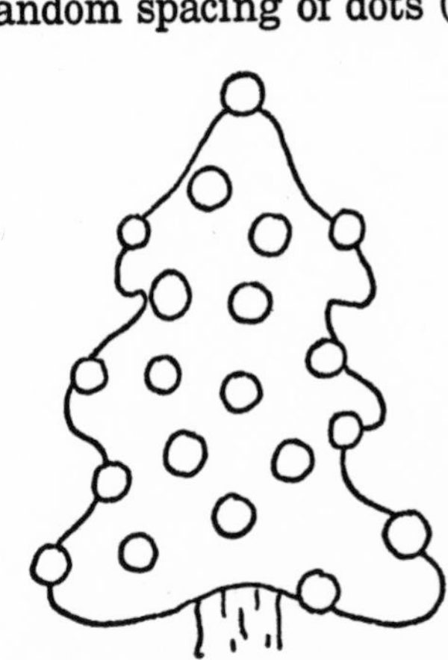

Steps for Students

1. Trace the tree pattern on your green construction paper.
2. Cut out the tree.
3. Dip the end of a straw into paint and touch to your tree.
4. Repeat using all your colors.

Variation

Paint dots can be "pulled" with the end of the straw to make interesting line patterns by placing dipped straw onto paper and dragging it along. Here is an example:

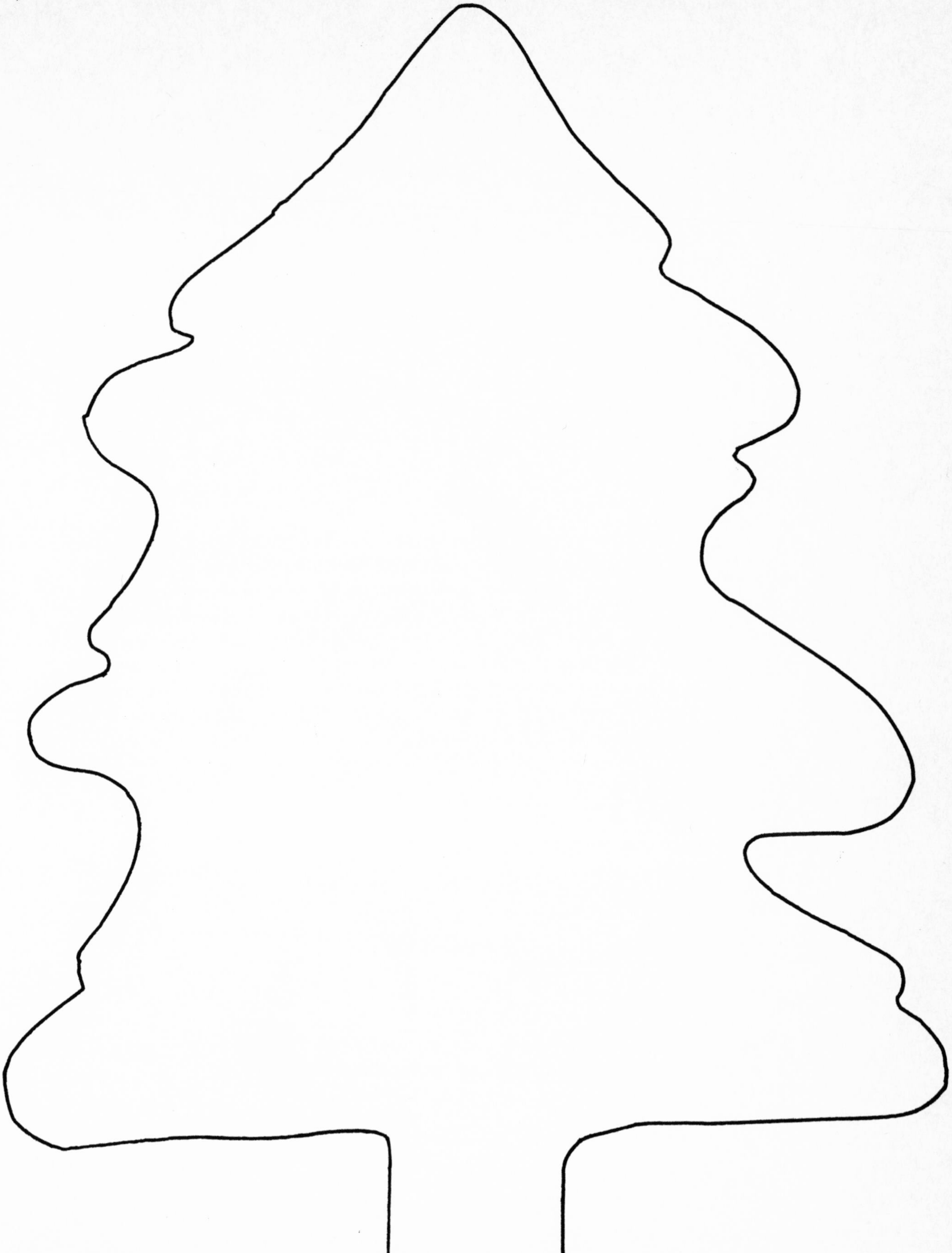

6-11 "WAGS" THE CHRISTMAS PUPPY

Theme Christmas

Skills Conceptual development—animals
Eye-hand coordination
Small-muscle control
Creative dramatics

Ages 4–7

Dog Facts

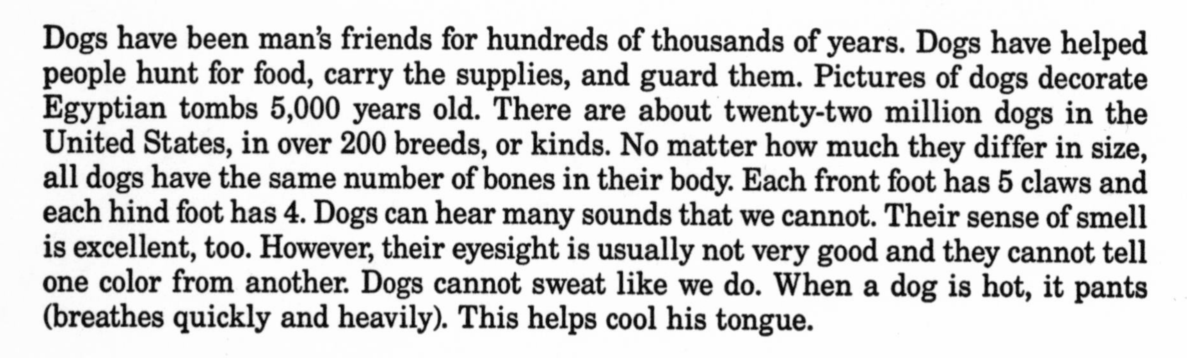

Dogs have been man's friends for hundreds of thousands of years. Dogs have helped people hunt for food, carry the supplies, and guard them. Pictures of dogs decorate Egyptian tombs 5,000 years old. There are about twenty-two million dogs in the United States, in over 200 breeds, or kinds. No matter how much they differ in size, all dogs have the same number of bones in their body. Each front foot has 5 claws and each hind foot has 4. Dogs can hear many sounds that we cannot. Their sense of smell is excellent, too. However, their eyesight is usually not very good and they cannot tell one color from another. Dogs cannot sweat like we do. When a dog is hot, it pants (breathes quickly and heavily). This helps cool his tongue.

Materials for Each Child

- 9″ x 12″ white construction paper or oaktag
- Felt-tipped pens or crayons
- Paper fastener (brad)
- Scissors

Teacher Directions

This is an easy, fun project that children love because Wags' tail and tongue move. You may wish to cut the slit for the mouth and insert the paper fastener.

Steps for Students

1. Trace the two patterns on your paper.
2. Color Wags' tail brown and tongue red:

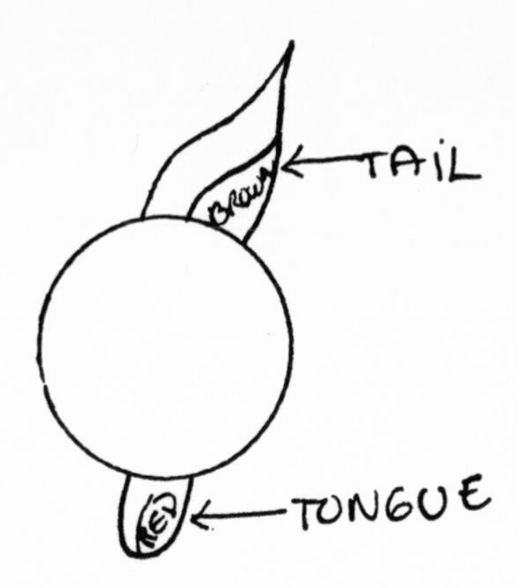

3. Draw Wags' two cute eyes and eyelashes.
4. You can color either all of Wags or just draw and color spots on him.
5. Cut out both patterns.
6. Lay the circle pattern on the back of Wags' head.

7. Trace a line to the right and left of Wags' tongue halfway around the circle.

8. Pick up the circle and connect the two lines.

9. With a scissor cut along this line; then cut back to the other side, cutting out a sliver of the paper, leaving a small mouth opening. Color the mouth on the front of Wags.
10. Put the circle back behind Wags' head, stick the tongue through the mouth opening.
11. Push the paper fastener, from front to back, into the center of the circle (at the point of Wags' nose).
12. Move Wags' tail back and forth and watch his tongue move too!
13. Use Wags to tell some dog stories.

Variation

Look at pictures of different kinds of dogs in the encyclopedia or in a dog book. Pick out one you like and try to make Wags look like him. Or, use your imagination and make up your own kind of dog!

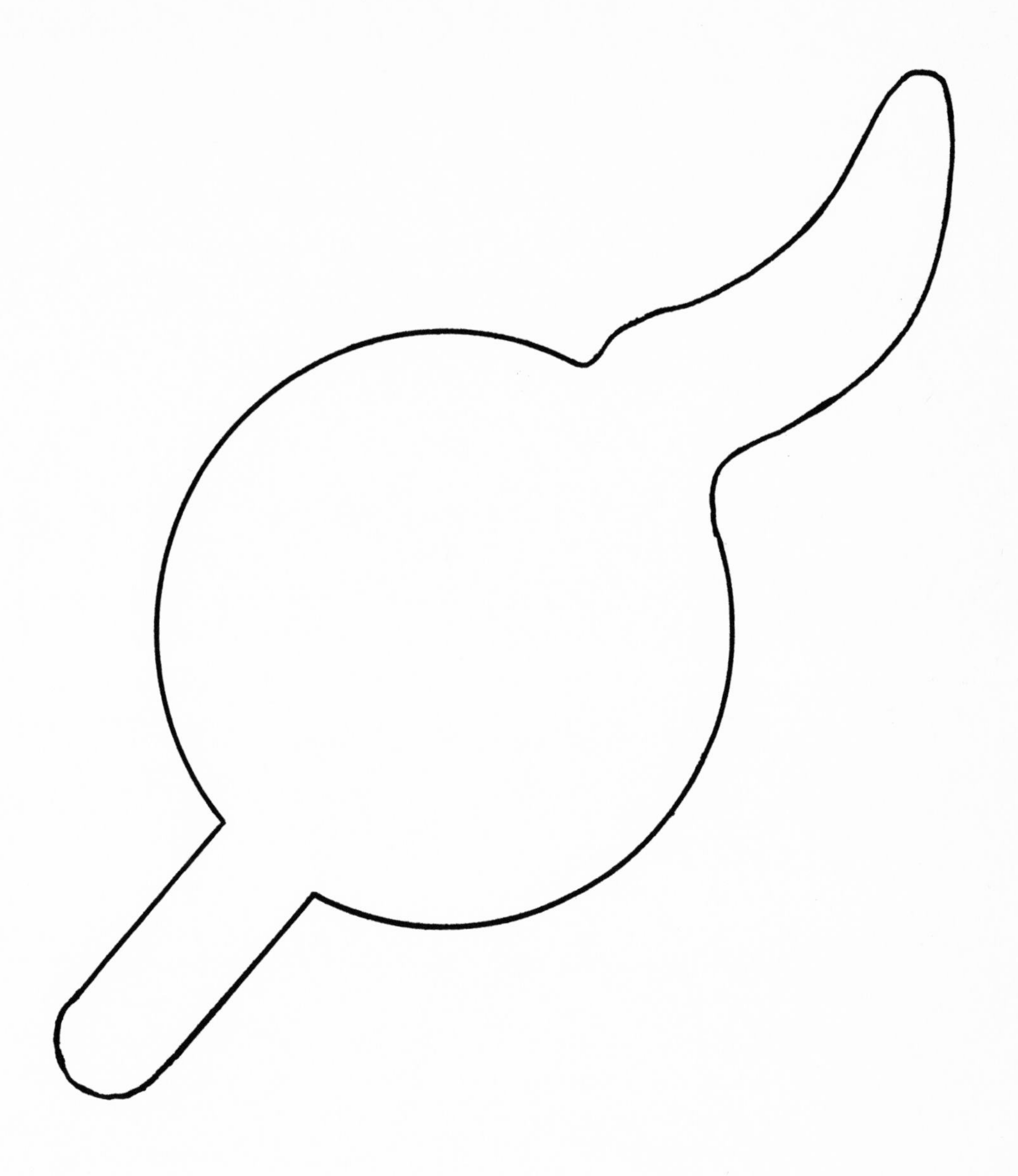

7-1 MENORAH

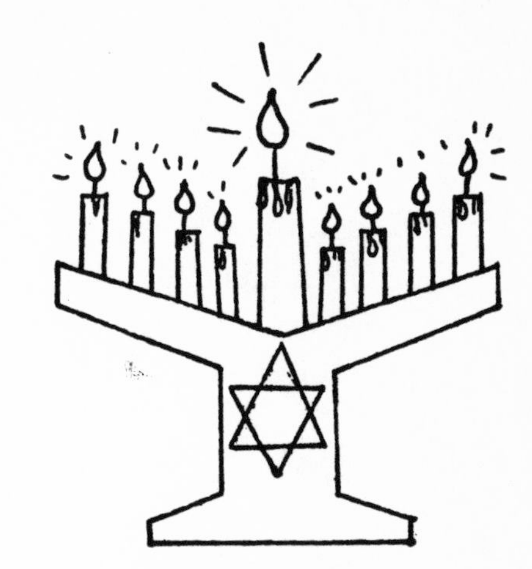

Theme Hanukkah

Skills Conceptual development—religion
Eye-hand coordination
Small-muscle control
Spatial relationships

Ages 4–8

Hanukkah Facts

Hanukkah is often called the Festival of Lights because candles are lit in Jewish homes and synagogues (a place where Jewish people gather to worship) during this eight-day celebration. The candles are held in a special candle holder called the Hanukkah menorah, which holds eight candles plus one in the center. During Hanukkah, Jewish people remember the victory of Jewish people who lived long ago (in the 2nd century B.C.). These brave people fought to be able to worship their own God. Judah Maccabee led the Jews in their battle against Antiochus IV. Maccabee inspired his people with these words: "Victory in battle does not depend on the size of an army, but on strength from Heaven." The Maccabees won their very hard struggle. The Jews rebuilt their temple and celebrated for eight days. Jewish people believe that when Judah Maccabee searched for oil to relight the menorah in the temple, he could only find enough oil to last for one day. Instead of lasting for one day, the oil lasted for eight days!

Materials for Each Child

- 9″ x 12″ yellow construction paper
- 9″ x 12″ blue construction paper
- 4 ½″ x 12″ (½ of a 9″ x 12″) white construction paper
- Felt-tipped pens or markers
- Glue
- Scissors

Teacher Directions

Explain that Hanukkah is a happy celebration and that the children should use bright, "happy" colors when decorating their candles. This is an easy craft, children should be able to complete it with little help.

Steps for Students

1. Trace the menorah, the Star of David, and the center candle on yellow construction paper. Cut them out.
2. Color the Star of David and glue it on the menorah.
3. Decorate the center candle with stripes, dots, and so on.
4. Glue the menorah and candle on the the blue paper.
5. Fold the 4 ½″ x 12″ white construction paper in half three times.
6. Open and cut on fold lines.
7. Decorate the candles and glue in place on menorah. Add orange and yellow flames.

Follow-ups

1. Make a menorah for the classroom. Add a flame to a candle each of eight school days available before or during Hanukkah.
2. During your in-school Hanukkah, have the children sample some of the foods eaten by Jewish people at this festive time of the year:

   Latkes (small potato cakes) found in the
   frozen food department of most supermarkets

   Applesauce

   Sour cream

   Butter cookies

   Cheese

7-2 POP-UP HANUKKAH CARD

Theme Hanukkah

Skills Conceptual development—religion
Small-muscle control
Eye-hand coordination

Ages 6–9

Hanukkah Facts

See project 7-1, "Menorah."

Materials for Each Child

- 9″ x 12″ yellow construction paper
- Scissors
- Glue
- Felt-tipped pens or crayons

Teacher Directions

If the skill level of the children makes it difficult for them to cut out candles while they are attached to the menorah, they can cut out the menorah, and then cut out candles separately and glue them on the menorah. (For younger children, this project should be photocopied or traced onto a ditto.)

Steps for Students

1. Cut the construction paper in half on the 12″ side.
2. Trace the menorah on one-half of your construction paper.
3. Color the menorah, candles, and flames.
4. Cut it out.
5. Fold the other half of the construction paper in half, then open it.

6. Fold the menorah as shown, then glue it onto the card:

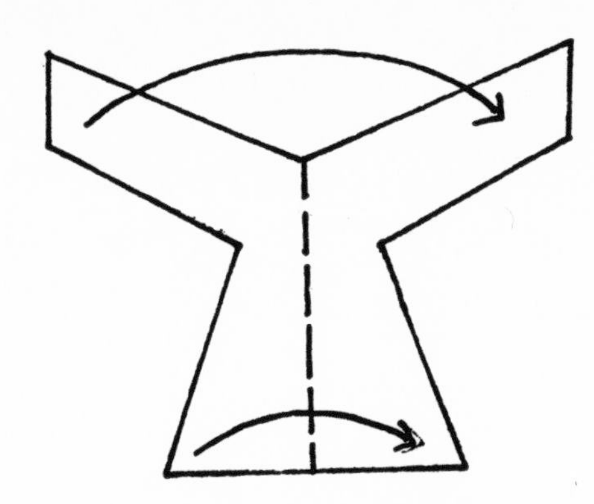

1 – FOLD FACE IN.

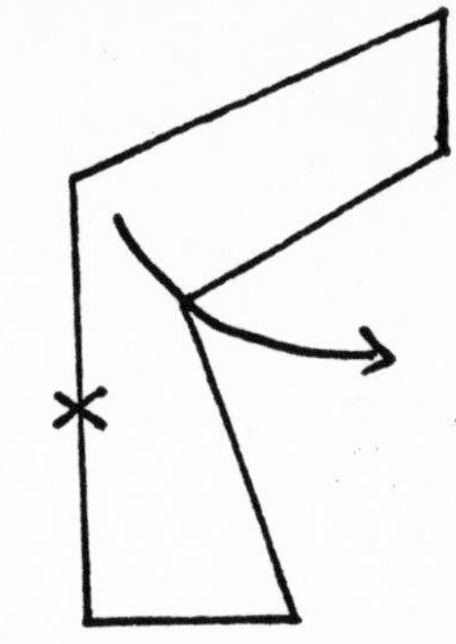

2 – AT POINT "X"
HALF WAY DOWN
FOLD MENORAH AT A
90° ANGLE TO ITSELF

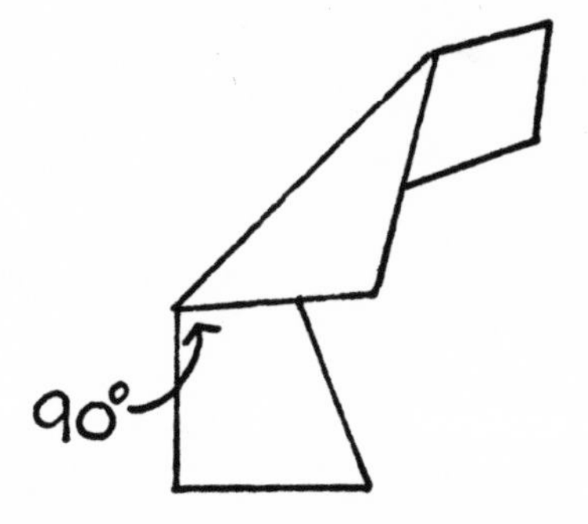

3 – FOLDED MENORAH
SHOULD RESEMBLE
THIS MODEL.

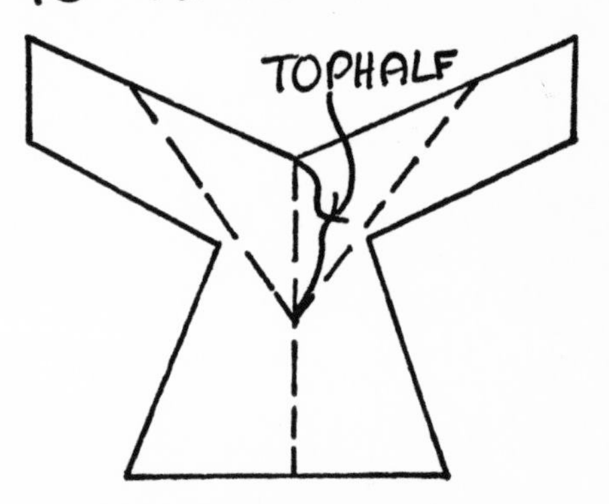

4 – UNFOLD, THEN
REFOLD BY FOLDING
THE TOP HALF IN (YOU
ARE REVERSING THAT FOLD)

7. Decorate the front of your card.

8-1 NEW YEAR'S HAT

Theme New Year's Eve

Skills Conceptual development—traditions
Eye-hand coordination
Small-muscle control

Ages 5–8

New Year Facts

Celebrating the first day of the year has been popular throughout the world for thousands of years. The date for celebrating the "New Year" is not the same in all countries. The ancient Egyptians and Persians began their year in the fall, on September 21. The Jews also celebrate their New Year in the fall. Long ago the Roman people used to celebrate the first day of the year on December 21 with masked processions. The Romans would parade around in masks, have big parties, and exchange gifts. In the past, in most Christian countries, March 25 was the first day of the year. In 1582, the first of January was made New Year's Day. In Scotland, New Year's Day is the most celebrated day of the year.

Materials for Each Child

- 9″ x 12″ oaktag or light colored construction paper
- Two 10″ pieces of yarn
- 4″ x 4″ piece of colored tissue paper
- Felt-tipped pens or crayons
- Scissors
- Tape or stapler

Teacher Directions

This is an easy project. Demonstrate different ways of decorating the hat: stripes, dots, zig-zags, and so on.

Steps for Students

1. Trace the circle pattern on your paper.
2. With your felt-tipped markers or crayons, decorate your hat with bright colors.

3. Cut to the center as shown:

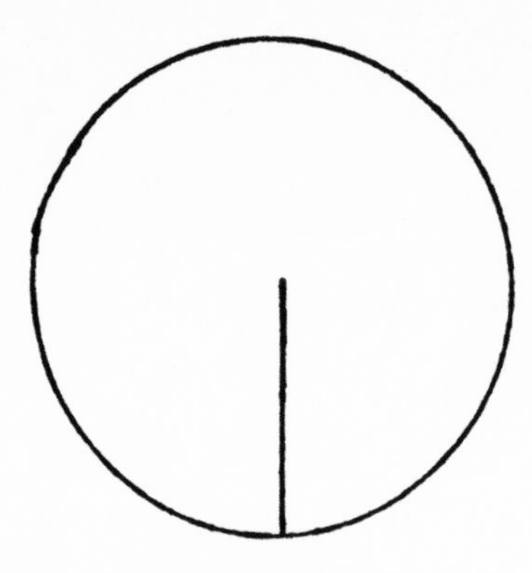

4. Fold the tissue paper in half three times; make cuts in the tissue three quarters of the way:

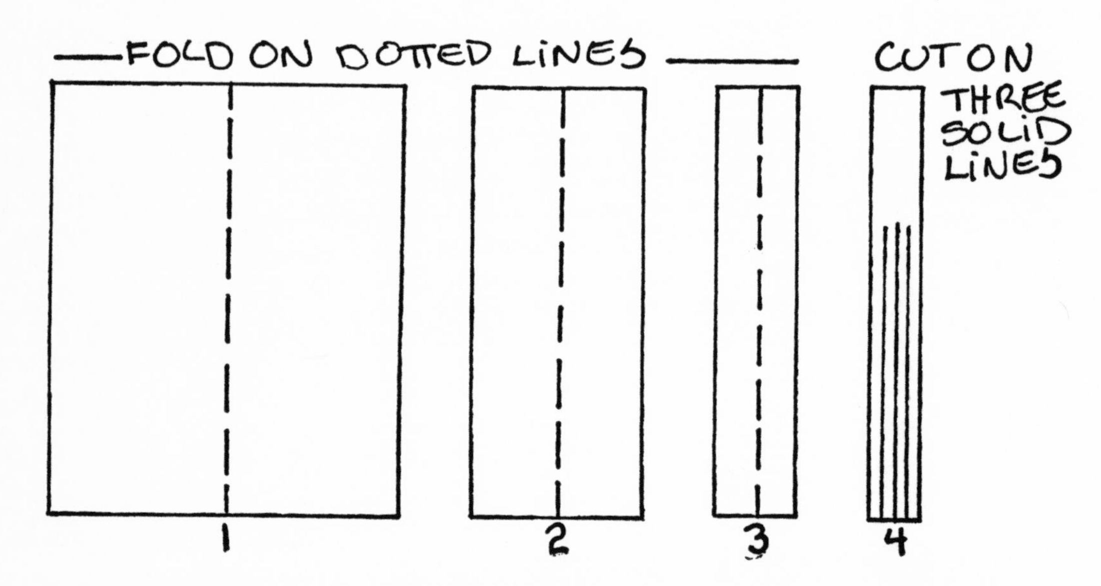

5. Tape or staple uncut end of the tissue paper in the center of the inside of the hat:

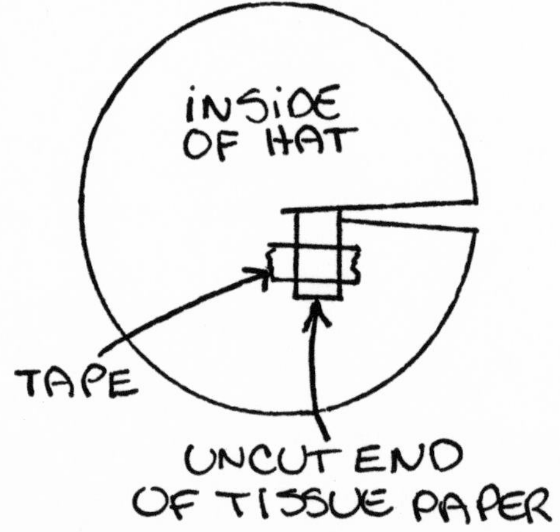

6. Staple into a cone shape:

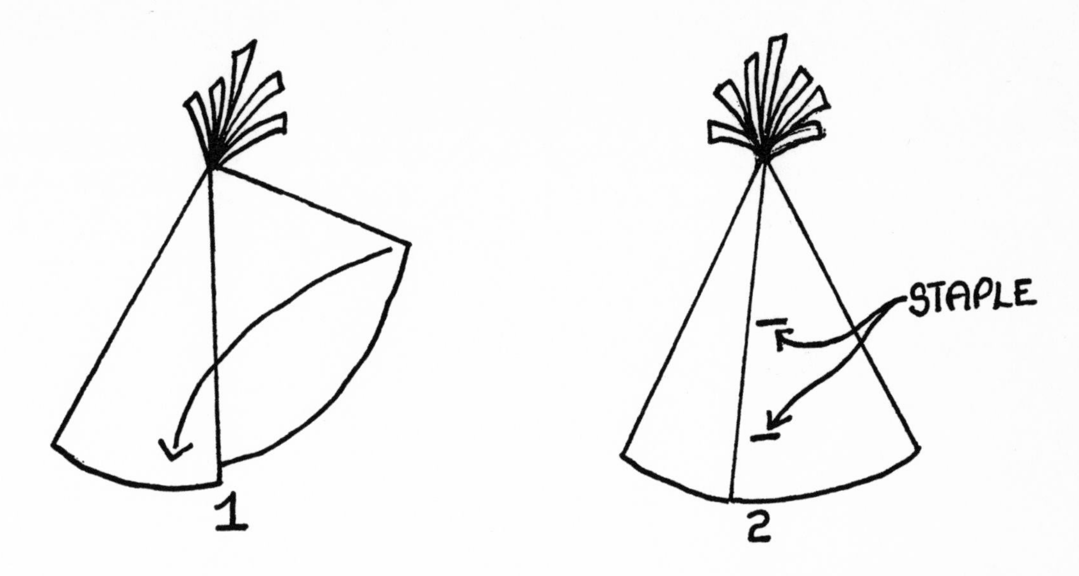

7. Punch holes in sides of hat or make holes with a scissor point.
8. String with yarn.
9. Tie the hat on your head and celebrate!

Follow-up

Make a hat for each member of your family and wear them at your next "New Year's" meal.

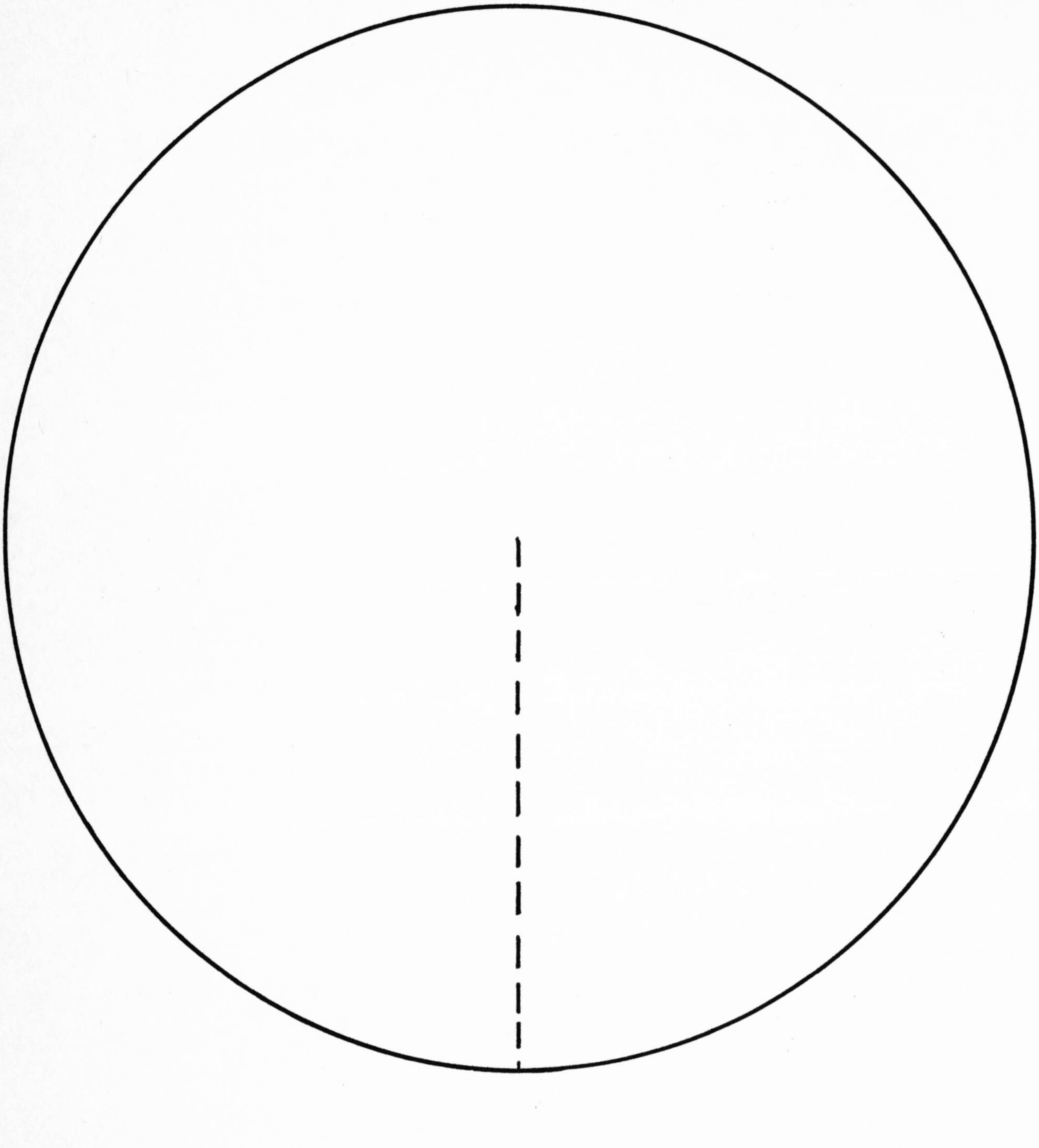

9-1 SUN-GLOW HEART

Theme Valentine's Day

Skills Conceptual development—history
Eye-hand coordination
Small-muscle control
Spatial relationships
Patterning
Color awareness

Ages 3–8

Valentine Facts

February 14 is the day we remember St. Valentine and give cards to people we love. Actually there were different St. Valentines, from five countries! No one knows exactly why these saints are connected with sending messages of love. Some people feel that celebrating St. Valentine's Day began long ago in Rome. Each February young Roman men and women held a carnival. They would put the names of all the women in a box; if a young man wanted a date for the carnival, he would pick a name out of the box. Christian priests thought this was foolish. So, they put the names of saints in the box, and called the celebration St. Valentine's Day. After a young man picked a name from the box, he would have to say prayers to that saint. The young Romans did not like this idea and refused to pick from the box. The name of this February holiday is still called St. Valentine's Day and people still celebrate it with messages of love.

Materials for Each Child

- 9″ x 12″ tracing paper
- Red and white tissue paper squares, approximately 1½″ square
- Glue mix: half white glue and half water in small bowl or cup (can be shared by 2 or 3 children)
- Small paint brush
- 8″ piece of red, white, or pink yarn
- Scissors
- Hole puncher

Teacher Directions

Discuss with children the concept that black and white are not colors, but rather, that they are shades. When added to color, they can make the color lighter or deeper. White added to red makes the red lighter producing pink. When the children overlap the red and white tissue squares on their project, they will see what you mean.

Show children what painting a small area, approximately 2″ x 2″, looks like.

Steps for Students

1. Trace the heart on the tracing paper.
2. Paint a small area with the glue mix.
3. Lay on tissue squares (red and white) to cover the glue mix. Overlapping is desirable. Continue until you have covered the heart.

4. Paint a light coat of glue mix over the surface of the tissue paper heart.
5. Let the heart dry.
6. Cut out the heart on the traced line.
7. Punch two holes in the top of the heart and string with yarn. Hang in a window and watch it glow!

Variation

Instead of tracing paper, use white construction paper. Proceed as above. When the heart is dry, you can write a special message with a black felt-tipped pen.

9-2 "I LOVE YOU" PULL CARD

Theme Valentine's Day

Skills Conceptual development—legends
Sequencing
Small-muscle control
Spatial relationships

Ages 3–8

St. Valentine Facts

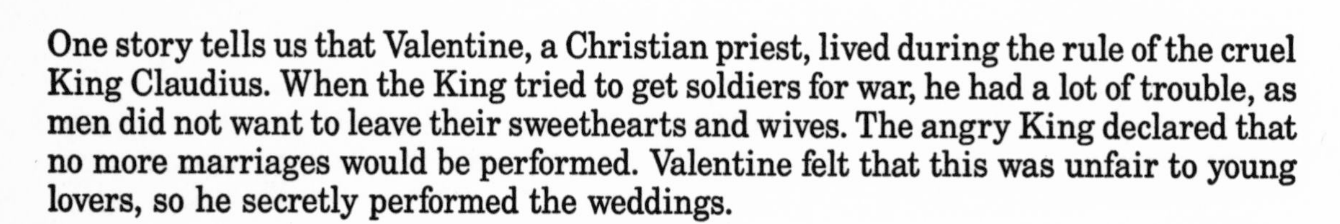

One story tells us that Valentine, a Christian priest, lived during the rule of the cruel King Claudius. When the King tried to get soldiers for war, he had a lot of trouble, as men did not want to leave their sweethearts and wives. The angry King declared that no more marriages would be performed. Valentine felt that this was unfair to young lovers, so he secretly performed the weddings.

Materials for Each Child

- 9″ x 12″ white construction paper
- Felt-tipped pens or crayons
- Scissors

Teacher Directions

The slits in this card are easy to make. Put the heart on top of some newspaper and use a single-edge razor and a ruler to make the slits straight. If you have young children, you may wish to write the "I LOVE YOU" lightly in pencil for them to trace over. Demonstrate placing the patterns so that they both fit on the paper. (*Alternative*: This project may be photocopied or traced onto a ditto.)

Steps for Students

1. Trace the heart and pull-strip on your construction paper.
2. Using your felt-tipped markers or crayons, decorate your heart with flowers, hearts, stripes, dots, and so on.

3. Write "I LOVE YOU" on your pull-strip as shown:

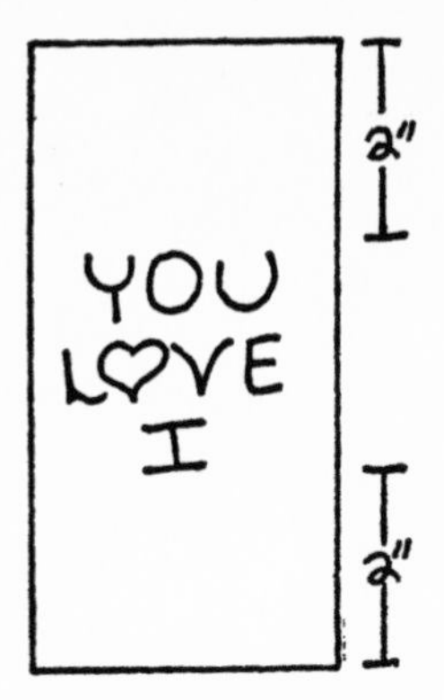

4. Color over the strip lightly with yellow or pink crayon.
5. Make two 3″ slits in the center of the card:

6. Insert the pull-strip from the back through top slit, then back through the bottom slit:

7. Pull the strip slowly to show the words I, LOVE, YOU.

Variation

Use your imagination, and think up other Valentine sayings for your pull-card.

9-3 "THIS MUCH" POP-UP CARD

Theme Valentine's Day

Skills Conceptual development—history
Eye-hand coordination
Small-muscle control
Body awareness
Detail awareness

Ages 5–8

Valentine Facts

Credit for the first Valentine card in this country goes to Miss Esther Howland, a student at Mount Holyoke College more than a century ago. Her father owned a stationery store in Worcester, Massachusetts. He used to buy Valentine cards from England to sell to people in his town. Esther decided to make her own Valentines. In 1830 she started a business that grew very fast. Her "Worcester Valentines" became very popular.

Materials for Each Child

- 9″ x 12″ pink construction paper
- Felt-tipped pens or crayons
- Scissors
- Glue

Teacher Directions

You may wish to write on the board Valentine phrases that you and the children create that would end with "this much," for example, I Love You..., I'm Thinking About You..., for the children to choose from and copy on their card. (*Alternative*: This project may be photocopied or traced onto a ditto.)

Steps for Students

1. Cut the construction paper in half on the 12″ side.
2. Trace your person pattern on one-half of your construction paper.

3. With your felt-tipped marker or crayons, color in your person. Make it look like you by matching your eye and hair color, and so on. Don't forget eyelashes, ears, and any other parts you have!
4. Cut out your person.
5. Fold the other half of your construction paper in half, then open it.
6. Fold your person as shown. Then glue it into the card:

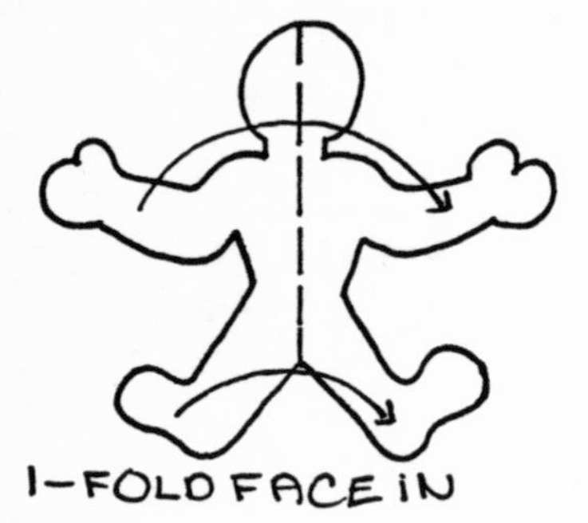

2-AT POINT "X" HALF WAY DOWN, FOLD PROJECT AT A 90° ANGLE TO ITSELF

90°
3-FOLD PROJECT. SHOULD RESEMBLE THIS MODEL

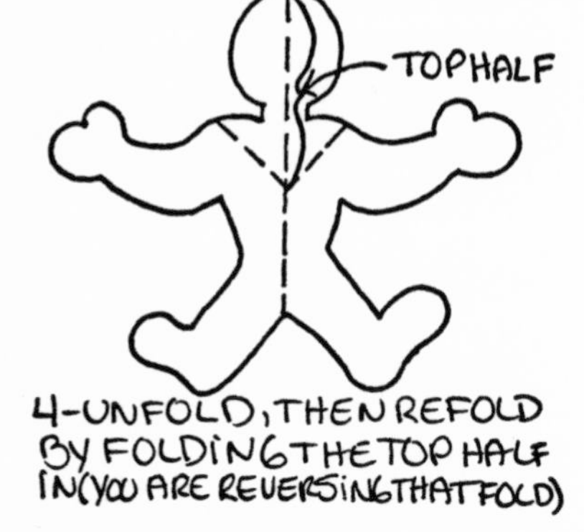

5-PROJECT IS FULLY FOLDED. SPREAD GLUE OVER SHADED AREA TURN PROJECT OVER AND SPREAD GLUE OVER THE SAME AREA ON THAT SIDE. PLACE PROJECT IN FOLD OF A CARD AND LET DRY.

7. Decorate the front of your card and write a Valentine greeting. Write "this much" inside.

9-4 MOSAIC HEART

Theme Valentine's Day

Skills Conceptual development—legends
Eye-hand coordination
Small-muscle control
Patterning

Ages 3–7

Valentine Facts

A legend about the origin of St. Valentine's Day is the story of a priest named Valentine who loved children and gave them flowers from his garden. He was put in prison by the emperor because he refused to pray to Roman gods. The children wrote notes to Valentine and attached flowers to them. While in prison, Valentine became friendly with the jailer's blind daughter. Valentine prayed for a miracle—and her sight was restored. After refusing to renounce Christianity, Valentine was beheaded by Emperor Claudius II.

Materials for Each Child

- 9″ x 12″ pink construction paper
- Red and white construction paper squares, approximately ½″ square
- Red crayon or felt-tipped pen
- Glue
- Scissors

Teacher Directions

Depending on the ages of your children, you may wish to write the "I ♥ You." Instruct the children that you only need a small drop of glue for each square.

Steps for Students

1. Trace the heart on your pink paper.

2. Write:

in the center of your heart. Use large printed letters.

3. Put a small drop of glue on the line of your heart and lay on a red or white square. Alternate colors and continue around your heart.
4. Cover the words "I" and "YOU" in the same way.
5. Color in the heart with your red crayon or felt-tipped marker.
6. Sign your name and give it to someone you love!

Variations

1. Before you mosaic the heart, go over the "I ♡ YOU" with glue, then glitter.
2. Instead of using construction paper squares, cut your squares from magazine pages.

9-5 VALENTINE PLACE CARD

Theme Valentine's Day

Skills Conceptual development—legends
Eye-hand coordination
Small-muscle control

Ages 4–7

Valentine Facts

When we think of St. Valentine's Day, we usually think of love and hearts. One story about why we think of hearts when we think of love tells about people who lived long ago who thought their souls (the part of them that they felt would never die) lived in their hearts. An old Greek story tells us about a chubby little god named Cupid who would shoot gold-tipped arrows into the hearts of those he wanted to fall in love.

Materials for Each Child

- 6″ x 9″ (½ of a 9″ x 12″) white construction paper
- Felt-tipped pens or crayons
- Glue
- Scissors

Teacher Directions

You may wish to demonstrate how to place the pattern and fold the place card.

Steps for Students

1. Trace the heart pattern on your construction paper:

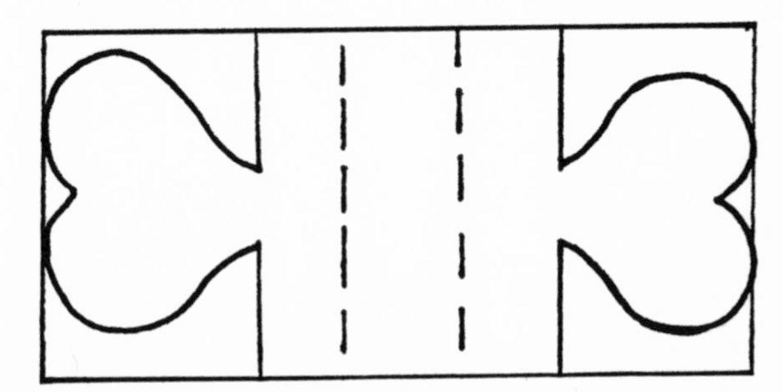

2. Cut out the place card only on lines shown, and fold on lines indicated:

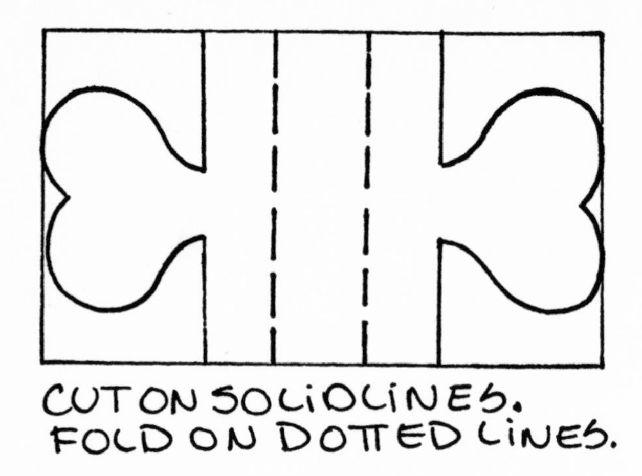

3. Lay your place card flat and write a name in the center of one heart.
4. Decorate the two hearts with red and pink swirls, dots, stripes, and so on.
5. Refold to upright position and glue the top of the hearts together.

Follow-up

Cut a big heart out of easel paper to use as a place mat.

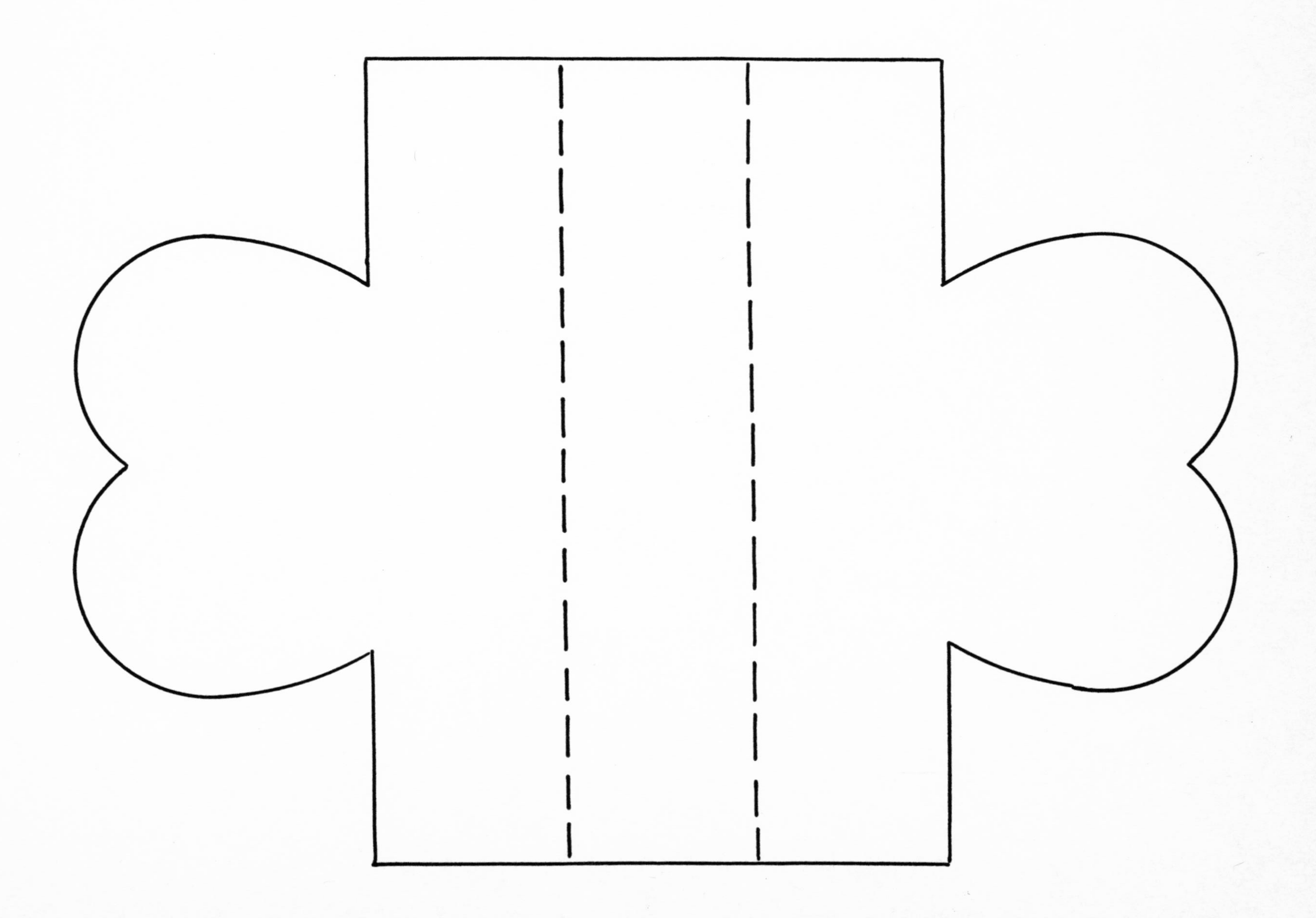

10-1 "LEAPIN' " THE LEPRECHAUN

Theme St. Patrick's Day

Skills Conceptual development—legends
Body awareness
Eye-hand coordination
Creative dramatics

Ages 4–7

Leprechaun Facts

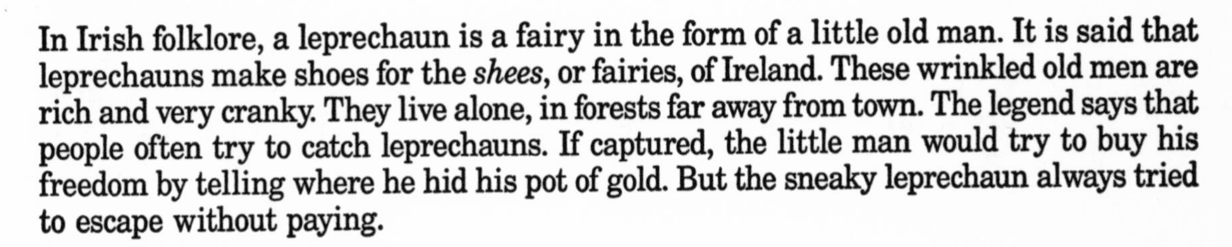

In Irish folklore, a leprechaun is a fairy in the form of a little old man. It is said that leprechauns make shoes for the *shees*, or fairies, of Ireland. These wrinkled old men are rich and very cranky. They live alone, in forests far away from town. The legend says that people often try to catch leprechauns. If captured, the little man would try to buy his freedom by telling where he hid his pot of gold. But the sneaky leprechaun always tried to escape without paying.

Materials for Each Child

- 6″ x 9″ (½ of a 9″ x 12″) oaktag or white construction paper
- Felt-tipped pens or crayons
- A rubber band
- Masking tape or paper saver
- Scissors
- Hole puncher

Teacher Directions

Depending on the skill level of your children, you may wish to cut out "Leapin'." If you are doing the cutting, you can cut three Leapin's at once.

Steps for Students

1. Trace Leapin' on oaktag or paper.

2. Draw lines to separate his head from his hat and beard.

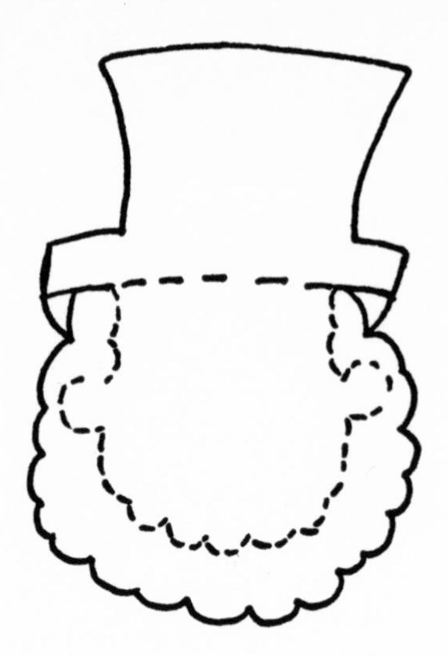

3. Cut him out.
4. With your crayons, or felt-tipped markers, color his hair rusty orange-red, give him a green suit (since green is the special color for St. Patrick's Day), and a happy face.
5. Punch a hole in the top of Leapin's hat and string a rubber band through as shown:

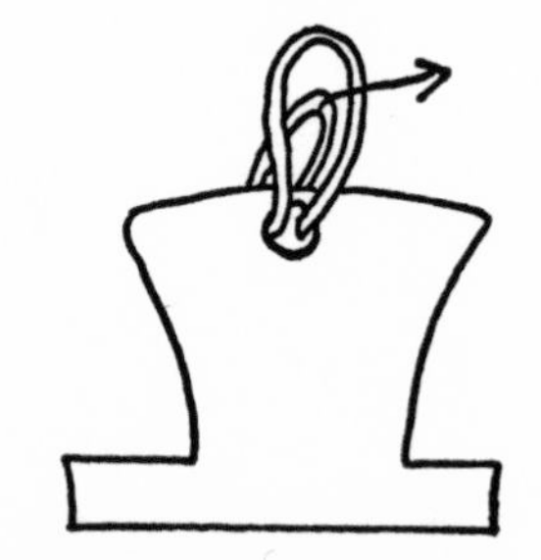

(If you are using construction paper, put a paper saver or piece of masking tape on top of hat before punching the hole.)

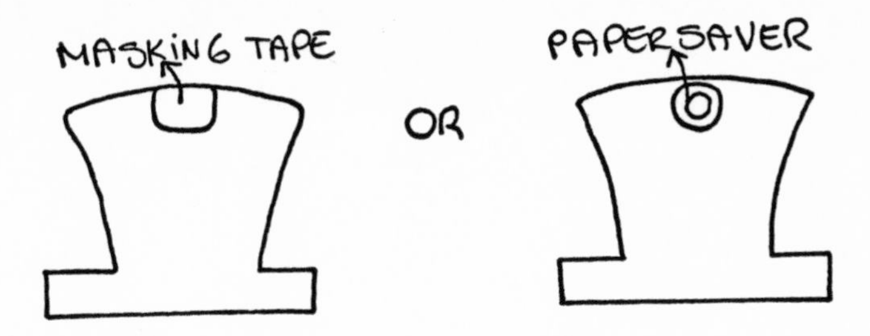

6. To make Leapin' leap, hold the end of the rubber band in one hand and pull Leapin' down by his boot. Then let go of his boot.

Variation

If you use elastic thread instead of a rubber band, Leapin' will really leap!

10-2 LEAPIN'S POT OF GOLD

Theme St. Patrick's Day

Skills: Conceptual development—history
Direction following
Eye-hand coordination
Manual dexterity

Ages 4–7

Gold Facts

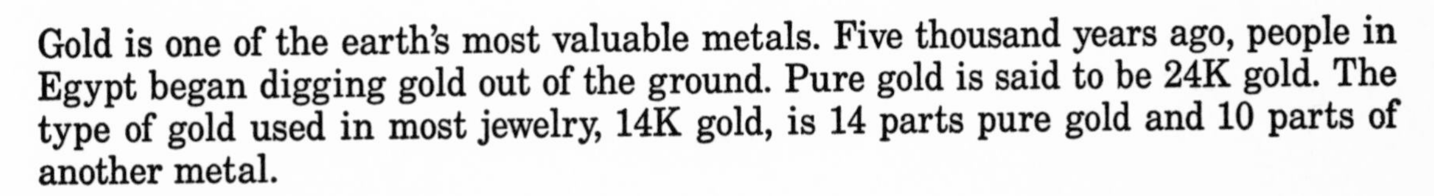

Gold is one of the earth's most valuable metals. Five thousand years ago, people in Egypt began digging gold out of the ground. Pure gold is said to be 24K gold. The type of gold used in most jewelry, 14K gold, is 14 parts pure gold and 10 parts of another metal.

Materials for Each Child

- 9″ x 12″ oaktag or white construction paper
- 6″ piece of yarn
- Felt-tipped pens or crayons
- Gold glitter (optional)
- Scissors
- Stapler

Teacher Directions

Demonstrate how to trace the pot on the fold of the construction paper, emphasizing that you do not cut on the fold.

Steps for Students

1. Fold construction paper on the 12″ side:

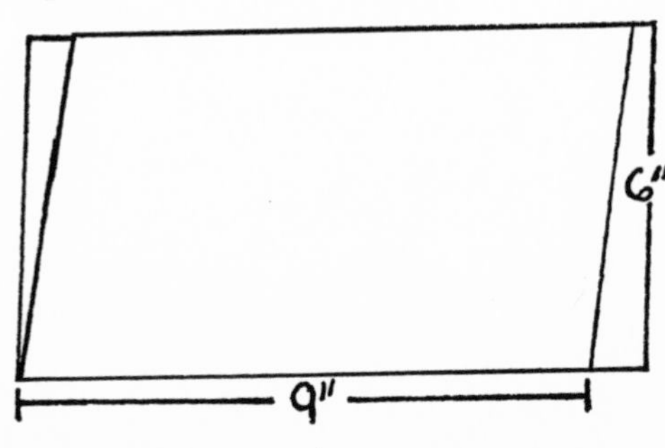

2. Trace the pot onto the paper with the bottom of the pot on the fold: (or, draw a pot of your own.)

3. Cut out the pot. Go slowly, you'll be cutting two pieces of paper at once. Do not cut on the fold mark.
4. Color both outsides of the pot black, in green and black stripes, or use your imagination.
5. Staple the sides of the pot together. Staple the piece of yarn between the top corners of the pot:

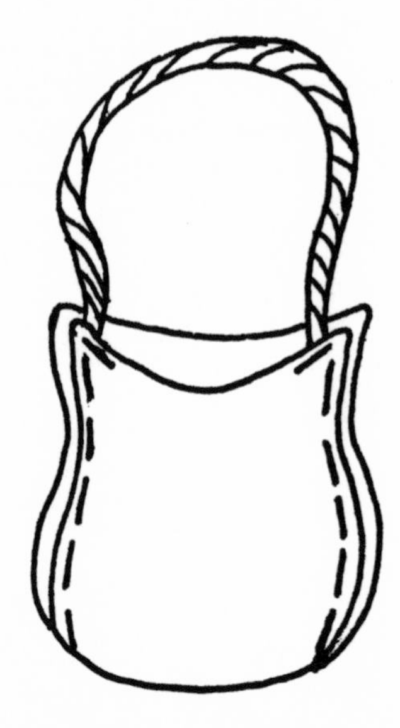

6. Stuff a small piece of newspaper into the bottom of the pot.
7. Trace the coins on the left over construction paper, and cut them out.
8. Color them yellow on both sides, or paint on some glue and sprinkle with gold glitter.
9. Put the coins in Leapin's pot.

Variations

Paint some small pebbles yellow or gold then let them dry. Use them as nuggets of gold, instead of the coins.

10-3 SUN-GLOW SHAMROCK

Theme St. Patrick's Day

Skills Conceptual development—religion, legends
Small-muscle control
Spatial relationships
Patterning
Eye-hand coordination

Ages 3–8

Shamrock Facts

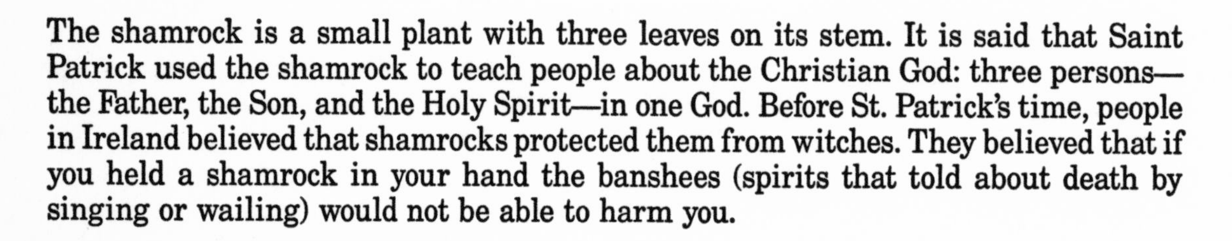

The shamrock is a small plant with three leaves on its stem. It is said that Saint Patrick used the shamrock to teach people about the Christian God: three persons—the Father, the Son, and the Holy Spirit—in one God. Before St. Patrick's time, people in Ireland believed that shamrocks protected them from witches. They believed that if you held a shamrock in your hand the banshees (spirits that told about death by singing or wailing) would not be able to harm you.

Materials for Each Child

- 9″ x 12″ tracing paper
- Green tissue paper squares approximately 1½″ square (varying shades, if available)
- Glue mix: half white glue and half water—in small bowl or cup (can be shared by 2 or 3 children)
- Small paint brush
- Scissors
- 6″ piece of yarn
- Hole puncher

Teacher Directions

Show children what painting a small area (approximately 2″ x 2″) looks like. (Remind them to wipe their brush on the side of the bowl each time before painting.)

Steps for Students

1. Trace shamrock on the tracing paper.
2. Paint a small area with the glue mix.
3. Lay on tissue squares to cover the glue mix. Overlapping is desirable. Continue until you have covered the shamrock.

4. Carefully paint a light coat of glue mix over the surface of the tissue paper shamrock.
5. Let the shamrock dry.
6. Cut out the shamrock on the traced line.
7. Punch two holes in the top of the shamrock and string with yarn. Hang in a window.

Variation

Instead of tracing paper use white construction paper. Proceed as above. This type of shamrock makes a great door decoration.

Follow-up

Find some clovers in your lawn. Press them in an old magazine. Glue them on a piece of construction paper. Paint a coat of glue mix over the clovers for permanence and shine. You may also use them on the front of a St. Patrick's card.

10-4 SAINT PATRICK

Theme St. Patrick's Day

Skills Conceptual development—religious history
Detail awareness
Eye-hand coordination
Small-muscle control
Spatial relationships

Ages 5–7

St. Patrick's Day Facts

St. Patrick is the patron saint of Ireland. He lived about 1500 years ago, and was the first man to spread Christianity throughout Ireland. St. Patrick was born in England. When he was sixteen years old, he was kidnapped by Irish outlaws and sold as a slave in Ireland. After six years as a slave he escaped to France. While he was in France, a voice came to him telling him to return to Ireland and tell people about the Christian religion. In Ireland he talked to many people about Christianity and founded many churches. Legend has it that St. Patrick drove the snakes out of Ireland; this may or may not be true. St. Patrick's feast day (the day he is honored by many Christians) is March 17.

Materials for Each Child

- 9″ x 12″ white construction paper
- Felt-tipped pens or crayons
- Stapler
- Scissors

Teacher Directions

Instruct children to trace the large pattern first and then fit in the smaller patterns. You may want to make the slits for the children with a single-edge razor or the point of a scissor.

Steps for Students

1. Trace the patterns on your paper.
2. Draw a line to separate St. Patrick's head from his body.

3. With your felt-tipped markers or crayons give St. Patrick a face, hair, and a nice green robe. Color the arms and hands, his bishop's hat, and his staff.
4. Cut out all the patterns.
5. Carefully make two slits in the body pattern and insert the arms, in one slit and out the other, as shown:

Make a slit in St. Patrick's staff and insert his hand into it.

6. Bend back the bottom edges of St. Patrick's robe and staple them together:

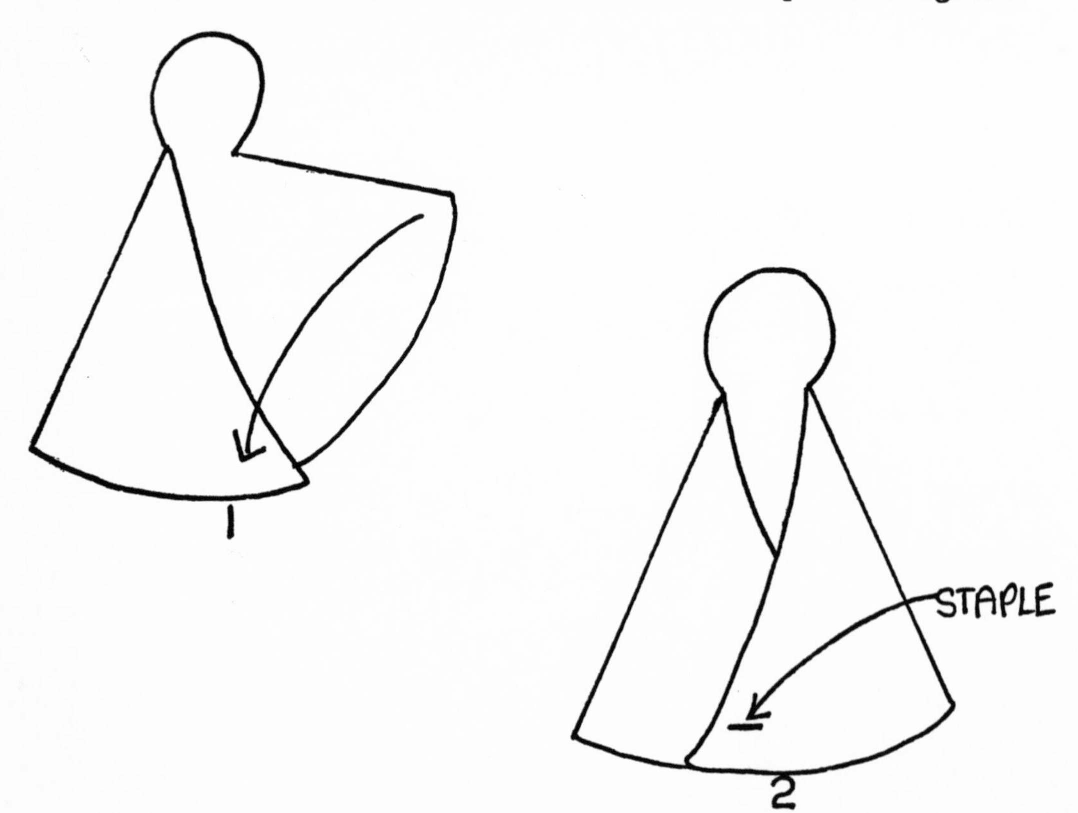

7. Make a slit in St. Patrick's hat (miter):

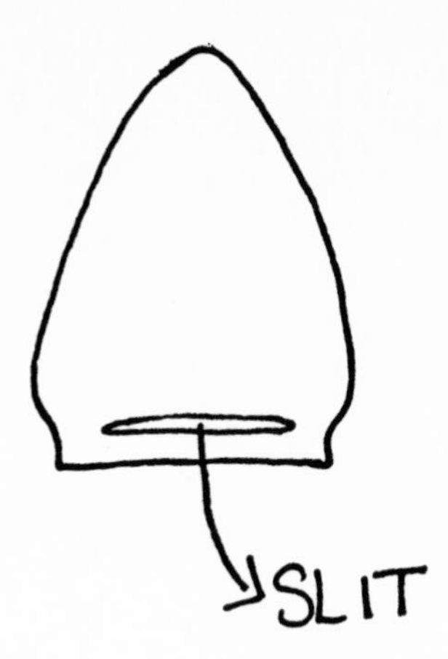

Insert it on St. Patrick's head.

Follow-up

Describe St. Patrick to the children. Encourage them to make a big painting or drawing of what they think St. Patrick looked like.

11-1 DRAGON

Theme Chinese New Year

Skills Conceptual development—cultural
Eye-hand coordination
Small muscle control
Creative dramatics

Ages 4–8

Chinese New Year Facts

The celebration of the Chinese New Year always attracts thousands of visitors to the Chinatowns in big cities. They come to see the fireworks and the dragon dance through the streets. To the Chinese, red is the color of this season. Sheets of red paper hang on the doors and gates of the Chinese homes during this holiday. The Chinese believe the red banners and flags will chase away the winter spirits.

Materials for Each Child

- 6″ x 9″ (½ of a 9″ x 12″) oaktag or light-colored construction paper
- 6″ x 9″ (½ of 9″ x 12″) red construction paper
- Craft stick
- Felt-tipped pens or crayons
- Scissors
- Hole puncher

Teacher Directions

When tracing the pattern, direct the children to place the head pattern against the side of paper, to leave room for the eyes and horns. (*Alternative*: This project may be photocopied or traced onto a ditto.)

Steps for Students

1. Trace the head, eyes, and horn patterns onto your oaktag or light-colored construction paper.
2. Cut them out.

3. Fold the eye patterns in half and draw in "dragon eyes."

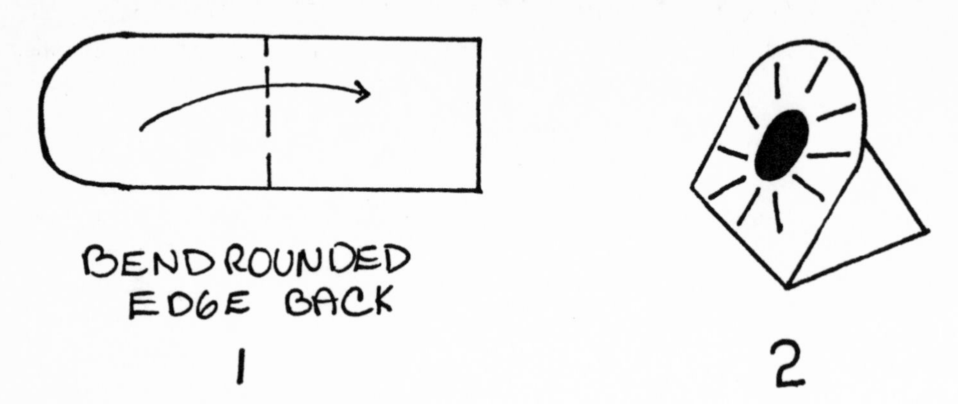

4. Fold head as shown:

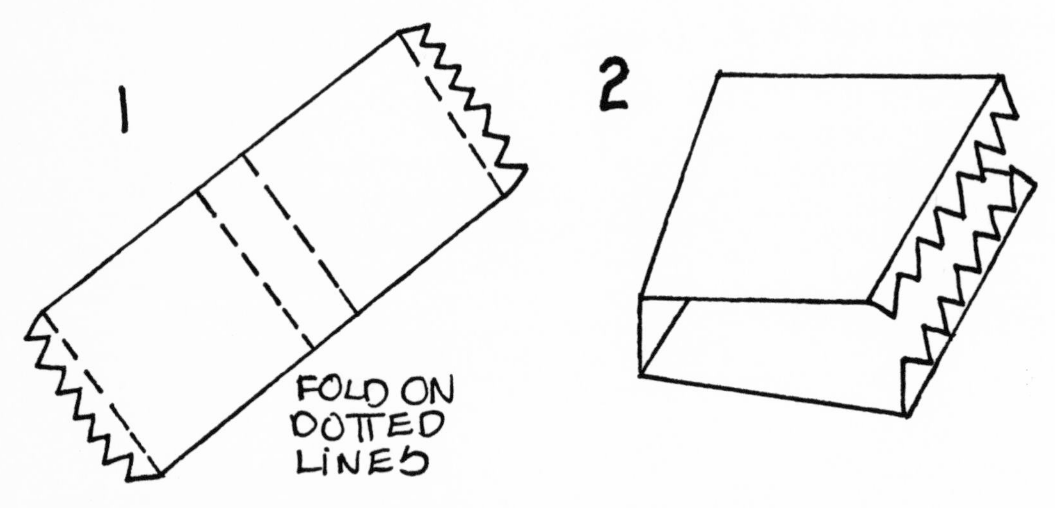

5. Open the head and lay it flat.
6. Color the teeth.
7. Color the head or pattern it with dots or stripes. Use bright fiery colors.
8. Color the horns.
9. Refold the head and glue on the eyes and horns as shown:

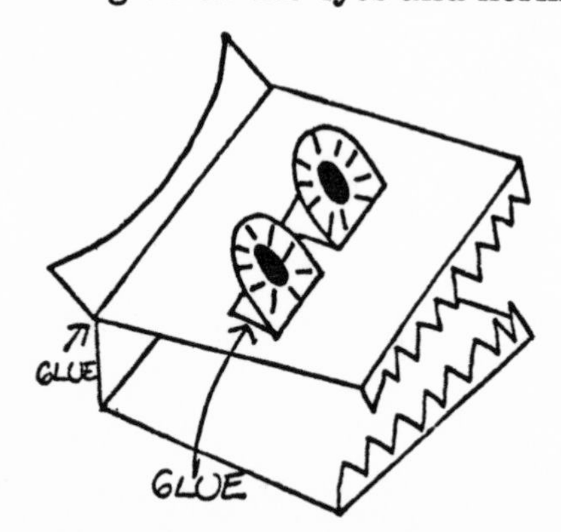

10. With a hole puncher, make holes where the dragon's nostrils would be. Weave small strips of colored tissue or construction paper in and out.
11. Trace the tongue pattern on the red construction paper and cut it out.
12. Glue or staple the dragon's tongue inside his mouth.

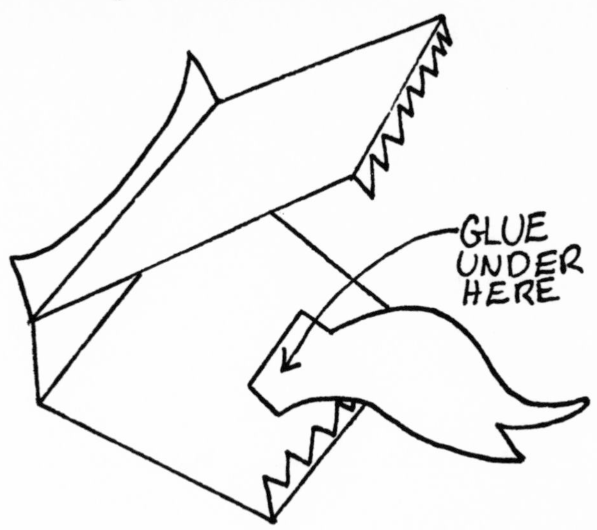

13. Glue or staple the craft stick to the back of the dragon's head.

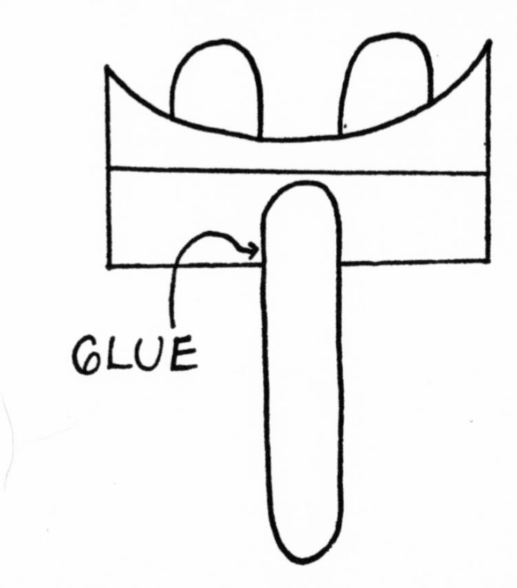

14. Hold the craft stick and move your arm up and down to make your dragon's mouth open and close.
15. Have a dragon parade!

Variation

1. Let the children have fun drawing and painting *lots* of dragons.
2. Use plasticine clay to build three-dimensional dragons!

SPRING

March 21 is the first day of spring. On this day, there are the same number of hours of light and darkness. Spring lasts for ninety-two days, twenty hours, and ends on June 21. As Spring goes on, the number of hours of light are more than the hours of dark. The earth begins to warm and nature begins a new growing season. Animals slowly come out of hibernation (their long winter sleep), and birds that have flown to warmer places come home.

12-1 THE INCREDIBLE SEED

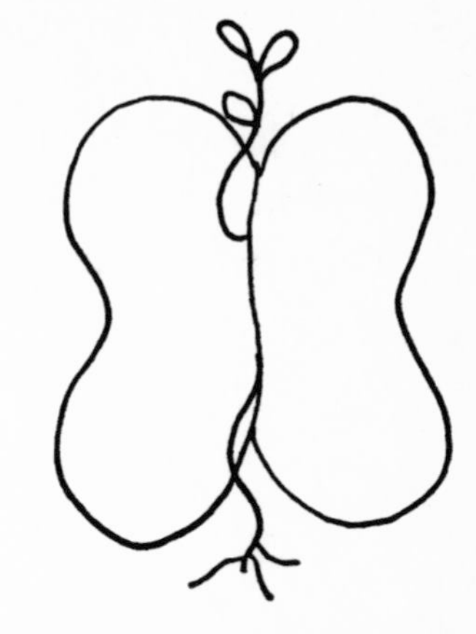

Theme Spring

Skills Conceptual development—nature
Eye-hand coordination
Small-muscle control

Ages 5–8

Seed Facts

A seed is the "egg" of a flowering plant. It has everything in it that is needed to make a new plant. At one end of the seed is a small stem, called the *hypocotol*, which grows downward to form the root. At the other end of the seed is a small bud, called the *plumule*, which grows upward to form the stem and leaves of the new sprout. The seed also contains a food supply that is used until the new plant's roots grow into the soil.

Materials for Each Child

- 9″ x 12″ white construction paper
- Felt-tipped pens or crayons
- Glue
- Scissors

Teacher Directions

Demonstrate for the children how to trace the pattern on the fold, and remind them that you do not cut on the fold line. You might wish to write the words "sprout" and "root" on the board for the children to copy.

Steps for Students

1. Fold your construction paper in half on the 12″ side.
2. Trace the seed pattern on the construction paper with its "back" on the fold:

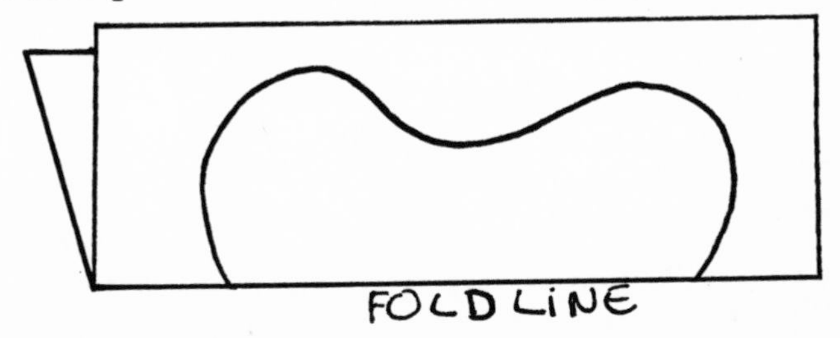

3. Cut out the seed. Do not cut on the fold line.
4. Color the seed brown, yellow, or the color you remember seeing in a seed.
5. Trace the root and the sprout on the leftover construction paper.
6. Cut them out.
7. Color the root light brown or yellow. Color the sprout green.
8. Fold the sprout and the root accordion-style if you can, or in half three times.
9. Glue the ends of the root and sprout inside the seed:

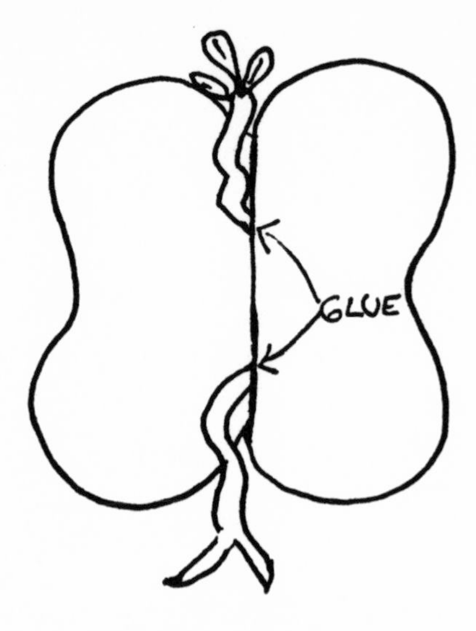

10. Label the sprout, root, and food of the seed.

Follow-ups

1. Soak lima bean seeds in water overnight. Stuff a glass with damp paper towels. Slide the seeds halfway down the side of the glass. Keep the towels moist. Observe the seed sending down a root and sending up a sprout.
2. Plant a lima bean seed (after soaking). When a sprout appears, gently dig the seed up. Observe the root and sprout. Gently replant and watch it grow!

12-2 APRIL SHOWERS UMBRELLA

Theme Spring

Skills Conceptual development—nature
Eye-hand coordination
Spatial relationships
Small-muscle control

Ages 4–7

Rain Facts

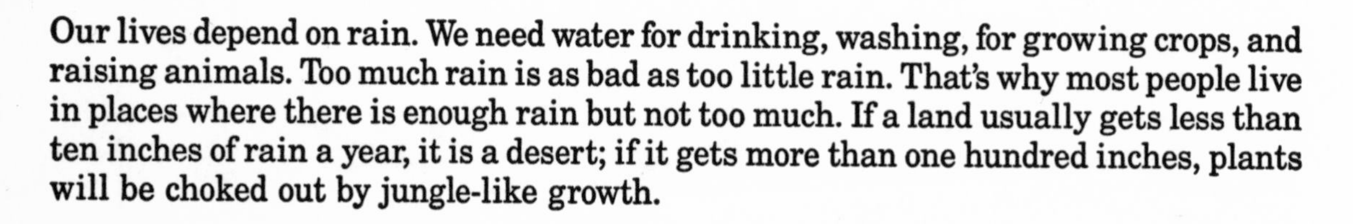

Our lives depend on rain. We need water for drinking, washing, for growing crops, and raising animals. Too much rain is as bad as too little rain. That's why most people live in places where there is enough rain but not too much. If a land usually gets less than ten inches of rain a year, it is a desert; if it gets more than one hundred inches, plants will be choked out by jungle-like growth.

Materials for Each Child

- 9″ x 12″ piece of white or yellow construction paper
- 2 feet of string, cut in varying lengths from 4″ to 6″
- Felt-tipped pens or crayons
- Glue
- Scissors

Teacher Directions

Show children how to place the patterns so that they both fit on the paper.

Steps for Students

1. Trace the two patterns on your construction paper.
2. With your crayons or felt-tipped pens, color the handle of the umbrella and decorate the top of the umbrella with flowers, sunshine, stripes, and so on.
3. Cut out the umbrella top and handle.

4. Glue the handle to the top of the umbrella from the back.

5. With the umbrella in this position, put four drops of glue on the umbrella's brim.
6. Lay the ends of string on the glue spots.

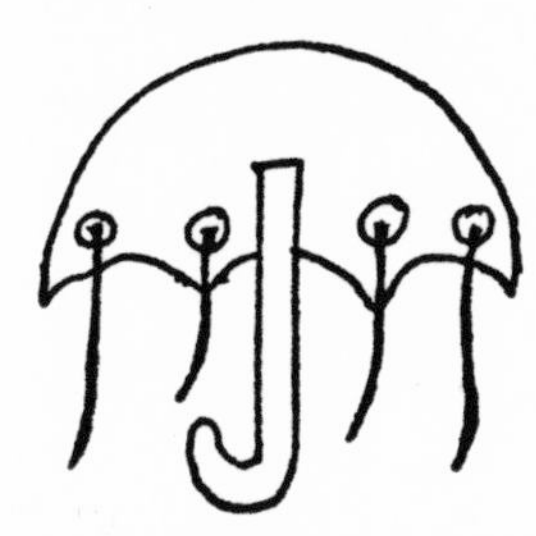

7. Cut out some raindrops from the scraps of paper. Try to make them look like drops. Color them blue.
8. Put a small drop of glue on the back of each rain drop and lay each under the strings:

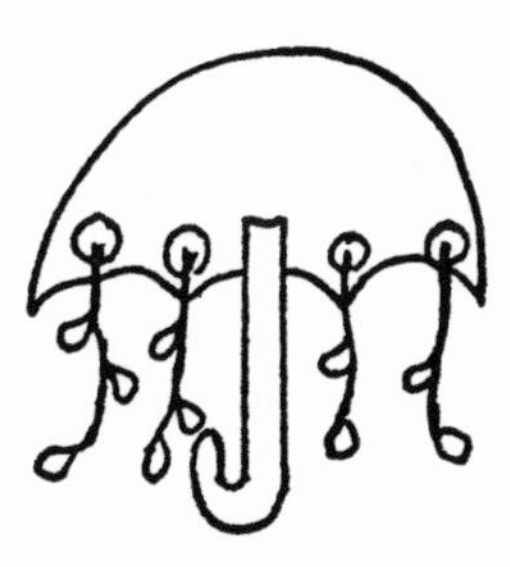

9. Let them dry before picking up your umbrella.

Follow-ups

1. Play the song "Singing in the Rain" and have children do an improvisational dance with an umbrella.
2. On rainy days, when you can't go to the playground or outside to play, discuss the positive aspects of rain. Draw pictures of rain falling on trees, flowers, vegetable plants, and into ponds with fish!

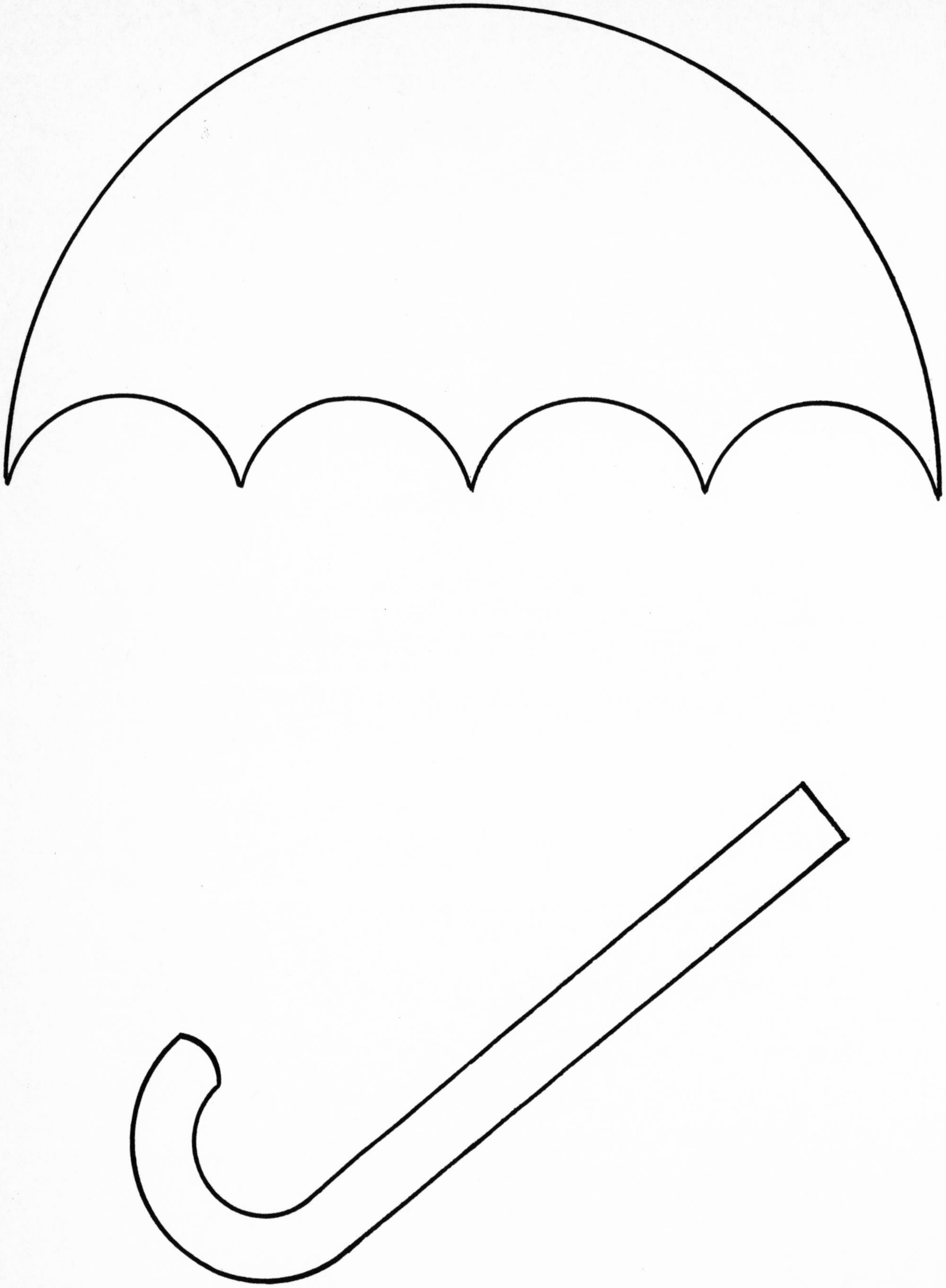

12-3 SPONGE-PAINTED RAINBOW

Theme Spring

Skills Conceptual development—nature
Eye-hand coordination
Color mixing

Ages 5–7

Rainbow Facts

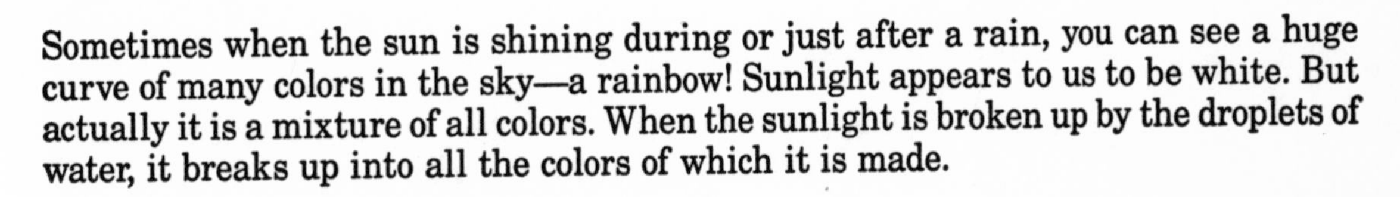

Sometimes when the sun is shining during or just after a rain, you can see a huge curve of many colors in the sky—a rainbow! Sunlight appears to us to be white. But actually it is a mixture of all colors. When the sunlight is broken up by the droplets of water, it breaks up into all the colors of which it is made.

Materials for Each Child

- 9″ x 12″ white construction paper
- Red, yellow, blue tempera paint
- Styrofoam or aluminum tray
- 3 small pieces of sponge
- Scissors

Teacher Directions

This project is good to use in connection with a lesson on primary/secondary colors. In the corners of the tray place small amounts of each of the primary paints. Demonstrate the tracing of the rainbow and the marking of the lines to separate the bands of color. (*Alternative*: This project may be photocopied or traced over onto a ditto.)

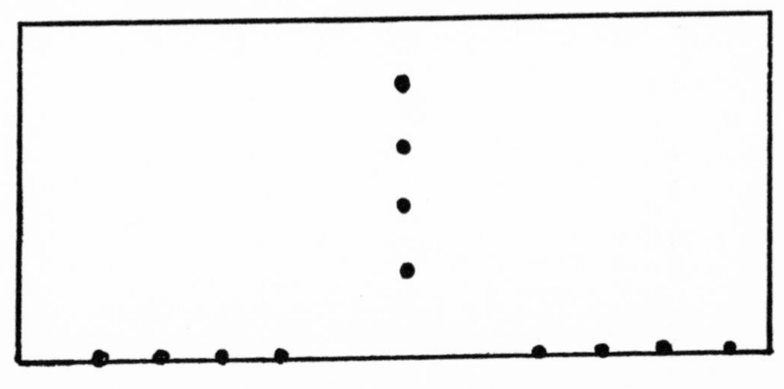

Steps for Students

1. Trace the rainbow pattern on your paper.
2. Mark the color bands beginning and ending dots.
3. Poke your pencil through the pattern to mark the center dots.
4. Draw lines to connect the dots:

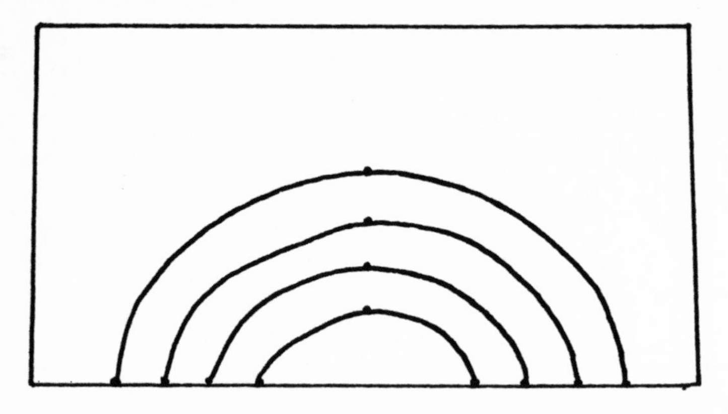

5. Dip a sponge in the red paint and slide it over the top band on your rainbow. Continue your red sliding until you fill the top band.
6. The next band make yellow, and the last one blue. Overlap the edge of the bands a little and you will see a new color appear!

Variation

Draw a sun, cut it out, and glue it to the back of your rainbow, so that it looks like it is peeking up over the rainbow. Draw a small cloud, cut it out and glue it on your rainbow.

Follow-ups

1. Get a prism from the science room. Slant it into a ray of sunlight so that a rainbow of color shows up on the wall. Explain that the prism breaks-up the sunlight like a droplet of water does.
2. Make a color wheel with the three primary colors on it. Show the children that the faster you spin the wheel, the more white it looks.

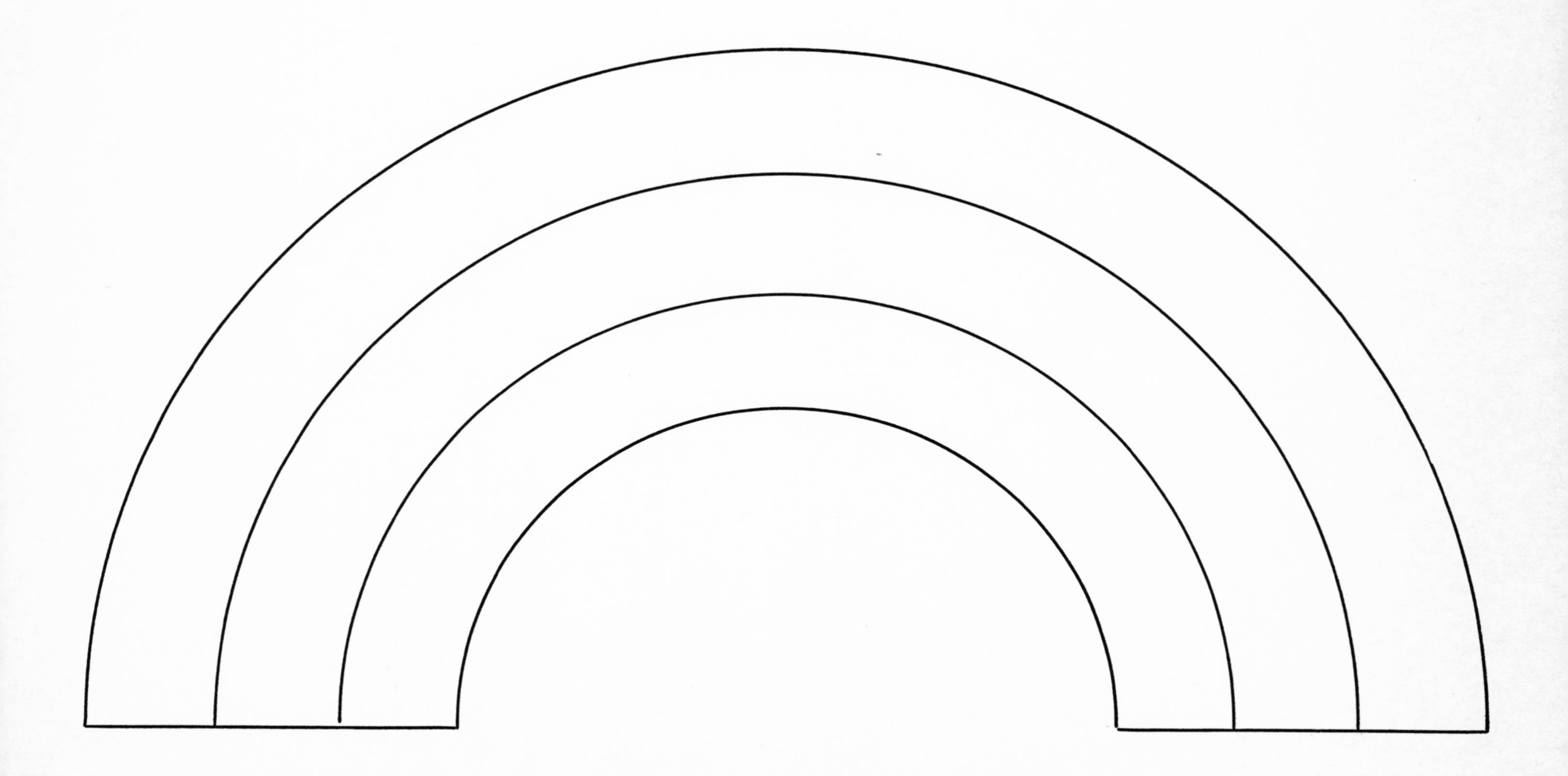

12-4 "CATHERINE" THE CATERPILLAR

Theme Spring

Skills Conceptual development—nature
Creative dramatics
Shape discrimination
Measuring skills

Ages 3–7

Caterpillar Facts

A caterpillar is a wormlike larva (a baby that will grow into an insect). Caterpillars hatch from butterfly or moth eggs. Usually the eggs are laid carefully on the leaves or twigs of the kind of plant the caterpillar will feed on. A single butterfly or moth may lay as many as a thousand eggs. The hatched baby caterpillars begin eating at once. Caterpillars have jaws for biting solid food. These hungry insects protect themselves from their enemies by feeding only at night and hiding during the day. As a caterpillar eats and grows fatter, its skin bursts and rolls off, and a new larger skin takes over. Caterpillars, like spiders, have a special organ in their bodies that produces silk. When a caterpillar has grown as large as it can, it goes into its resting stage (pupa). The caterpillar makes itself a cocoon. While in this state, all the insides of the caterpillar turn into liquid which feeds the butterfly or moth.

Materials for Each Child

- 3″ x 9″ (¼ of a 9″ x 12″) oaktag or white construction paper (you can get 4 caterpillars from one 9″ x 12″)
- 6″ pipe cleaner
- Felt-tipped pens or crayons
- Scissors

Teacher Directions

You may wish to tape the head and insert the pipe cleaner. Demonstrate the folding of the paper in fourths, noting that the squared end is the head.

Steps for Students

1. Trace the caterpillar on the oaktag or construction paper.
2. Cut it out.
3. Fold the caterpillar into four parts by folding it in half, and then in half again.
4. Unfold your caterpillar:

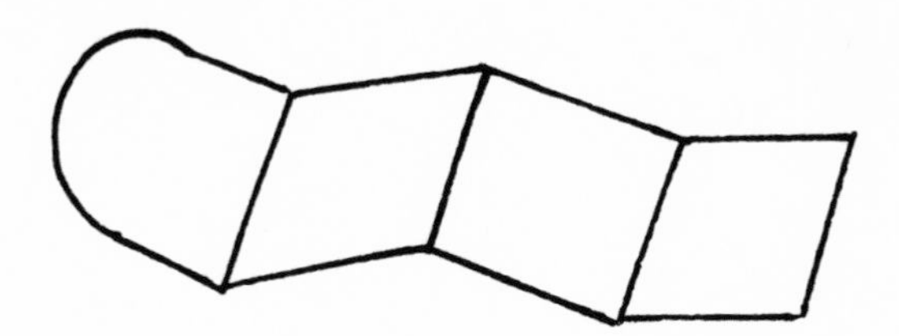

5. With your crayons or felt-tipped pens, color in each section a different color, or use your imagination to make your caterpillar look fancy.
6. On the end that is squared, add eyes.
7. With the point of a pencil, make two small holes above Catherine's eyes.
8. Bend the pipe cleaner in half and insert as shown:

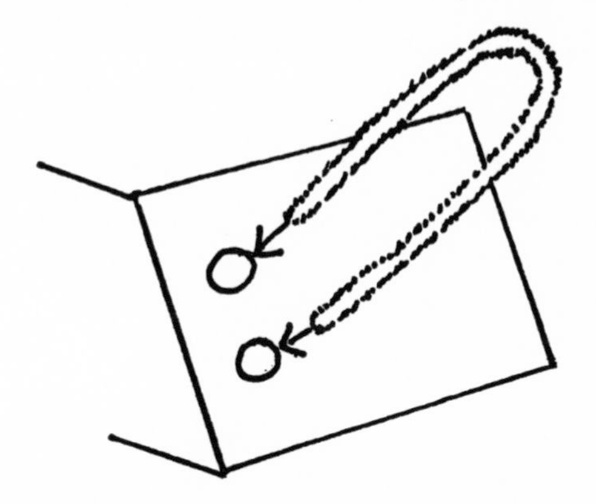

Leave enough room for an index finger.

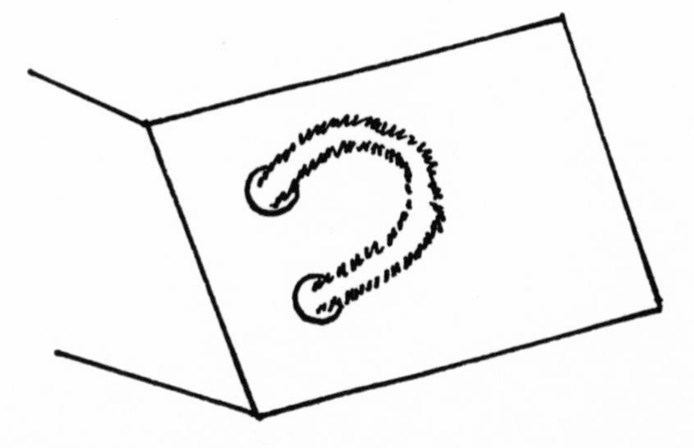

Twist once on top of Catherine's head.

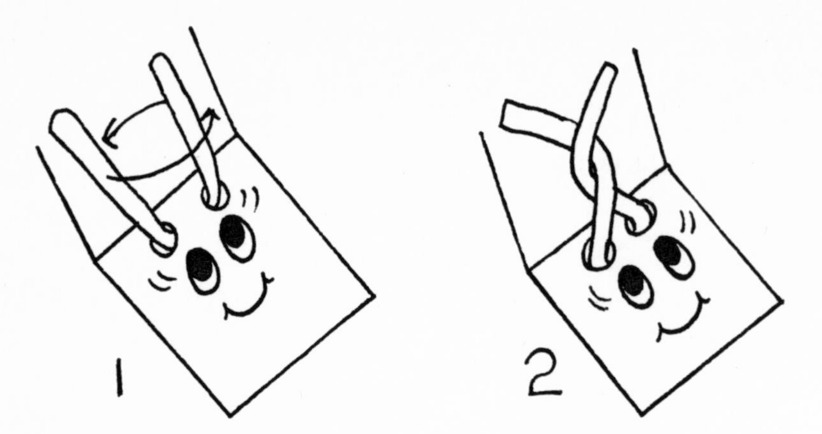

9. Turn in outside corners of Catherine's head and tape together:

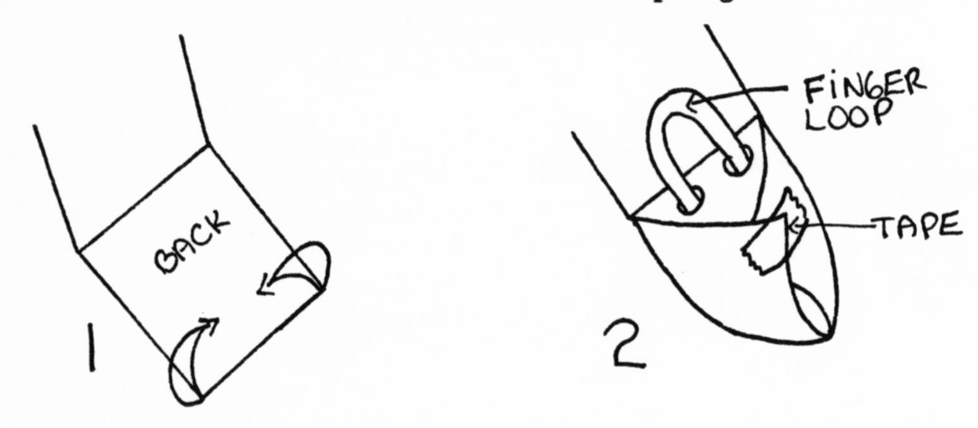

10. Slip your finger into the loop on the bottom of Catherine. Move your finger up and down to make Catherine move.

Follow-up

Put on a caterpillar play for the class next door: (with Catherine Caterpillar on a finger, have children each say one line). If you have more children than the lines that are here, look in the encyclopedia for more facts (there are lots of them), or continue into becoming liquid, emerging as butterfly, and so on.

1. "Hi, I'm Catherine the Caterpillar."
2. "When I hatched out of my egg, I was very hungry."
3. "My favorite food is leaves."
4. "Sometimes I eat aphids or ant grubs."
5. "So that birds don't eat me,"
   "I usually do my eating at night."
6. "I hide during the day in rolled up leaves or in special tents made of silk."

7. “Just like my friend the spider, I can make silk inside my body.”
8. “I use this silk to make my hiding place and I also use it as a lifeline to drop down from the branch I’m on if someone or something disturbs me.”
9. “I love to eat. But my skin cannot stretch like yours.”
10. “So, I pop my old skin off and grow a new one!”
11. “I keep eating and popping off my skin until I get as large as I can be.”
12. “Then, if I’m a butterfly caterpillar, I make a button of silk on a twig.”
13. “I attach myself to the button and pop my last skin.”
14. “I now look strange. I’m pointed at both ends and I have a smooth skin.”
15. “Yawn! I’m really tired. Goodnight. I’m going to sleep now.”
16. “You can call me a pupa now.”

12-5 MARVELOUS MONARCH

Theme Spring

Skills Conceptual development—nature
Eye-hand coordination
Color awareness
Measuring
Patterning

Ages 4–8

Butterfly Facts

Butterflies are small animals that fly about with lovely colored wings. They are insects, so they have six legs. Their bodies are divided into three parts. A butterfly's wings are covered with scales. If you touch a butterfly's wing, your finger becomes dusty. This dust is really thousands of tiny flat scales. Nearly all butterflies fly only during the day. When resting, butterflies fold their wings together overhead. Butterflies live entirely on liquid, such as the nectar of flowers.

Monarch butterflies appear in large numbers in Canada and the northern part of the United States. In the early fall they all begin to fly to warmer places, such as Florida, California, and the West Indies.

Materials for Each Child

- 9″ x 12″ white construction paper
- 3″ x 9″ (¼ of a 9″ x 12″) yellow construction paper
- One cup each of orange and black tempera paint (children can share cups)
- 2 plastic spoons
- Felt-tipped pens or crayon
- Newspaper
- Scissors

Teacher Directions

Spread newspaper on the project table. Demonstrate for the children how to make small drops of paint on the paper by taking a spoon of paint and touching it to the paper in various spots, allowing a drop to drip off the spoon. Remind them not to shake the paint off of the spoon as it will splatter on them.

Steps for Students

1. Fold the white paper in half.
2. Open the paper. Carefully spoon on drops of orange and black paint.
3. Close the paper on the fold and gently "push" the drops of paint with your fingers to spread and mix the paint.
4. Carefully rub a craft stick or ruler from top to bottom to squeeze out any excess paint.
5. Open the paper and let it dry.
6. Trace Marvelous Monarch's body on the yellow paper. Cut it out.
7. Give "Marvelous" a face and glue his body in the middle of his wings.

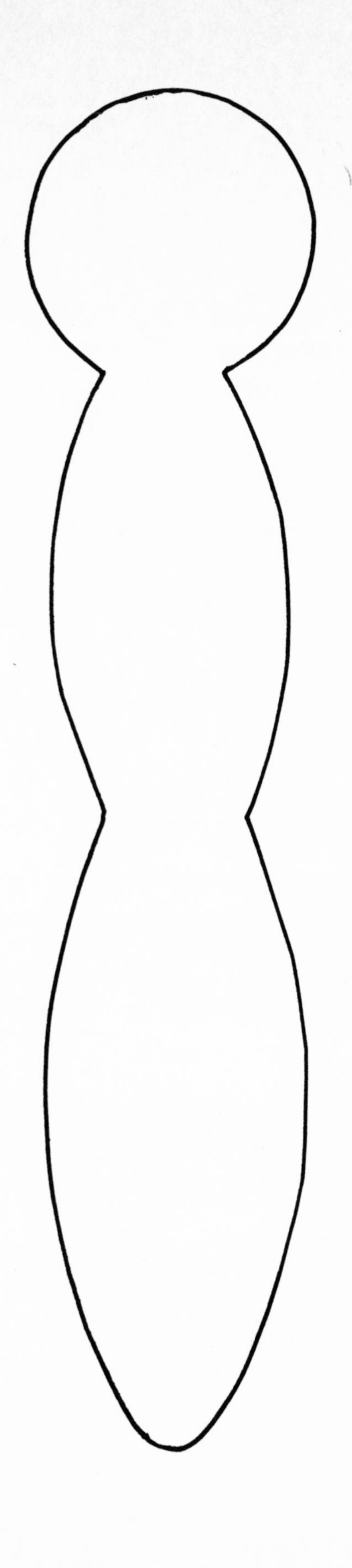

12-6 MOSAIC FLOWER

Theme Spring

Skills Conceptual development—history
Eye-hand coordination
Patterning

Ages 3–7

Mosaic Facts

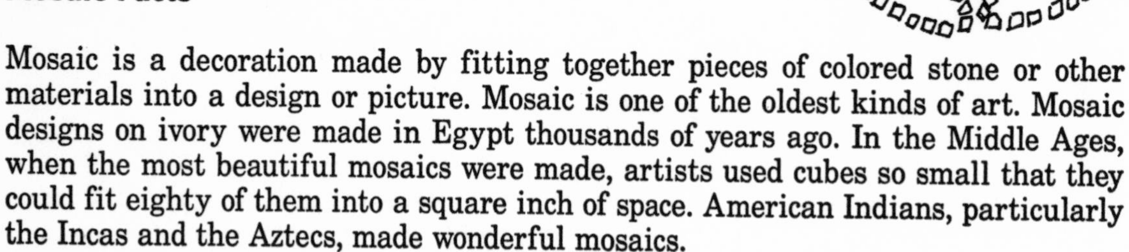

Mosaic is a decoration made by fitting together pieces of colored stone or other materials into a design or picture. Mosaic is one of the oldest kinds of art. Mosaic designs on ivory were made in Egypt thousands of years ago. In the Middle Ages, when the most beautiful mosaics were made, artists used cubes so small that they could fit eighty of them into a square inch of space. American Indians, particularly the Incas and the Aztecs, made wonderful mosaics.

Materials for Each Child

- 9″ x 12″ light colored construction paper
- Green and two pastel color paper squares, approximately ½″ square
- Glue
- Scissors

Teacher Directions

This is an easy project, with great results. The squares are easy and fast to cut with a paper cutter. (*Alternative*: This project may be photocopied or traced onto a ditto.)

Steps for Students

1. Trace the pattern on the construction paper.
2. Put a small drop of glue on the line at the top of the flower's stem:

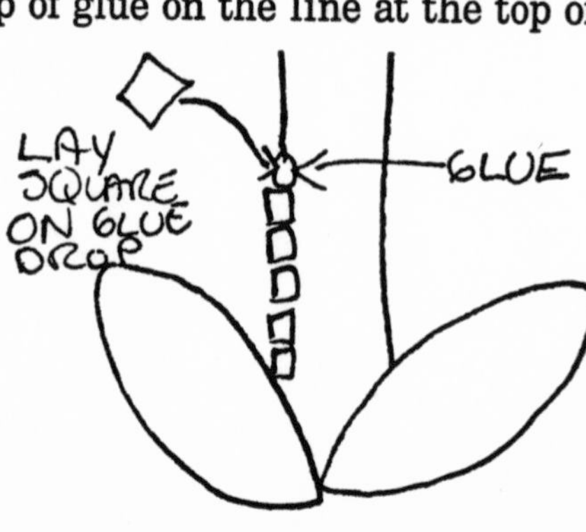

3. Lay on a green square. Continue down the stem and around each leaf, then up the stem.
4. Glue your pastel squares around the edge of the flower.

Variation

Instead of using construction paper squares, cut squares from a flower seed catalogue.

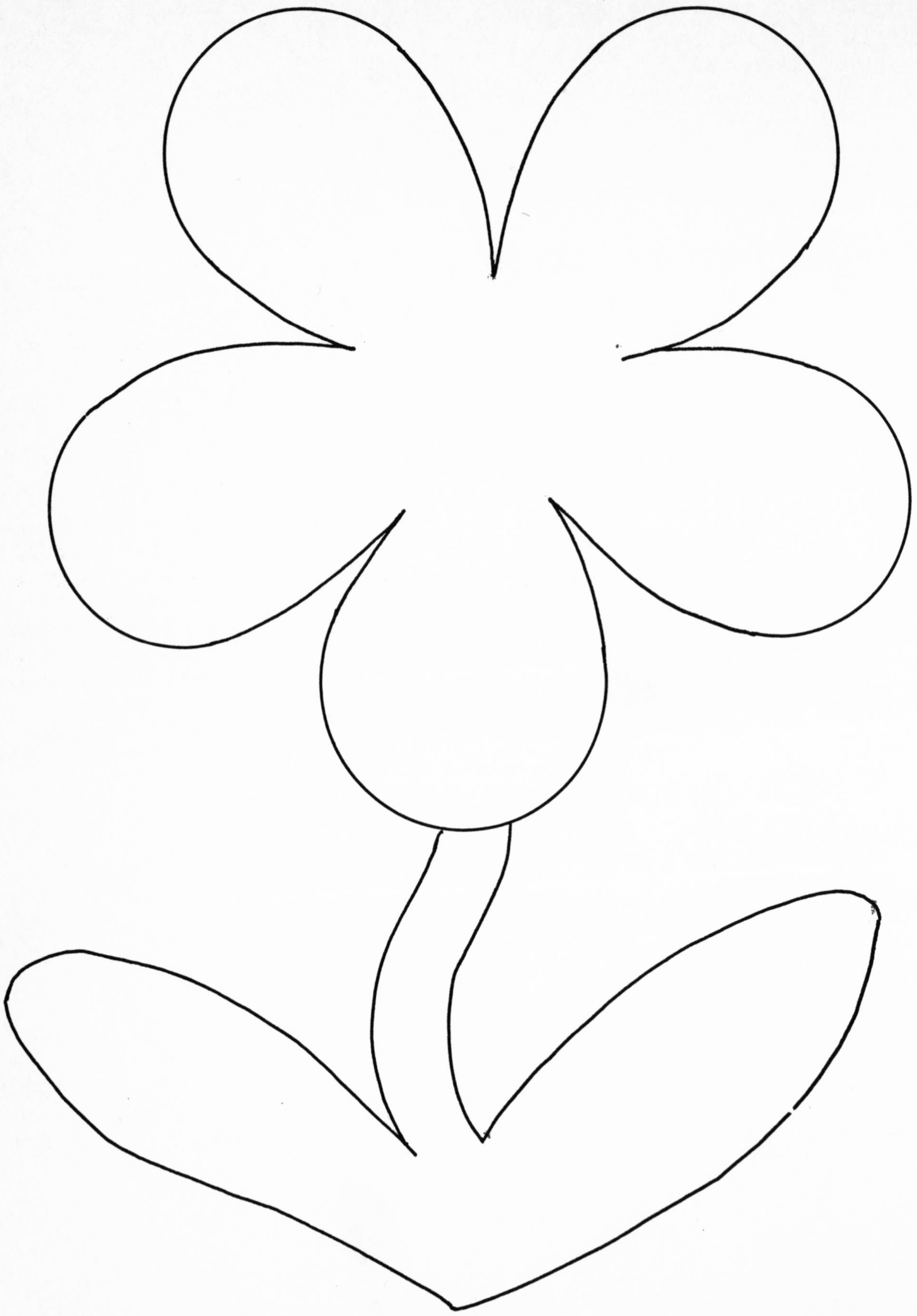

12-7 MOMMA ROBIN

Theme Spring

Skills Conceptual development—birds
Creative dramatics
Eye-hand coordination
Small-muscle control

Ages 4–6

Robin Facts

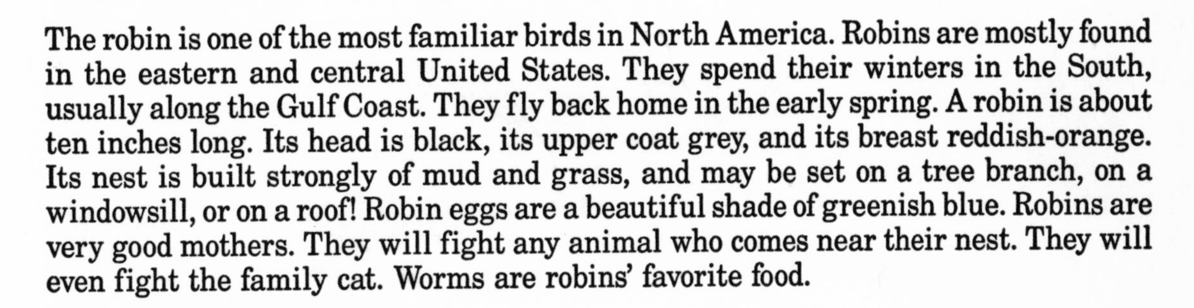

The robin is one of the most familiar birds in North America. Robins are mostly found in the eastern and central United States. They spend their winters in the South, usually along the Gulf Coast. They fly back home in the early spring. A robin is about ten inches long. Its head is black, its upper coat grey, and its breast reddish-orange. Its nest is built strongly of mud and grass, and may be set on a tree branch, on a windowsill, or on a roof! Robin eggs are a beautiful shade of greenish blue. Robins are very good mothers. They will fight any animal who comes near their nest. They will even fight the family cat. Worms are robins' favorite food.

Materials for Each Child

- 9″ x 12″ white construction paper
- Craft stick
- 2 2″ pieces of yarn
- Felt-tipped pens or crayons
- Glue
- Scissors

Teacher Directions

A good way to spark children's interest is to examine the construction of a real nest. You may look in the early spring for returning birds. Demonstrate the placing of the patterns so that they all fit on the paper. (*Alternative*: This project may be photocopied or traced onto a ditto.)

Steps for Students

1. Trace all patterns on your paper.
2. Draw lines to separate the heads, breasts, and beaks of the three birds.
3. Give all your birds one eye, as you are seeing them in profile.
4. Color their beaks yellow, heads black, backs brown, and breasts red.
5. Color the nest a mixture of gray and brown.
6. Cut out all the patterns.
7. Glue the two baby birds in the left hand corner of the nest.
8. Cut a slit just below the babies to within 1½″ of each side of the nest:

9. Glue the craft stick half-way up the mother robin's back. When dry, insert Momma Robin into the nest from the front. Grasp the craft stick from behind.
10. Lay a yarn worm in Momma's beak. See if you can feed the babies by moving Momma by her handle. No fair touching the worm with your hand!

Variation

Instead of coloring the nest, glue on tiny scraps of cloth, paper, twigs, grass, string, and so on to show what robins use to construct their nests.

Follow-up

Make a nest with the materials birds use. Gather scraps of paper, cloth, dried grass, or small twigs. In a bowl gather some mud, or make it, mix in the grass, or other nest material, and push the mixture against the sides of the bowl. Let it dry out. Then remove the nest. Compare it to a bird's nest. Now draw a picture of a (make-believe) bird that could be happy in your nest.

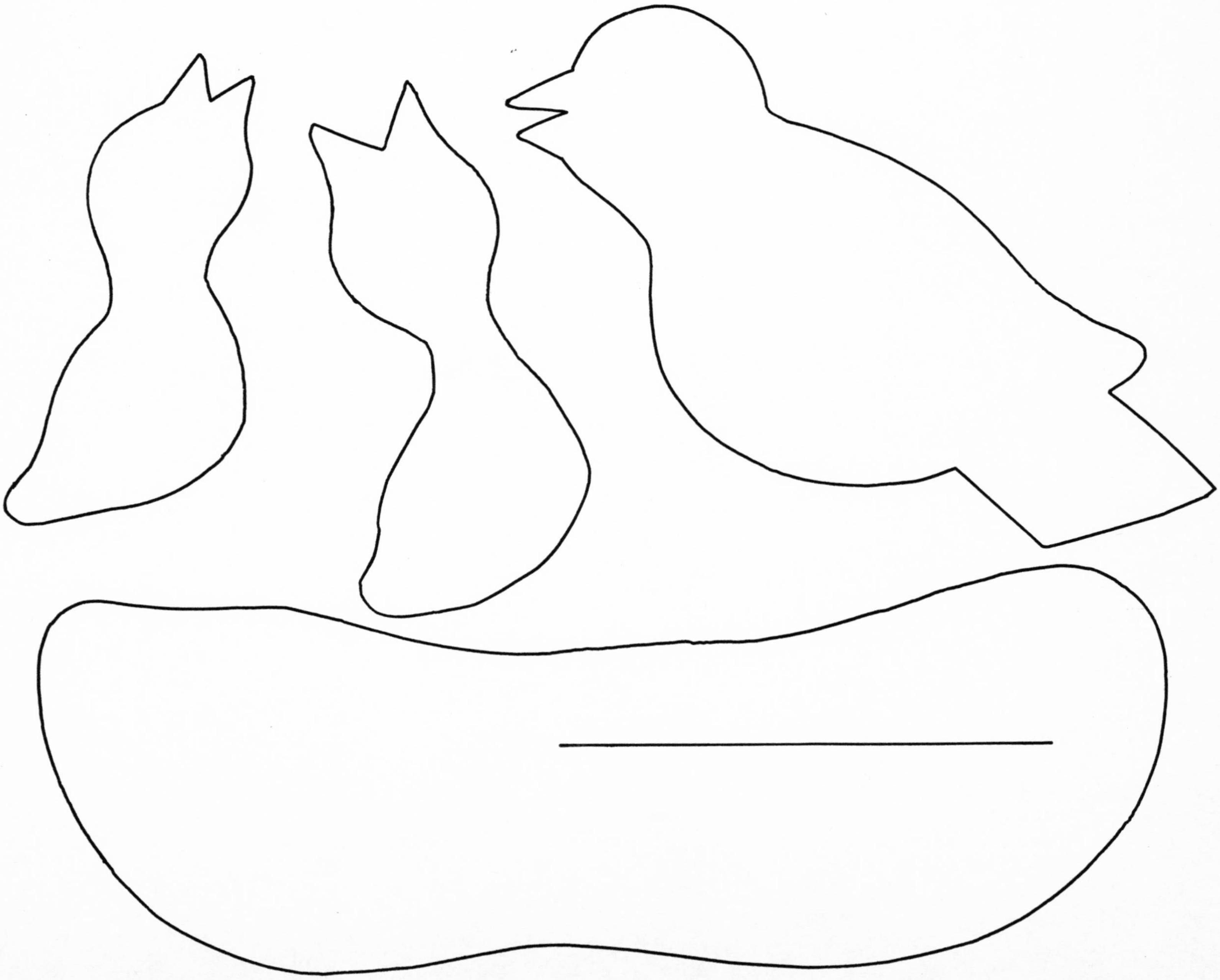

13-1 BUNNY BLUE

Theme Easter

Skills Conceptual development—animals
Eye-hand coordination
Small-muscle control
Creative dramatics

Ages 4–6

Bunny Facts

Rabbits are long-eared, large-eyed, four-legged animals found throughout the world. Their hind legs are long and very powerful, which enables them to move very quickly. Rabbits use their two long front teeth to gnaw at vegetables, shrubs, and tree bark. Most rabbits weigh two to four pounds. Most rabbits do not live together. They like to live alone in nests or in holes under the ground, under logs or rocks.

Materials for Each Child

- 9″ x 12″ oaktag or white construction paper
- Paper fastener (brad)
- Felt-tipped pens or crayons
- 2″ piece of masking tape
- Six 2″ pieces of yarn
- Scissors

Teacher Directions

Teach this brief poem to your students to promote excitement:

"Say hello to Bunny Blue
And he'll change his eyes for you."

You should insert the paper fastener and cut out the eyes.

Steps for Students

1. Trace the bunny and the circle pattern on your oaktag or paper.
2. With your blue felt-tipped pen or crayon color your bunny. Give him a mouth, but not a nose as the paper fastener will be his nose. You can color in a ribbon around his neck, and some pink inside his ears, if you like.

3. Make a "Y" in the circle and color each section a different color.
4. Cut out the bunny, his eyes, and the circle.
5. Place the circle in back of the bunny's head so that you can see the colors through his eyes.
6. Mark the middle of the circle from the back. Make a small hole there with a scissor point or the point of the paper fastener. Insert the paper fastener from the front of your bunny through the circle.
7. Glue on the pieces of yarn, three on each side of the paper fastener, for Bunny Blue's whiskers.
8. Make a handle for turning Bunny Blue's eyes as shown:

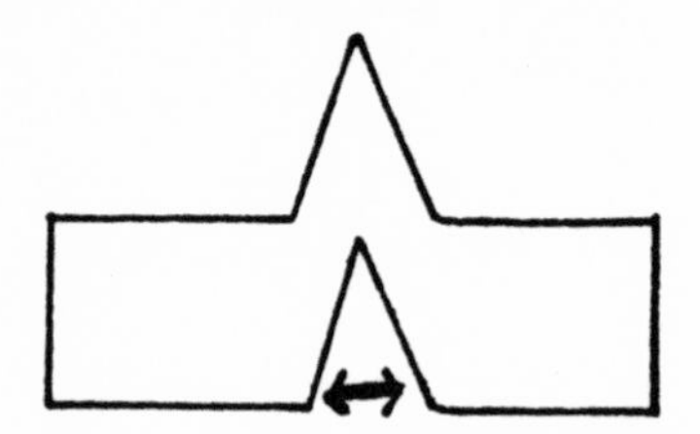

CUT ONE 2" PIECE OF MASKING TAPE. 'PINCH' TOGETHER, LEAVING ENOUGH STICKY TAPE TO ALLOW YOU TO PRESS HANDLE ON TO CIRCLE

13-2 SPONGE-PAINTED EGG

Theme Easter

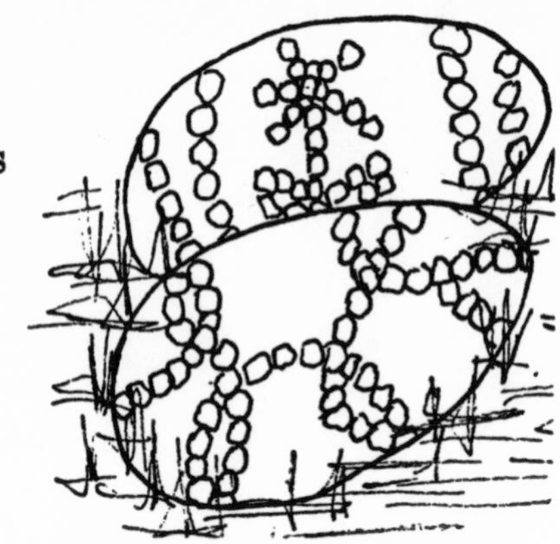

Skills Conceptual development—religious traditions
Eye-hand coordination
Patterning

Ages 3–7

Easter Egg Facts

Eggs stand for a new beginning, or birth. To Christians, Easter is a celebration of the rebirth of Jesus. The shell of the egg is made just a short time before the egg is laid. Bird eggs can be very small or very large. The ostrich lays between twelve and sixteen eggs at one time. Each egg weighs about three pounds. An ant will lay about one million tiny eggs a year, while an oyster may lay sixty million eggs in a year. The most expensive eggs to buy come from the sturgeon fish—they are called caviar! The Chinese bury a year's supply of eggs. The eggs become hard, as if they are hard-boiled. They do not spoil and are supposed to be delicious! Although the eggs are only buried for a year, the Chinese call them "hundred-year eggs."

Materials for Each Child

- 9″ x 12″ light colored construction paper
- Three pastel colored tempera paints
- Three small pieces of sponge
- Styrofoam or aluminum tray covered with aluminum foil for throw-away ease. (2 or 3 children can share one tray)
- Scissors

Teacher Directions

This project needs little of your attention other than to set up the paint trays and inspire the children to make their own creative designs.

Steps for Students

1. Trace the egg pattern onto your construction paper.
2. Dip your sponge into one of the color paints and dab it up and down around the egg line.

3. Take another sponge, dip it in another color paint and decorate the inside of the egg. Use all three colors, and your imagination, to make a beautiful Easter egg.

Variation

You can draw a lot of little eggs on your construction paper and sponge paint the entire other side. When dry, cut out the eggs, draw a basket, and glue them in.

13-3 "QUACKY"

Theme Easter

Skills Conceptual development—animals
Creative dramatics
Eye-hand coordination
Small-muscle control

Ages 4–6

Duck Facts

Ducks are water birds, found in all parts of the world. Ducks have webbed feet and are excellent swimmers. They are also powerful fliers. Some ducks have been known to fly as fast as sixty miles an hour. Wild ducks live on snails, water plants, and small insects. Ducks' feathers are covered with a natural oil that keeps the water from soaking them. Baby ducks leave their nests as soon as they are hatched and follow their mothers to the water. They can swim without lessons!

Materials for Each Child

- 9″ x 12″ white construction paper
- Felt-tipped pens or crayons
- Glue
- Scissors

Teacher Directions

For inspiration visit a duck pond or show the children pictures of ducks. Have the children "quack" and "waddle" like ducks.

You may wish to make the slit for the duck's bill. This is easily done with a single-edge razor. (Remember to put newspaper under the duck.) Show the children how to place the patterns so that they all fit on the construction paper.

Steps for Students

1. Trace Quacky's head and upper and lower bill on your construction paper.
2. Color the duck's head. Give him two big bright eyes.

3. Cut out all the patterns. Cut a slit for Quacky's bill:

4. Fold the top bill as shown: and glue just above the mouth slit.

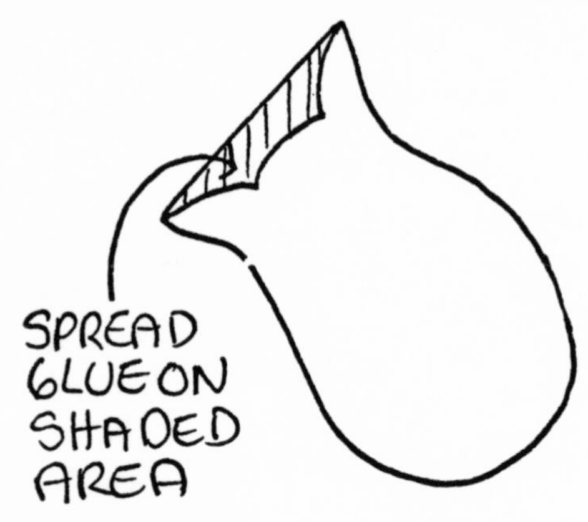

5. Insert the bottom half of the bill into the slot, from the front to the back.
6. Move the bottom half of the bill up and down from the back of Quacky's head.

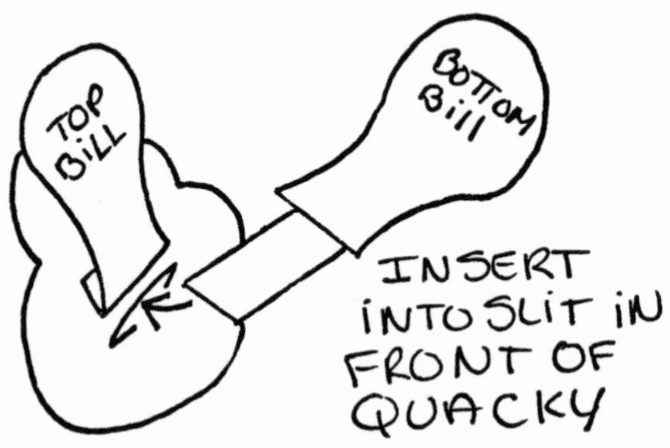

7 Think of some ducky stories to make him quack about!

Follow-up

Make a fuzzy duckling swimming in a pond! Take a piece of dark blue construction paper. Make it look like a pond by cutting off the corners of the paper. With yellow chalk draw a duckling in the middle. Spray the duckling with hair spray so that it doesn't smudge.

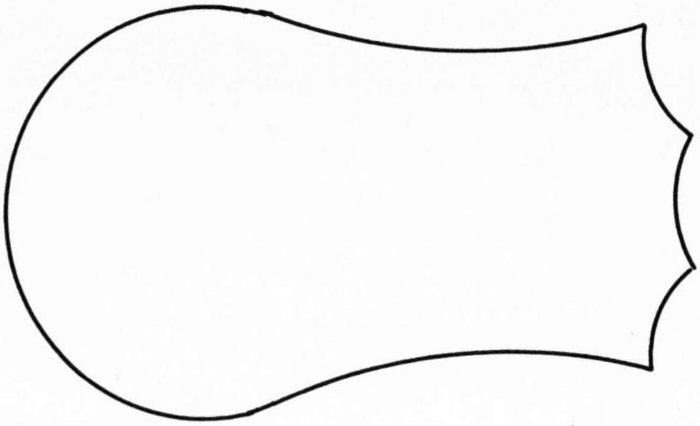

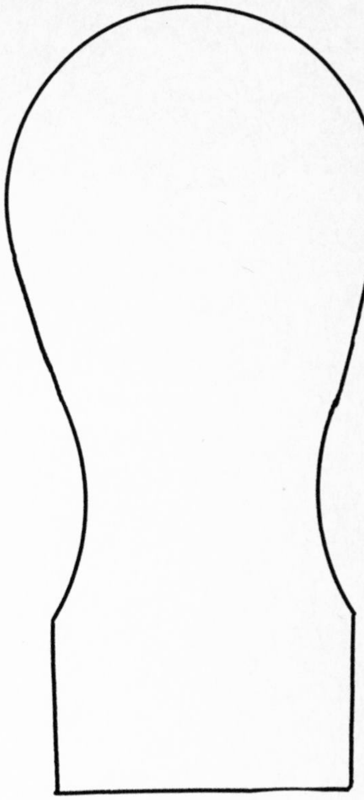

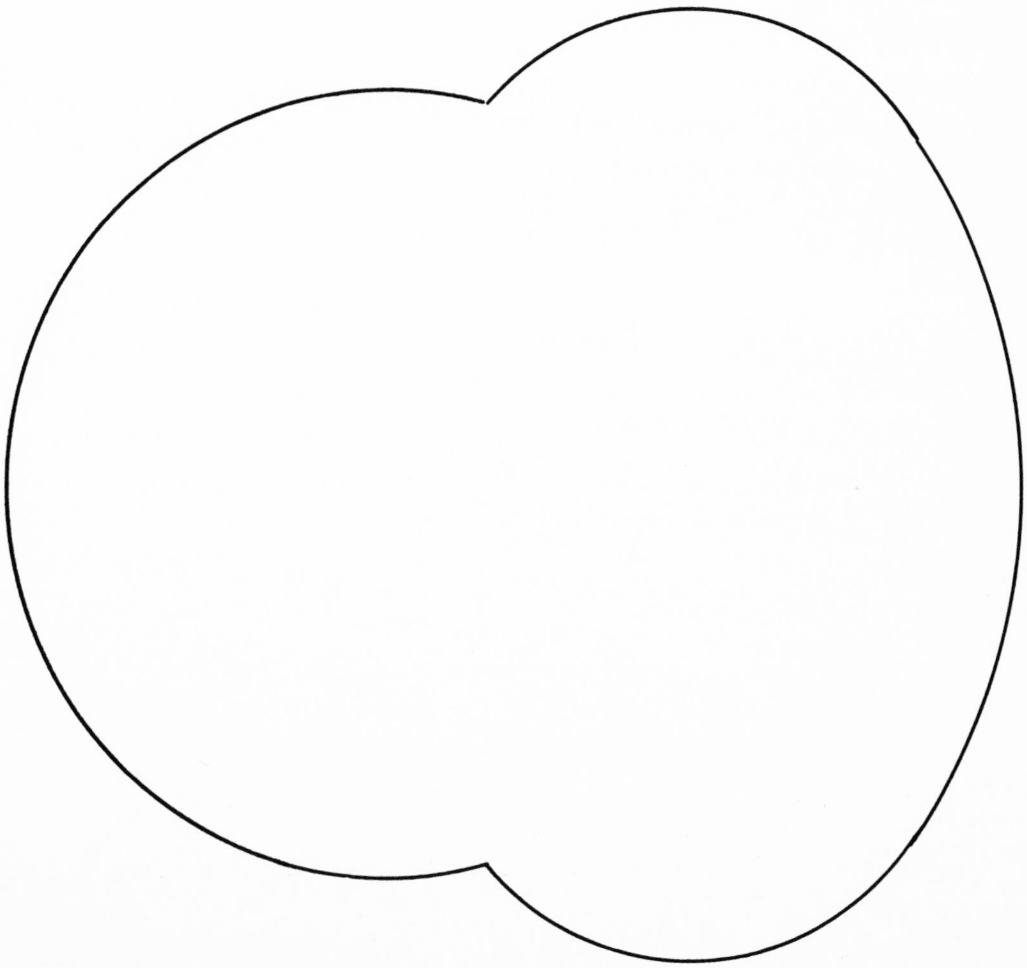

13-4 BUNNY MASK

Theme Easter

Skills Conceptual development—animals
Creative dramatics
Small-muscle control
Eye-hand coordination
Patterning
Spatial relationships

Ages 4–7

Bunny Facts

See projects 13-1, "Bunny Blue," and 13-7, "Bunny Pop-Up Card."

Materials for Each Child

- 9″ x 12″ white construction paper or oaktag
- Pink tissue paper squares, approximately 1½″ square
- Craft stick or a 1″ x 4″ piece of cardboard
- Glue mix: one-half white glue and one-half water in a small bowl or cup (can be shared by 2 or 3 children)
- Small paintbrush
- Scissors

Teacher Directions

Show children what painting a small area (approximately 2″ x 2″) looks like. (Remind them to wipe their brush on the side of the bowl before painting.)

Steps for Students

1. Trace the bunny pattern on your construction paper or oaktag.
2. With your glue mix, paint a small area of your bunny.
3. Lay on pink tissue squares to cover the glue mix. Repeat to cover entire bunny. Overlapping is desirable.

4. Carefully paint a light coat of glue mix over the surface of the tissue paper bunny.
5. Let the bunny dry.
6. Cut out the bunny on the traced lines. Cut out the holes for your eyes.
7. Glue the craft stick to the back of your bunny's head:

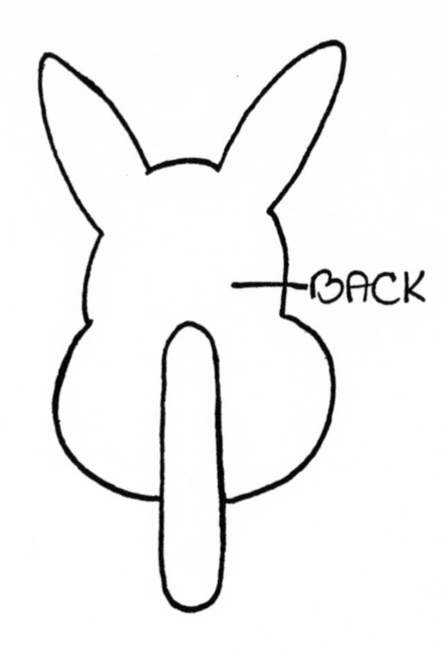

8. Let it dry.
9. Now, be Peter Rabbit for your friends and family!

13-5 WET CHALK EGG

Theme Easter

Skills Conceptual development—science, traditions
Small muscle control
Spatial relationships
Eye-hand coordination
Patterning

Ages 4–8

Egg Facts

The Easter bunny does not take Easter eggs to every country. In France, you get your Easter eggs from bells! There people say that the church bells fly away to Italy before Easter. When the bells fly back, they drop eggs for you to find.

Materials for Each Child

- Pastel colored chalk
- 8 ½″ x 11″ ditto or typing paper
- Small cup or bowl of water (can be shared by 2 or 3 children)
- Stapler
- Scissors

Teacher Directions

Wet chalk drawing gives a very vibrant result. Demonstrate for the children a number of ways to design their egg, for example, start the design at the outer edge and work your way in, start in the center and work out, use random patterning, etc. Discuss Easter and spring symbols for inspiration.

Steps for Students

1. Trace the egg patterns on your paper.
2. Think about how you are going to decorate your egg.
3. Dip the end of your chalk in the water and color your two egg halves. When the chalk dries out, dip again.

4. Let the egg halves dry.
5. Cut out the egg halves.
6. Staple the two egg halves halfway around the bottom of the egg:

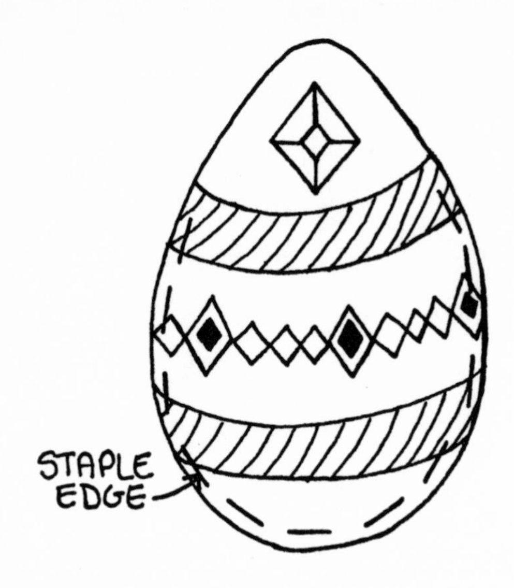

7. Stuff the scraps of paper, that were left over after cutting out the egg halves, into the egg.
8. Continue to staple the egg closed.

13-6 BUNNY POP-UP CARD

Theme Easter

Skills Conceptual development—animals
Detail awareness
Eye-hand coordination
Small-muscle control

Ages 4–7

Bunny Facts

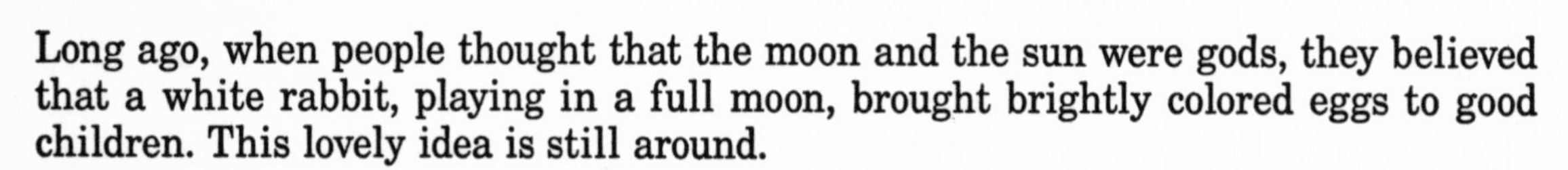

Long ago, when people thought that the moon and the sun were gods, they believed that a white rabbit, playing in a full moon, brought brightly colored eggs to good children. This lovely idea is still around.

Materials for Each Child

- 9" x 12" white construction paper
- Felt-tipped pens or crayons
- Glue
- Scissors

Teacher Directions

You may wish to write on the board Easter greetings that you and your children create, and let them choose one to copy on their card. (*Alternative*: This project may be photocopies or traced onto a ditto.)

Steps for Students

1. Cut your construction paper in half on the 12" side.
2. Trace your bunny pattern on one half of your construction paper.
3. Remembering all your details, give your bunny a face, whiskers, paws, feet, and so on.
4. Cut out your bunny.
5. Fold the other half of your construction paper in half, then open it.

6. Fold your bunny as shown and glue it into the card:

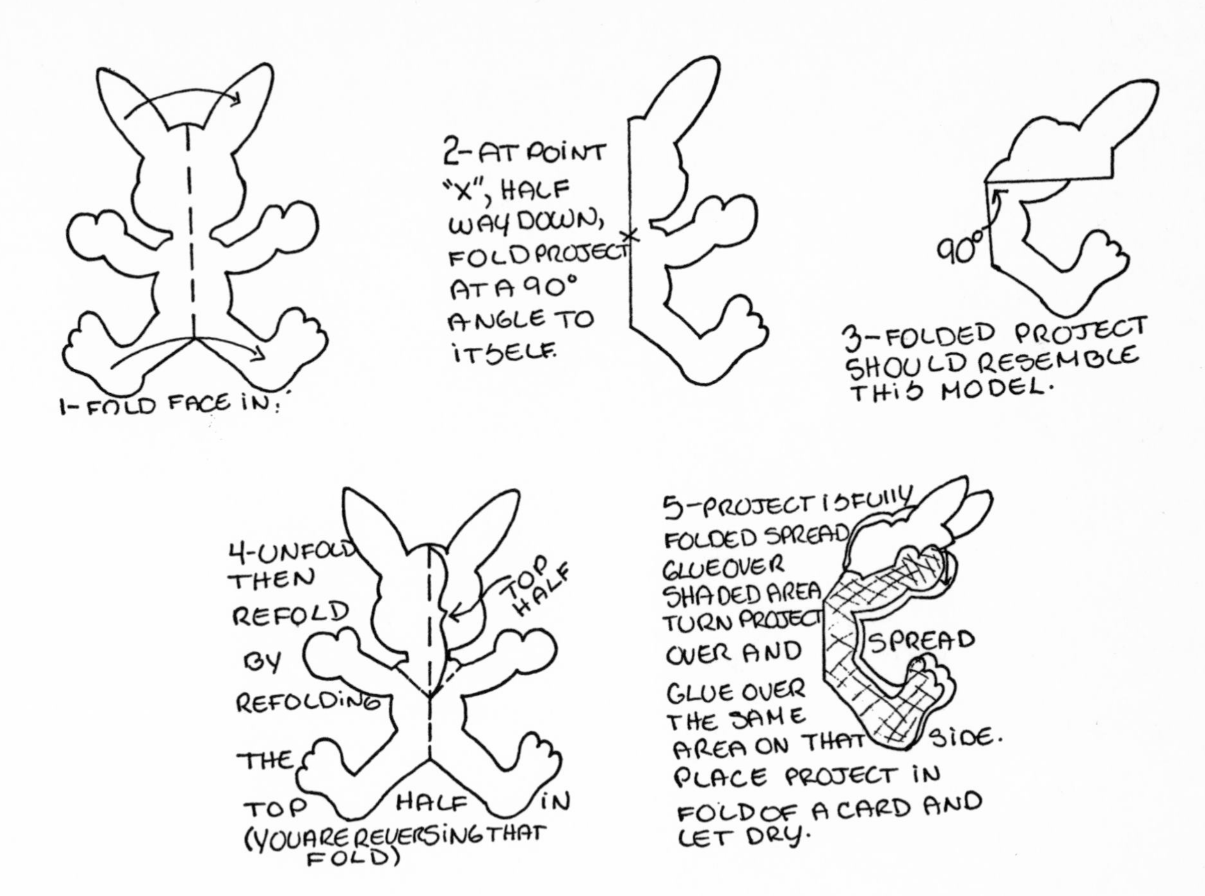

7. Decorate the front of your card and write an Easter greeting on it.

14-1 SUN-GLOW ELIJAH'S CUP

Theme Passover

Skills Conceptual development—religion
Eye-hand coordination
Patterning
Small-muscle control

Ages 3–8

Elijah Cup Facts

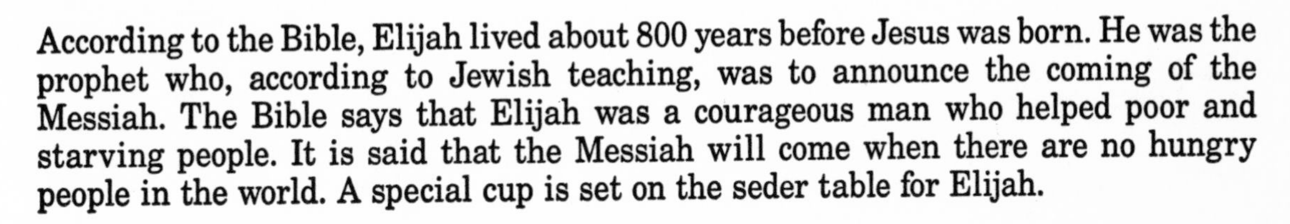

According to the Bible, Elijah lived about 800 years before Jesus was born. He was the prophet who, according to Jewish teaching, was to announce the coming of the Messiah. The Bible says that Elijah was a courageous man who helped poor and starving people. It is said that the Messiah will come when there are no hungry people in the world. A special cup is set on the seder table for Elijah.

Materials for Each Child

- 9″ x 12″ tracing paper
- Glue mix: one-half water and one half white glue (bowl can be shared by 2 or 3 children)
- Small brush
- Colored tissue squares (approximately 1″ square)
- Scissors

Teacher Directions

Show children what painting a small area (approximately 2″ x 2″) looks like. (Remind them to wipe their brush on the side of their bowl before painting.)

Steps for Students

1. Trace Elijah's cup on the tracing paper.
2. With glue mixture paint a small section of the cup, lay on a tissue square. Repeat to cover cup. Overlapping of squares is fine.

3. Give finished cup a light coat of glue mix.
4. Let dry. Cut out the cup.
5. Hang or tape the cup in a window and watch it glow!

Variation

This project also comes out very well using light-colored construction paper. However, you do lose the translucency.

14-2 SEDER PLACE CARD

Theme Passover

Skills Conceptual development—religion
Small-muscle control
Eye-hand coordination

Ages 4–7

Passover Facts

Passover is the Jewish festival of freedom. It celebrates the Israelites' journey (Exodus) from slavery to freedom three thousand years ago. The Bible tells us that Moses told the Pharaoh that God would kill the firstborn in every Egyptian household, if he didn't let the Israelites leave. Moses then instructed each of the Jewish families to sprinkle lamb's blood on the doorposts of their homes so that the angel of the Lord would "pass over" and leave their children unharmed. After this was done, Moses led the Jewish people, with their few belongings including bread that didn't have time to rise (matzoth), out of Egypt. When they got to the Red Sea, they heard the Pharaoh's army behind them. They thought they'd all be killed by the soldiers. God parted the sea, allowing the Jews to walk on the floor of the sea to the other far bank. When the Egyptian soldiers tried to do the same, the sea walls closed and the Egyptians drowned.

On the first and/or second nights of Passover a supper called a *Seder* is served. Special foods are served and the story of the Exodus is told.

Materials for Each Child

- 9″ x 12″ white construction paper
- Crayons or felt-tipped pens
- Scissors
- Glue

Teacher Directions

After the children have traced their Seder cups, draw a rectangle in the center of each cup. This rectangle is not to be colored, as it will be used for the name.

Steps for Students

1. Trace the place card pattern at the top and bottom of your paper:

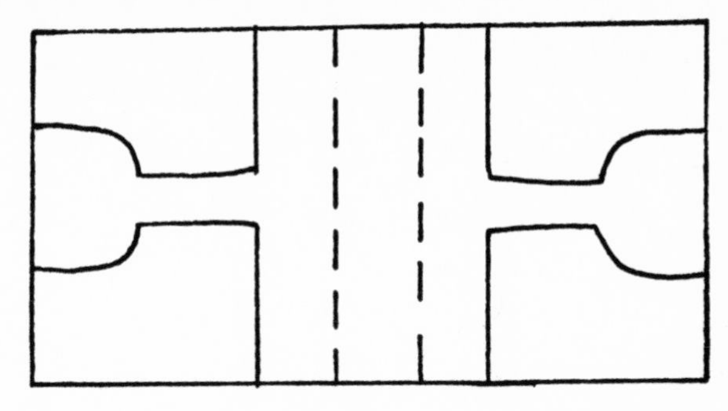

2. Cut out the place card only on the lines shown and fold on lines indicated:

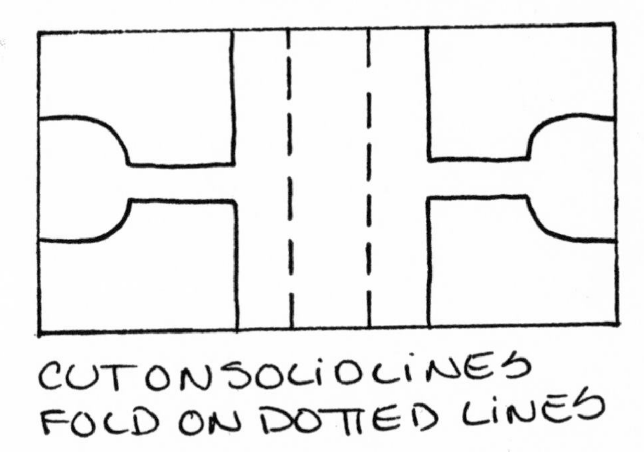

3. Lay your place card flat and write a name in the center of the Seder cup.
4. Decorate the cup.
5. On the rectangle at the bottom of the cup draw some Seder foods: eggs, matzoth, bitter herbs, lamb shankbone.
6. Refold to upright position and glue the top of the cups together.

14-3 PASSOVER CANDLE

Theme Passover

Skills Conceptual development—religion
Eye-hand coordination
Small-muscle control
Patterning

Ages 4–7

Passover Candle Facts

The first step of the Passover Seder is the lighting and blessing of the candles at sundown. The lighting of the candles signals the light of freedom that comes after the darkness of slavery.

Materials for Each Child

- 9″ x 12″ white or yellow construction paper
- Felt-tipped pens or crayons
- Glue
- Scissors

Teacher Directions

Discuss some of the simple Passover symbols for the children as inspiration for their designing their candle.

Steps for Students

1. Trace your candle and flame on your construction paper.
2. Color the flame with red, orange, and yellow.
3. Think about the patterning of your candle.
4. Decorate your candle with Passover symbols, lines, dots, and so on.
5. Turn your candle into a cylinder form and glue or tape it closed.
6. Fold the flame as shown and glue inside the candle:

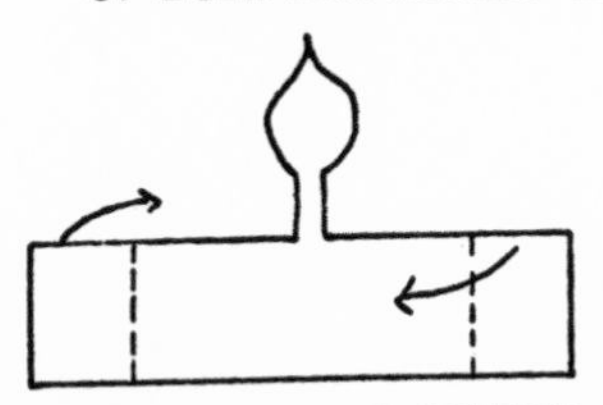

1-FOLD ON DOTTED LINES IN THE INDICATED DIRECTIONS

GLUE
GLUE

2-SPREAD GLUE OVER THE TWO FOLDED TABS

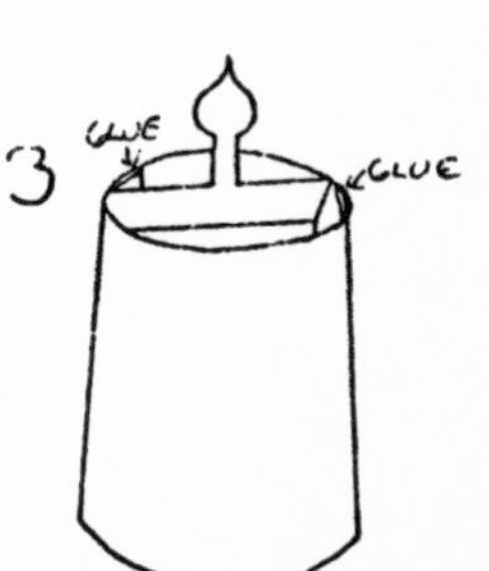

SUMMER

The longest day of the year is the first day of summer. On this day, June 21, there is more light and less darkness than any other day. Summer lasts for ninety three days and fifteen hours, and ends September 23. In the summer, birds, snakes, and lizards hatch from eggs, and caterpillars spin cocoons of silk around themselves.

15-1 THE GRAND SEAL

Theme Summer

Skills Conceptual development—animals
Eye-hand coordination
Small-muscle control

Ages 3–7

Seal Facts

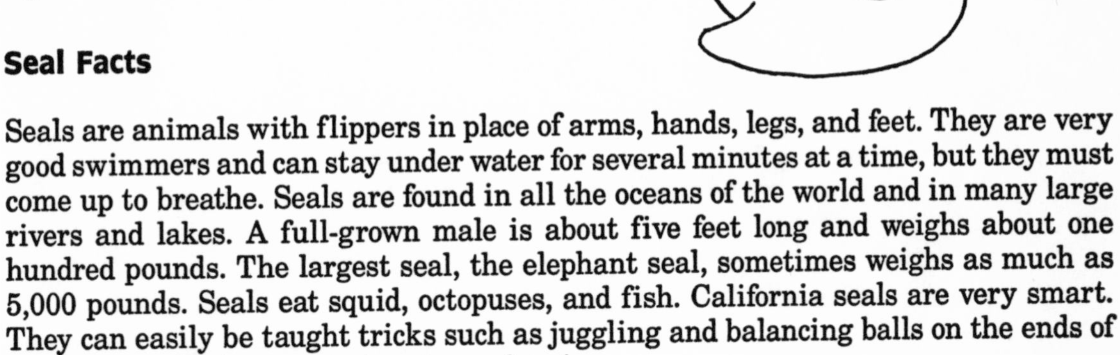

Seals are animals with flippers in place of arms, hands, legs, and feet. They are very good swimmers and can stay under water for several minutes at a time, but they must come up to breathe. Seals are found in all the oceans of the world and in many large rivers and lakes. A full-grown male is about five feet long and weighs about one hundred pounds. The largest seal, the elephant seal, sometimes weighs as much as 5,000 pounds. Seals eat squid, octopuses, and fish. California seals are very smart. They can easily be taught tricks such as juggling and balancing balls on the ends of their noses. Seals seem to love to perform!

Materials for Each Child

- 6″ x 9″ (½ of 9″ x 12″) white construction paper
- Felt-tipped pens or crayons
- Scissors

Teacher Directions

Show the children how to place the three patterns so that they all fit on the construction paper. You may wish to make the slit for the seal's flipper with a single-edge razor. (Put newspaper under the seal so that you don't slit the table!) The seal is in profile. Demonstrate that in profile you only see half a face. (*Alternative*: This project may be photocopied or traced onto a ditto.)

Steps for Students

1. Trace the three patterns on your construction paper.
2. With your crayons give your seal an eye and mouth.
3. Color your seal with gray crayon or, if you don't have gray, use your black lightly. Color the flipper on both sides.

4. Make your seal's ball fancy by using bright colors and an interesting pattern.
5. Cut out all the pieces.
6. Make a slit in your seal's body as shown and insert the flipper.

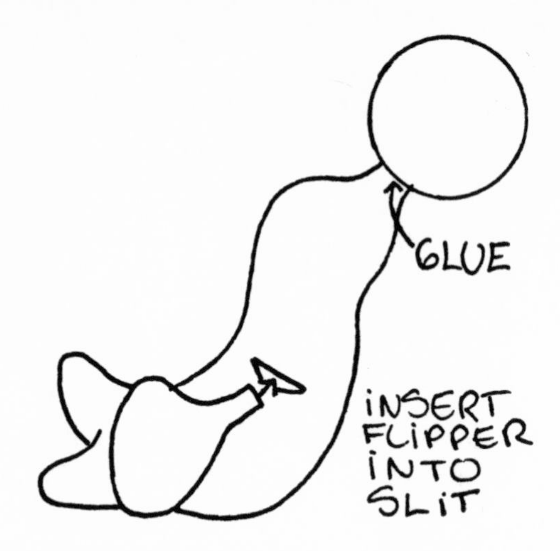

7. Glue the ball on the seal's nose.
8. From the back of the seal move the flipper up and down —— and make some seal noises —— "arf, arf!"

15-2 "AL E. GATOR"

Theme Summer

Skills Conceptual development—animals
Eye-hand coordination
Small-muscle control
Creative dramatics

Ages 4–8

Alligator Facts

Alligators can grow to as much as fifteen to nineteen feet long and weigh up to 600 pounds! Alligators live in fresh water streams only in the southern United States and China. They live between thirty and fifty years. Their babies are hatched from oval white eggs. Mother alligators lay twenty to ninety eggs in nests on dry land. The eggs are left there to be hatched by the heat of the sun. Although alligators eat mostly fish, they sometimes capture, drown, and eat animals as large as deer.

Materials for Each Child

- 9″ x 12″ white construction paper
- Felt-tipped pens or crayons
- Stapler
- Glue
- Scissors

Teacher Directions

Depending on the skill level of your children, you may want to do the stapling. Show the children how to place the patterns so that they all fit on their paper.

Steps for Students

1. Trace the patterns on your paper.
2. With your felt-tipped pens or crayons color the top and bottom of Al's head

green. (If you are using crayons, do not color where the eyes are going to be glued, as the crayon wax sometimes resists the glue.)

3. On the pattern that is the inside of Al's mouth, draw teeth and a tongue:

4. Draw eyeballs on the two eye patterns and then fold in half.

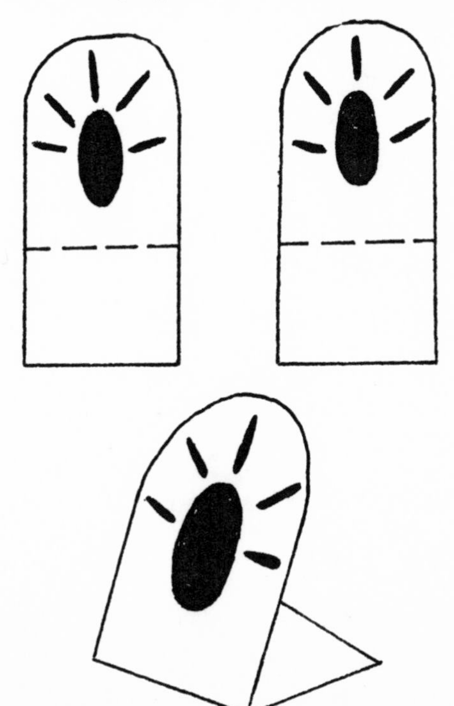

5. Glue the eyes on one of your green patterns:

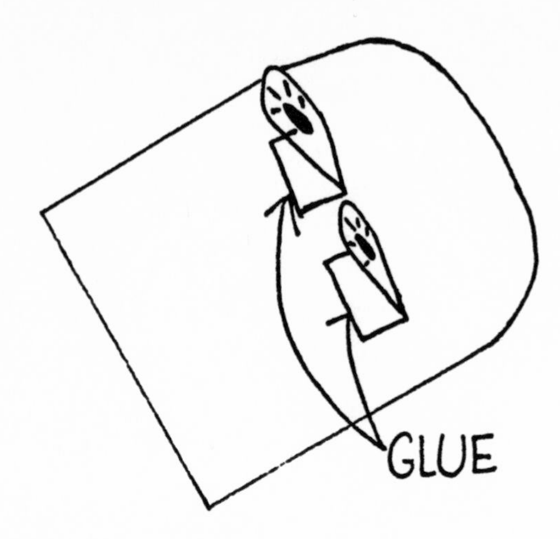

6. Staple parts together (all colored surfaces face out) as shown. (Make sure the tongue end is on the opposite end to the eyes.)

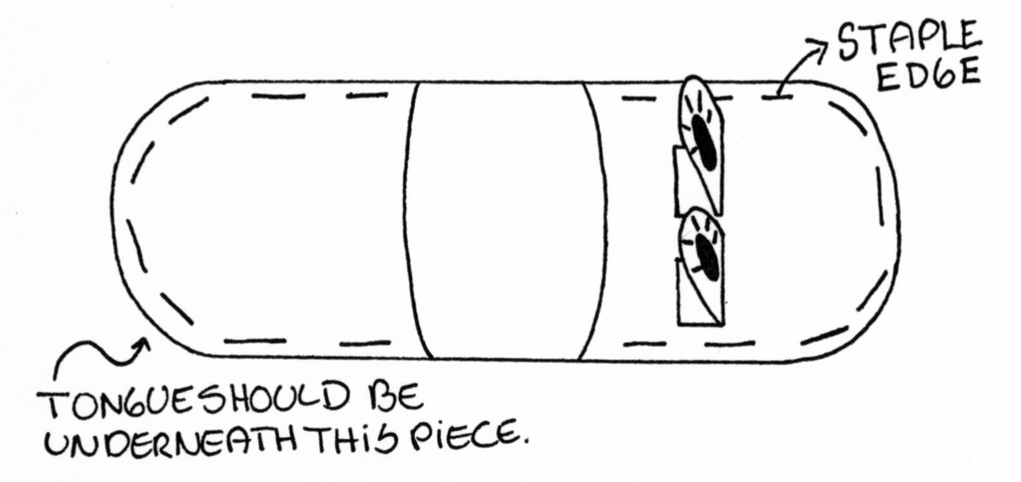

7. Insert your thumb in the pocket that has the tongue on it, and your other fingers in the other pocket.
8. Move your fingers in an open and close movement to make Al talk.

Follow-up

Make two Al E. Gators, one for each hand. Make up a little story and use your Al E. Gators like hand puppets to tell the story and talk to each other.

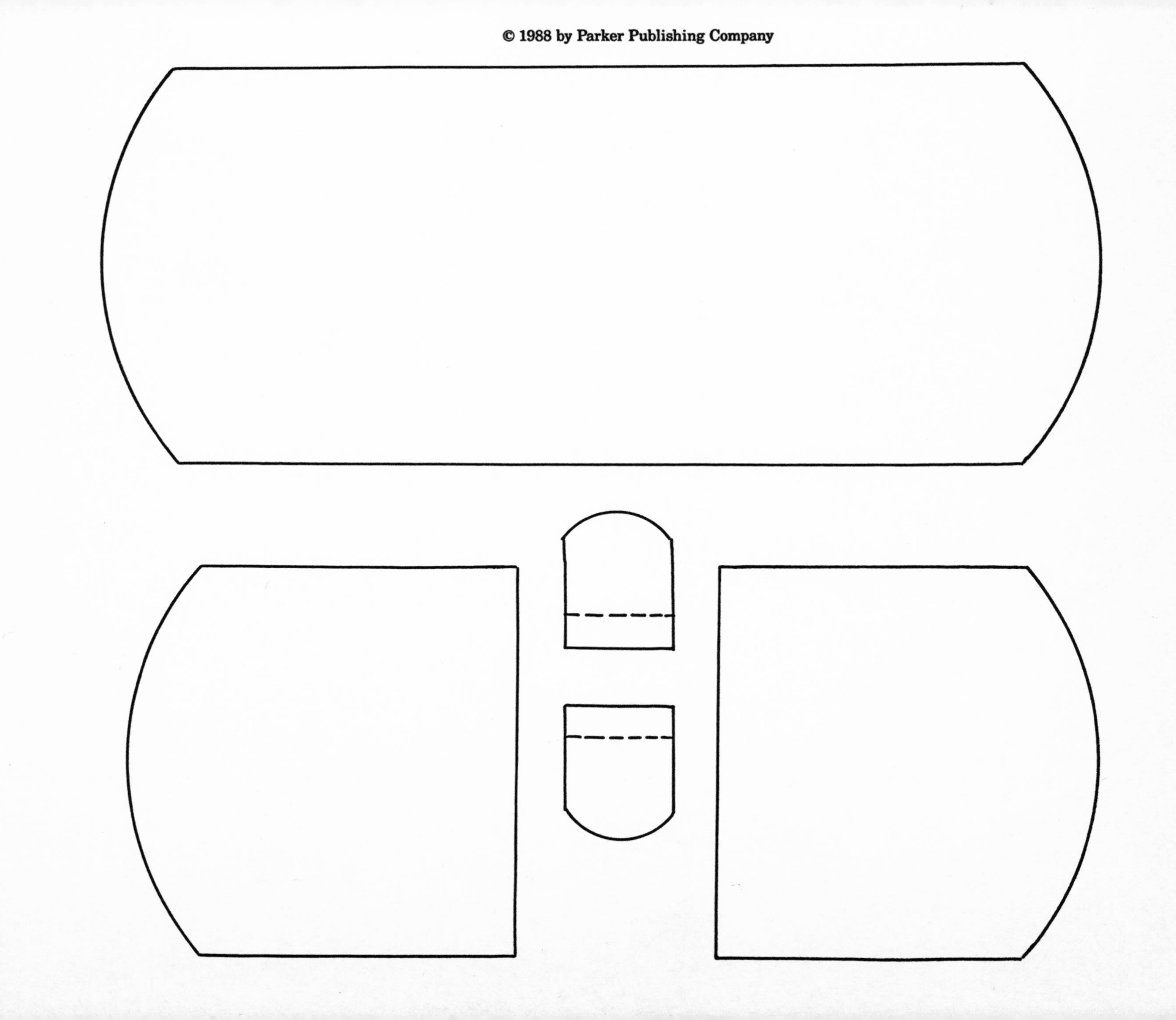

15-3 "GILLY" THE FISH

Theme Summer

Skills Conceptual development—fish
Creative dramatics
Eye-hand coordination
Small-muscle control

Ages 4–8

Fish Facts

Fish are animals that have gills, scales, and fins. Scientists say that there are nearly thirty thousand different kinds of fish that live in the waters that cover three-quarters of the earth's surface. Like every other living thing, fish need oxygen to live. Fish breathe through their gills. They take in water that contains oxygen through their mouths. The blood vessels in the gills absorb the oxygen and let the water out. Fins are the arms and legs of fish. The fins enable the fish to swim, to steer, and to balance themselves.

Materials for Each Child

- 9″ x 12″ light-colored construction paper
- Felt-tipped pens or crayons
- Stapler
- Scissors

Teacher Directions

Show children how to place patterns on their paper so that they all fit.

Steps for Students

1. Trace all the patterns on your construction paper. Or, draw a big fish by yourself.
2. Draw a line to separate the fish's face from his body.
3. On both body patterns give Gilly an eye. Since fish come in so many beautiful colors and patterns, use your imagination to make Gilly special. Color the two gills.

4. Cut out all the patterns. Save the scraps.
5. Glue or staple the rounded side of Gilly's gill to the center of his body. Bend the other end out.
6. Staple the two body parts as shown:

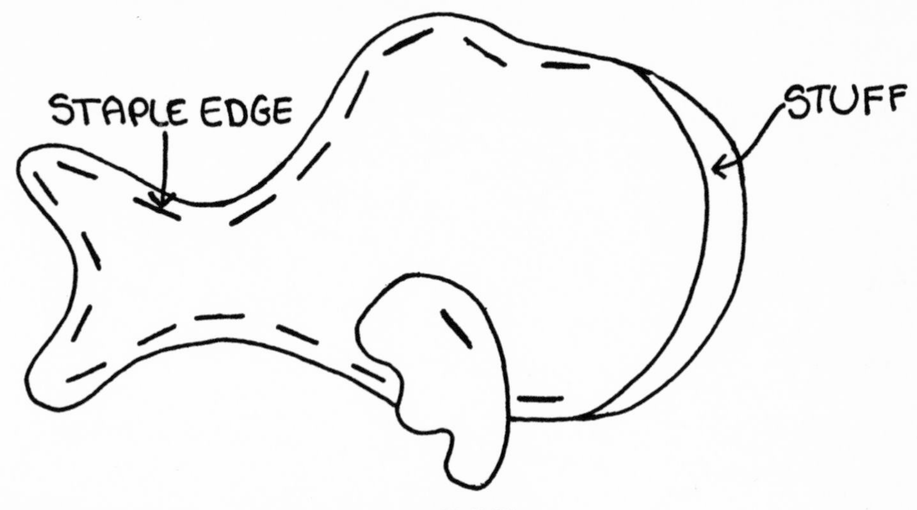

7. Crumble up your scraps and stuff Gilly.
8. Continue to staple around head to close Gilly.

Follow-ups

1. String the children's Gillys and tie them to a string across the room. Make the strings attached to Gilly of varying lengths. Your classroom will look like an aquarium.
2. Have the children learn the traditional little song "Three Little Fishes":

Three little fishes
In an itsy bitsy brook
"Swim," said the mother
"Swim, if you can"
And they swam and they swam
All over the dam.

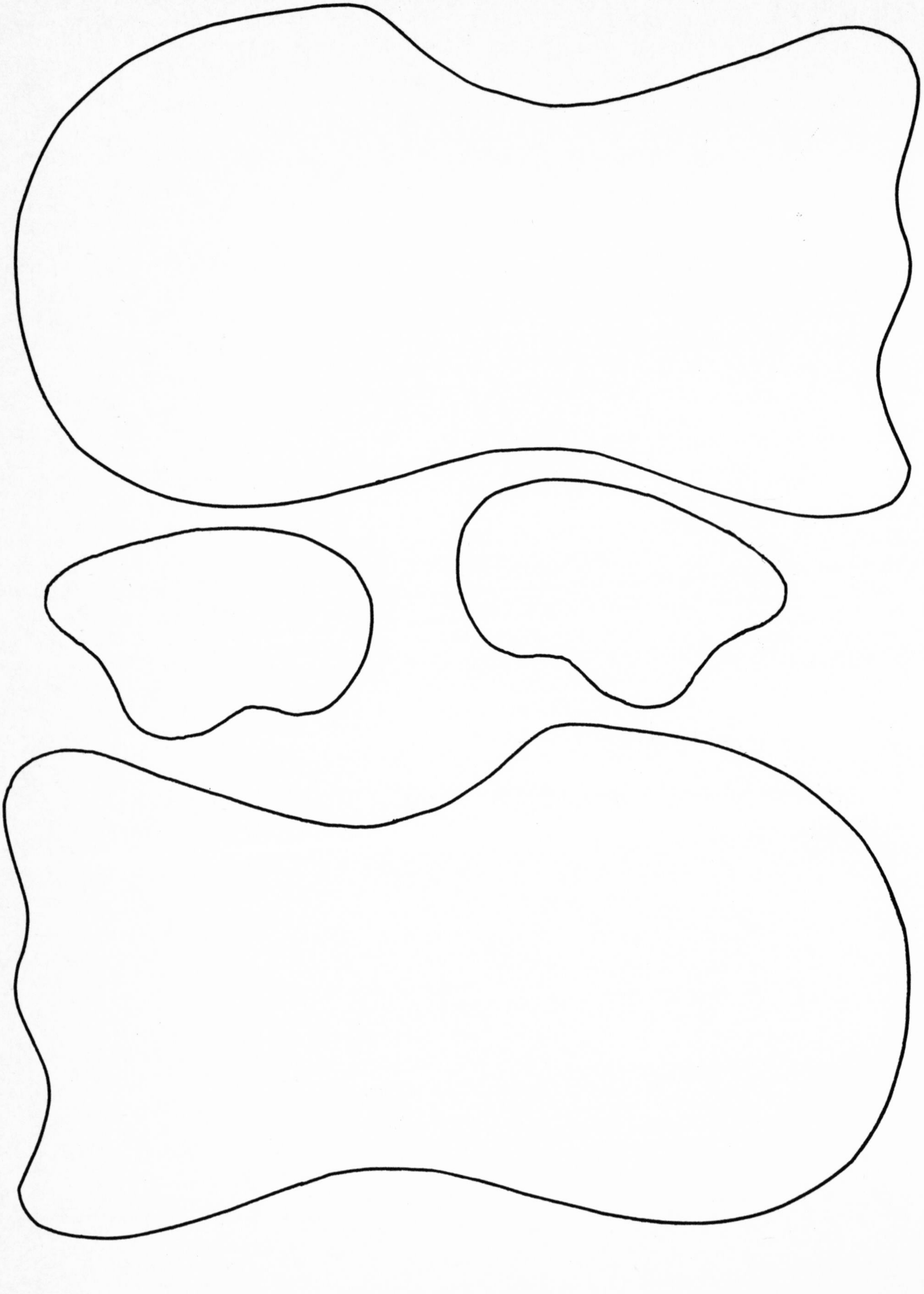

15-4 "CRABBY"

Theme Summer

Skills Conceptual development—animals
Creative dramatics
Eye-hand coordination
Small-muscle control
Spatial relationships
Concrete counting

Ages 5–8

Crab Facts

Crabs are hard-shelled animals with roundish, flattened bodies, and ten legs. There are more than 1,000 different kinds of crabs. The pea crab is less than one inch across. The Japanese giant crab can grow up to twelve feet across! The blue-claw crab has claws at the ends of its front legs and its back pair of legs are flattened into paddles for swimming. Crabs have eyes on stalks which they can make stick out. They are famous for their way of swimming sideways.

Materials for Each Child

- 9″ x 12″ white construction paper
- 12″ piece of string
- Felt-tipped pens or crayons
- Glue
- Scissors
- Hole puncher

Teacher Directions

Discuss Crabby's ten legs, emphasizing that the front two are claws and the back two are paddles. (*Alternative*: This project may be photocopied or traced onto a ditto.)

Steps for Students

1. Trace all the patterns on your construction paper.
2. With your felt-tipped pens or crayons, color Crabby's shell and ten legs.

3. Cut out all the patterns.
4. Fold the small ovals in half. Draw eye balls on one side of each half:

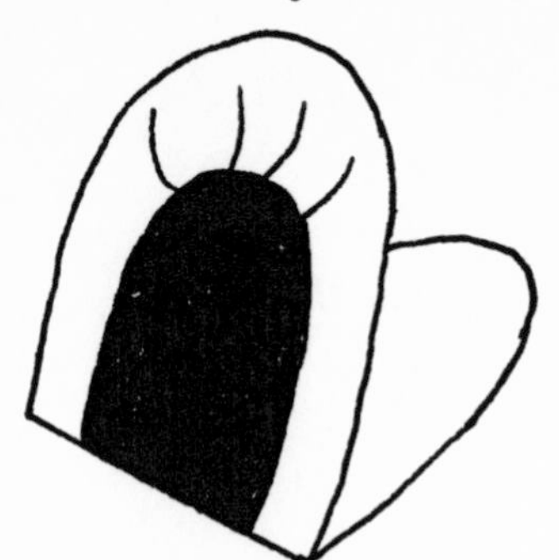

5. Glue Crabby's legs on the underside of his shell:

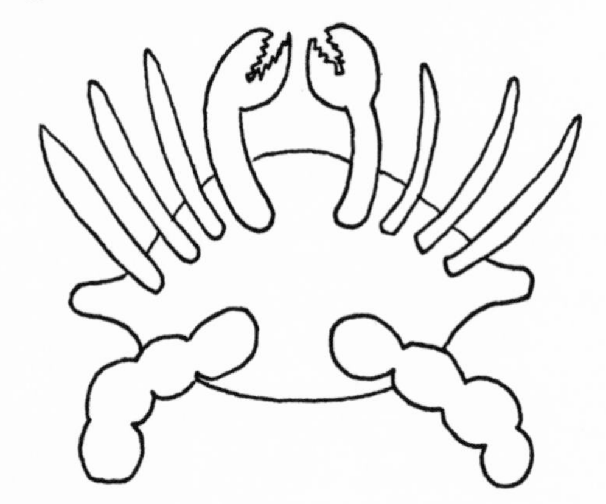

6. Cut a 1″ slit at each end of Crabby's shell, fold and glue as shown:

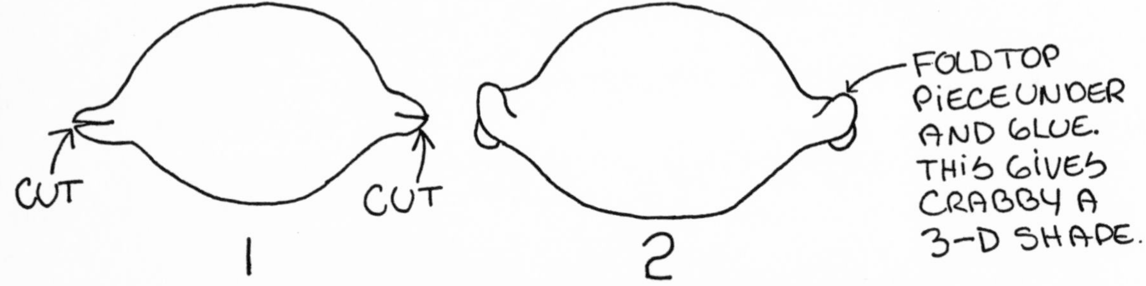

7. Glue Crabby's eyes close together on the top side of his shell.
8. Make two small holes in the top of Crabby's shell, about 2" apart. Put the string in the holes from the top, and tie knots underneath so that the string does not pull back.
9. Use Crabby as a puppet and make up a story about life in the deep blue sea.

Follow-up

Make a picture of Crabby under water! On white construction paper draw and color in a crab with crayons. Make a blue wash—½ cup of water, ½ teaspoon blue paint or ink. Brush the wash over the whole piece of construction paper. The wash won't stick to Crabby, and it will look like the deep, blue sea.

16-1 UNCLE SAM

Theme Fourth of July

Skills Conceptual development—legends
Eye-hand coordination
Detail awareness
Patterning
Shape discrimination

Ages 4–7

Uncle Sam Facts

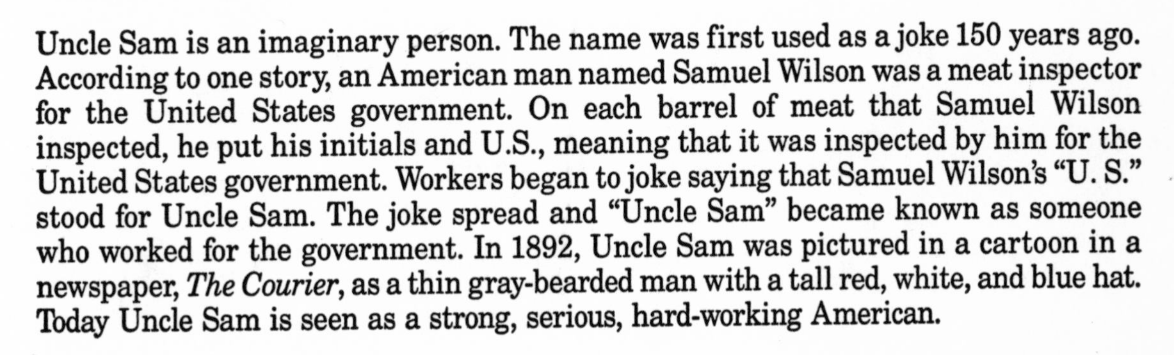

Uncle Sam is an imaginary person. The name was first used as a joke 150 years ago. According to one story, an American man named Samuel Wilson was a meat inspector for the United States government. On each barrel of meat that Samuel Wilson inspected, he put his initials and U.S., meaning that it was inspected by him for the United States government. Workers began to joke saying that Samuel Wilson's "U. S." stood for Uncle Sam. The joke spread and "Uncle Sam" became known as someone who worked for the government. In 1892, Uncle Sam was pictured in a cartoon in a newspaper, *The Courier*, as a thin gray-bearded man with a tall red, white, and blue hat. Today Uncle Sam is seen as a strong, serious, hard-working American.

Materials for Each Child

- 6″ x 9″ (½ of 9″ x 12″) white construction paper
- 6″ x 9″ (½ of 9″ x 12″) light colored construction paper
- 9″ x 12″ red, white or blue construction paper
- Cotton ball
- Glue
- Felt-tipped pens or crayons
- Scissors

Teacher Directions

Although this is an easy project, you may wish to demonstrate how to bend and glue the tabs of Uncle Sam's hat.

Steps for Students

1. Trace the circle pattern on your light-colored construction paper.
2. Draw a face on the circle. Remember to put as many face details as you can think of (eyelashes, eyebrows, ears, and so on).
3. Cut out the circle and glue it on the lower half of your 9″ x 12″ construction paper.
4. Pull apart your cotton ball into long thin strips. Put glue around Uncle Sam's chin. Lay the cotton in place to make him a beard.
5. Trace the two hat patterns on the white construction paper. With your felt-tipped pens or crayons draw lines of red and blue, leaving a line of white in the middle. Have the lines go the long way on the rectangle pattern.
6. Fold the tab up on the rounded pattern (the brim of his hat) and glue on the top of Uncle Sam's head.
7. Bend the tabs of the top of his hat, arc the rectangle and glue as shown:

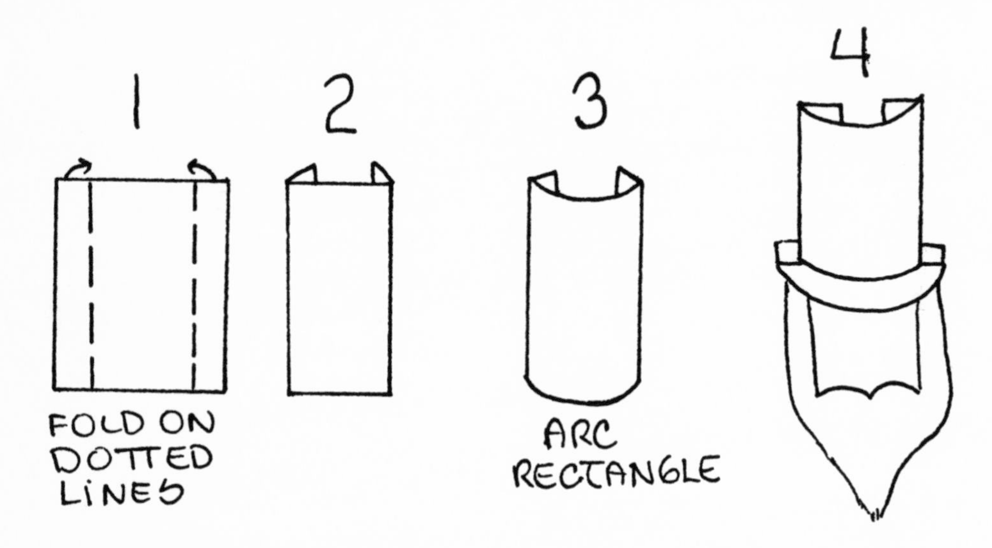

16-2 STATUE OF LIBERTY'S CROWN

Theme Fourth of July

Skills Conceptual development—history
Creative dramatics
Spatial relationships
Eye-hand coordination

Ages 5–8

Statue of Liberty Crown Facts

The young french sculptor, Frederic Auguste Bartholdi, who made our Statue of Liberty, thought of how his mother Charlotte looked while he was making this wonderful statue. Miss Liberty's head was finished in time to go to the Paris World Fair in 1878. The head was taken to the fair grounds in a wagon pulled by twelve horses. The reason for this exhibit was to raise money so that the rest of the statue could be built. The statue was finally completed in 1884. It weighed 225 tons! It was packed in 214 crates to travel to America by ship.

Materials for Each Child

- 4 8 ½″ x 11″ white ditto paper, or trace onto a ditto and run four sheets (seven spires) for each child
- 3″ x 18″ (¼ of a 12″ x 18″) construction paper
- Felt-tipped pens or crayons
- Glue
- Tape
- Scissors

Teacher Directions

Demonstrate the careful folding of the spires and the taping of them to the headband.

Steps for Students

1. Trace seven spires on your paper. Two will fit on each 8 ½″ x 11″ paper.
2. Decorate Miss Liberty's spires. Be creative. Decorate the spires in your own design or alternating red, white, and blue sections of each spire.

3. Cut out all seven spires
4. Fold each spire in half. Then, in half again. Unfold.

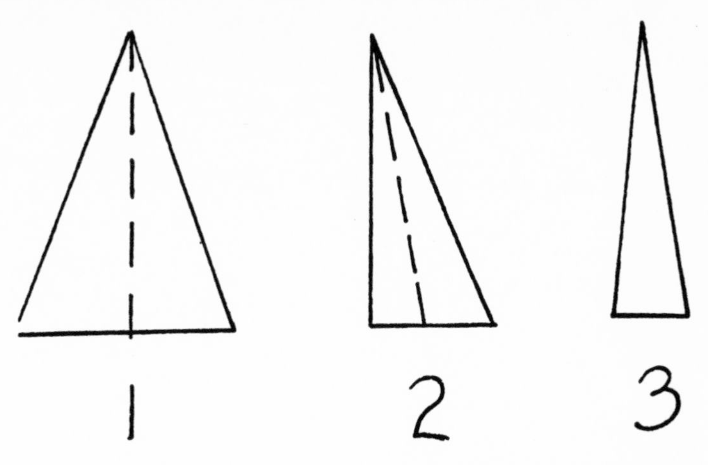

5. Bend the left section back toward the middle along its same fold line.
6. Close the two end sections over each other and glue together.
7. Do the same for the other spires.
8. Fold the 3″ x 18″ paper in half and glue together.
9. The part of the spire that is glued together is going to be taped to the headband as shown:

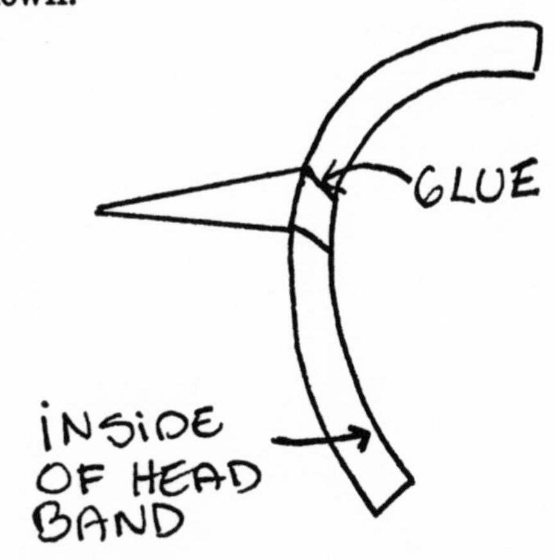

10. Continue to attach all seven spires. The bottom edge of the spire need not be taped as the end opening rests against the band for support.
11. Staple a piece of paper to each side of the band to adjust it to each child's head, or, punch a hole at each end of the band and tie them together with a cut rubber band.

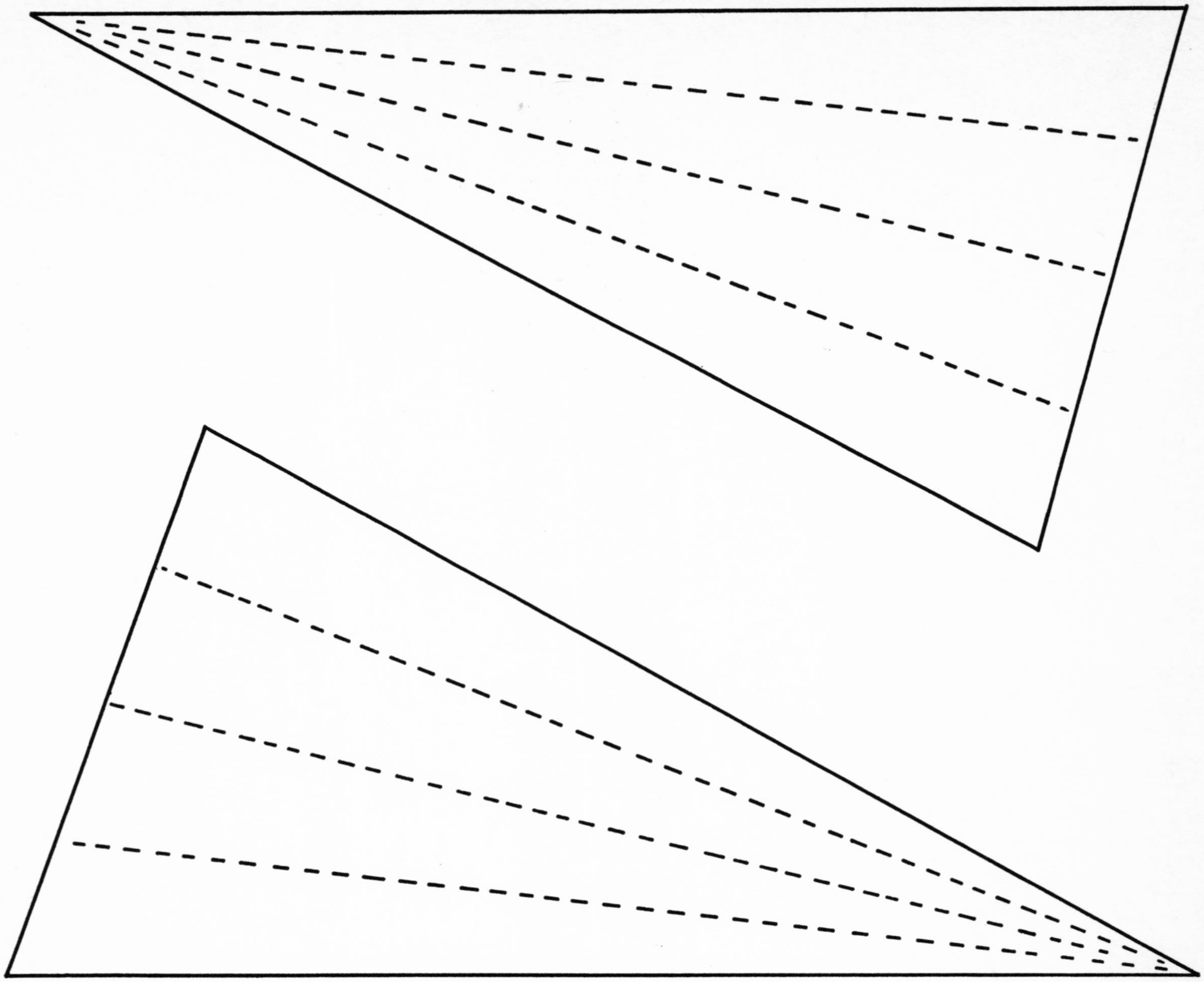

16-3 FOURTH OF JULY CARD

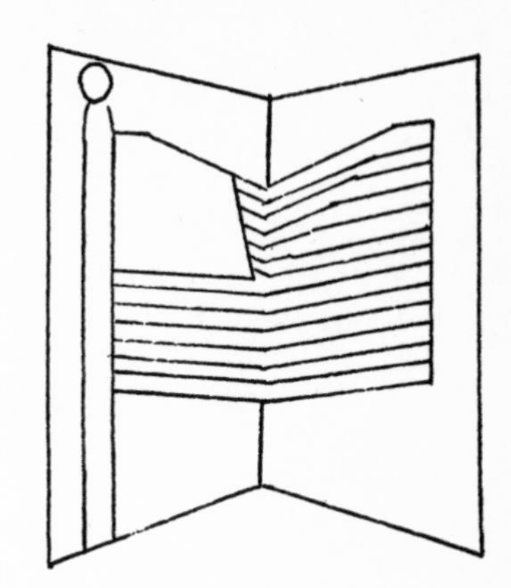

Theme Fourth of July

Skills Conceptual development—history
Small-muscle control
Eye-hand coordination
Patterning

Ages 5–8

Flag Facts

The first cloth flag was the invention of the Romans in the Middle Ages, 600 years ago. On June 14, 1777, the Continental Congress approved the Stars and Stripes as the national flag of the United States. This flag had thirteen red and white stipes, one for each colony, and thirteen stars on a field of blue. Red was used for the blood of the brave men who died fighting for us. Blue stood for courage and bravery. The white represented hope for our future. In 1791 and 1792, when two more states joined the union, Congress voted to add two more stars and two more stripes. As more and more states joined the union, a different design had to be thought up or our flag would have gotten much too big. In 1818 Congress passed a law saying that the flag should have thirteen stripes and that a star would be added for each new state.

Materials for Each Child

- 9″ x 12″ white construction paper
- Felt-tipped pens or crayons
- Glue
- Scissors

Teacher Directions

You may wish to write on the board and then discuss briefly some patriotic sayings for the children to choose from and copy on their cards, for example, have a Flag-Waving Fourth, Happy Birthday America! (*Alternative*: This project may be photocopied or traced onto a ditto.)

Steps for Students

1. Cut the construction paper in half on the 12″ side.
2. On one half of the construction paper trace the flag.
3. With your felt-tipped pens or crayons give your flag stripes, by making red lines that go from one edge of the flag to the other. Make stars by starting with an "x" then add more cross lines. Or, draw a small circle, and make small lines sticking out from around the edge of the circle.
4. Cut out the flag.
5. Fold the other half of the construction paper in half, then open it.
6. Fold your flag as shown, then glue it into your card:

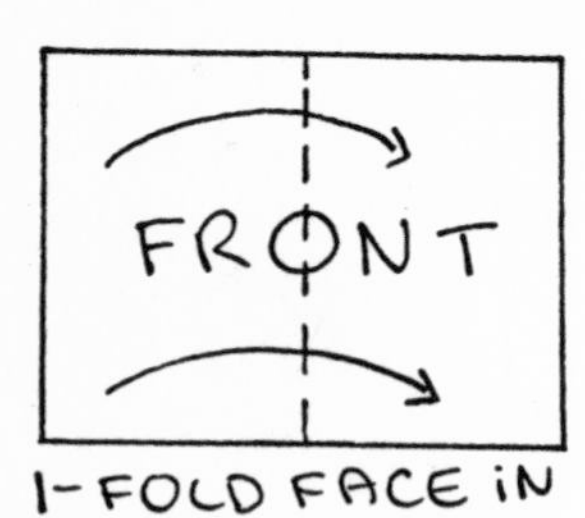

1-FOLD FACE IN

2-AT POINT "X" HALF WAY DOWN, FOLD FLAG AT A 90° ANGLE TO ITSELF

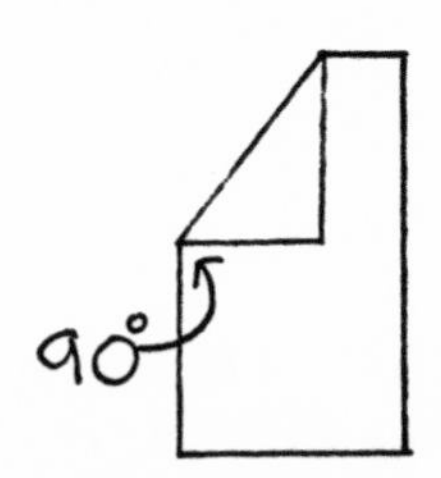

3-FOLDED FLAG SHOULD RESEMBLE THIS MODEL

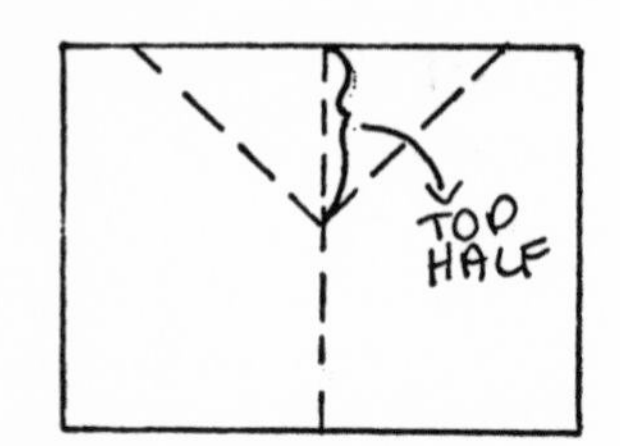

4-UNFOLD, THEN REFOLD BY REFOLDING THE TOP HALF IN (YOU ARE REVERSING THAT FOLD)

5-PROJECT IS FULLY FOLDED. SPREAD GLUE OVER SHADED AREA, TURN PROJECT OVER AND GLUE THE SAME AREA ON THAT SIDE. PLACE PROJECT IN FOLD OF A CARD AND LET DRY.

7. Decorate the front of your card.

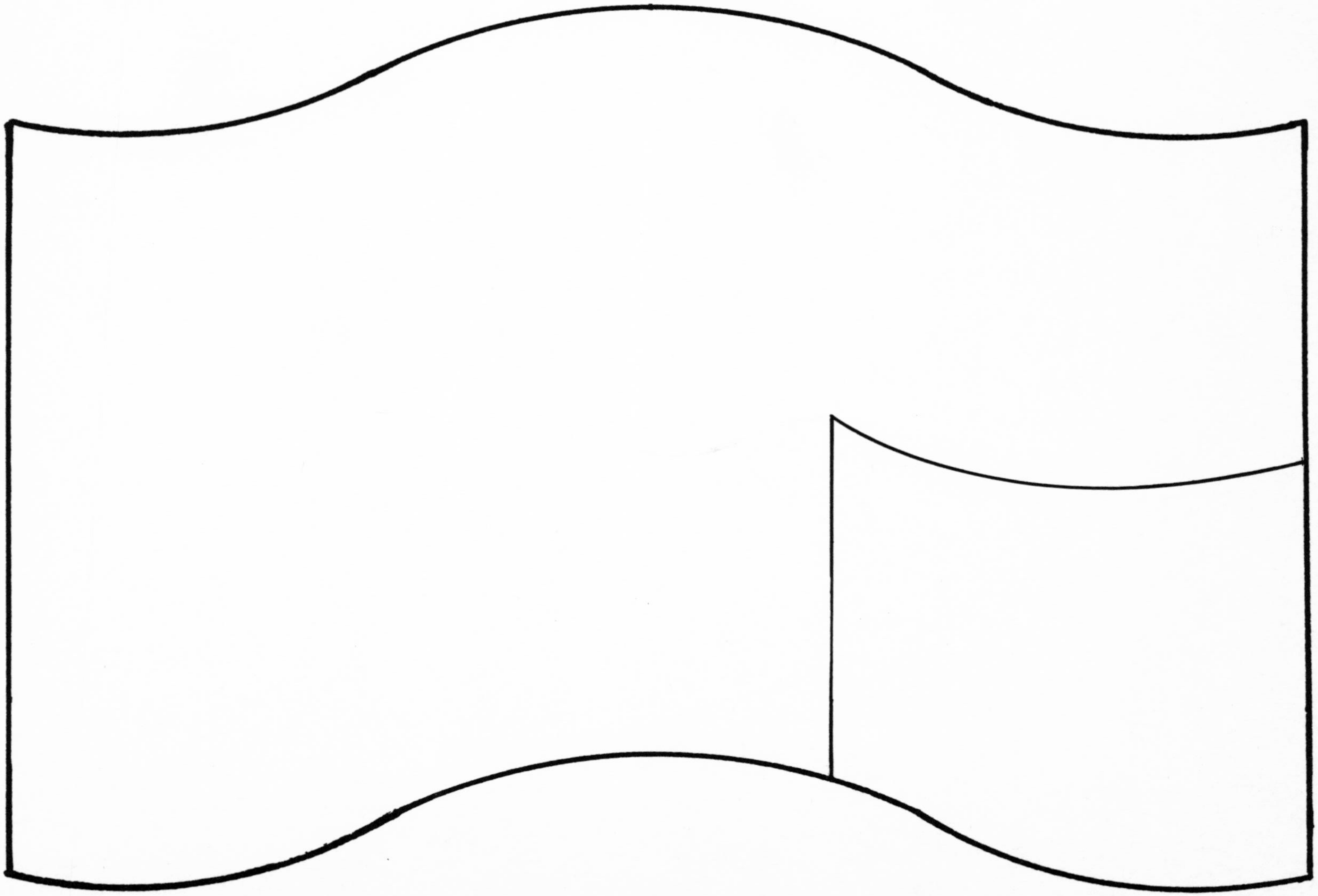

17-1 SPACE SHUTTLE COLUMBIA

Theme Space Flight

Skills Conceptual development—space flight
Creative dramatics
Eye-hand coordination
Small muscle control

Ages 4–8

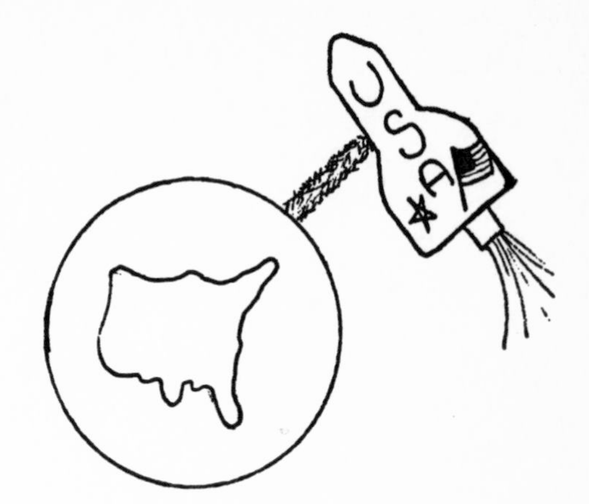

Space Flight Facts

Human travel in space began on April 12, 1961 when Russian cosmonaut Yuri Gagarin made a single orbit around the earth. John H. Glenn, Jr., in 1962, was the first American astronaut to orbit the earth. He went around the earth three times. In the early 1970s United States engineers and scientists began working to design a spaceship that could be used more than once. On April 12, 1981, the United States launched the Columbia, the first space shuttle. It took off like a rocket and landed like an airplane. Shuttles are built to be used one hundred times. They can orbit the earth at speeds up to 17,000 miles per hour—that is 245 miles a minute, and 4 miles every second!

Materials for Each Child

- 9″ x 12″ oaktag
- Paper fastener (brad)
- 6″ pipe cleaner
- Felt-tipped pens or crayons
- Glue
- Scissors

Teacher Directions

Demonstrate how to place the patterns so that they all fit on the paper. You may wish to insert the paper fastener and twist the pipe cleaner.

Steps for Students

1. Trace the rocket ship and the circle patterns on your oaktag.
2. Trace the pattern of America in the center of the circle.
3. With your felt-tipped pens or crayons, color the land green and the water blue. Color your rocketship and write the letters U.S.A. on it.
4. Push the paper fastener through the center of the circle front to back. Wrap one end of the pipe cleaner around the end of the paper fastener. Spread the legs of the paper fastener. Turn the paper fastener around a few times to loosen.
5. Turn your earth and the rocketship over and glue the other end of the pipe cleaner to the back of the rocketship:

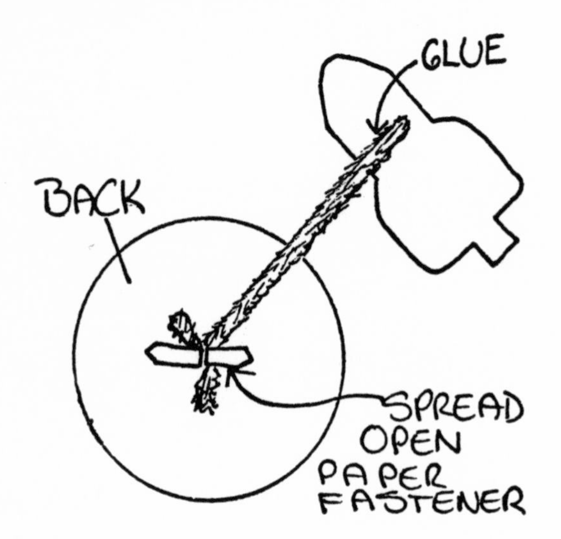

17-2 KATHRYN SULLIVAN

Theme Space Flight

Skills Conceptual development—space flight
Creative dramatics
Eye-hand coordination
Small-muscle control
Detail awareness

Ages 4–8

Kathryn Sullivan Facts

The space shuttle Challenger was launched for the sixth time on October 5, 1985. It had a crew of seven, including two women—Sally K. Ride and Kathryn D. Sullivan. It was during this flight that Kathy Sullivan became the first United States woman to walk in space. She and mission specialist, David Leestma, walked in space for three-and-a-half hours!

Materials for Each Child

- 9″ x 12″ white construction paper
- 6″ piece of yarn
- Felt-tipped pens or crayons
- Glue
- Scissors

Teacher Directions

Show the children a picture of astronauts in their space suits. (Most children's encyclopedias have good ones.) Discuss the most recent space venture.

You may wish to cut open the doors of the spacecraft. It's easy to do this with a single-edge razor. (Be sure to put a newspaper under the spacecraft before you cut.)

Steps for Students

1. Trace the spacecraft, the astronaut, and the rectangle on your construction paper.

2. Mark the doors of the spacecraft:

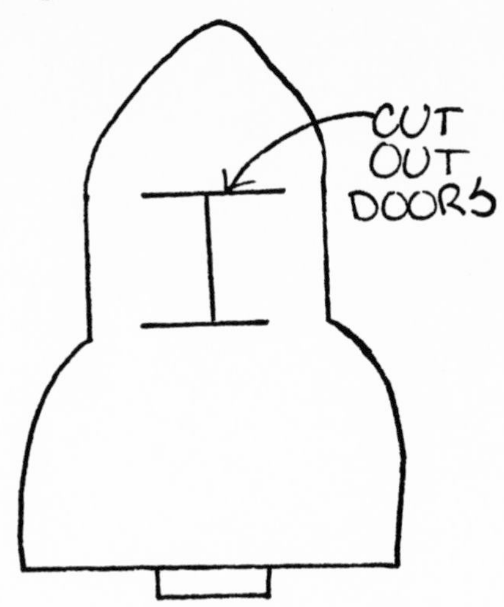

3. Give your astronaut a happy face and a nice space suit.
4. Color your spacecraft and write U.S.A. on it.
5. Cut out all the patterns.
6. Cut open the doors.
7. Glue the rectangle to the back of the rocket as shown:

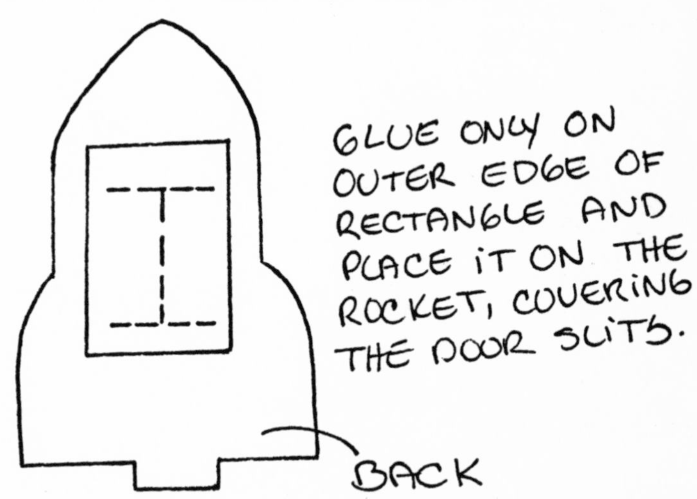

8. Glue one end of the yarn to the back of the astronaut. Open the doors of the spacecraft and glue the other end of the yarn in the center of the rectangle. Let the glue dry.
9. You can tuck your astronaut inside the spacecraft and close the doors while you are in flight. Open the doors and let him out for a space walk.

18-1 "BESSY"

Theme Animals

Skills Conceptual development — animals
Creative dramatics
Detail awareness
Eye-hand coordination
Small-muscle control

Ages 4–7

Cow Facts

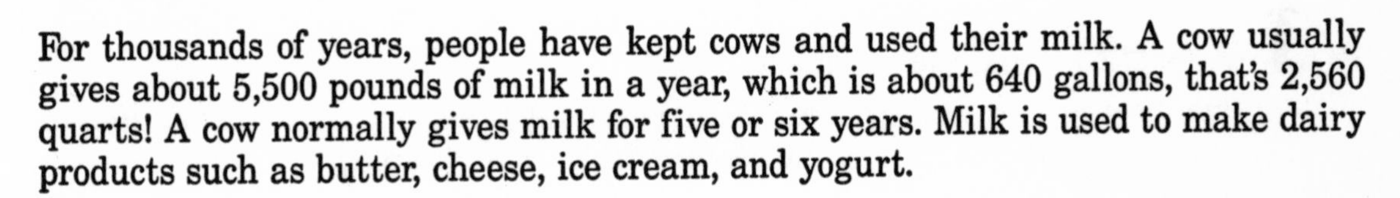

For thousands of years, people have kept cows and used their milk. A cow usually gives about 5,500 pounds of milk in a year, which is about 640 gallons, that's 2,560 quarts! A cow normally gives milk for five or six years. Milk is used to make dairy products such as butter, cheese, ice cream, and yogurt.

Materials for Each Child

- 9″ x 12″ white construction paper
- Paper fastener (brad)
- Felt-tipped pens or crayons
- Scissors

Teacher Directions

Demonstrate how to trace the patterns so that they both fit on the paper. You may wish to insert the paper fastener for the children. Making a hole with the tip of a scissor helps insertion.

Steps for Students

1. Trace both patterns on your construction paper.
2. Color Bessy's head pattern. You can color her all brown like Brown Swiss cows, in black and white spots like Holstein cows, redish-brown with white spots like Guernsey cows, or almost any color like Ayrshire cows.
3. Color the tongue that is attached to the circle pattern.

4. Cut out both patterns. Cut out Bessy's eyes.
5. Lay the circle pattern on top of Bessy's head and mark the line that you are going to cut out for Bessy's mouth:

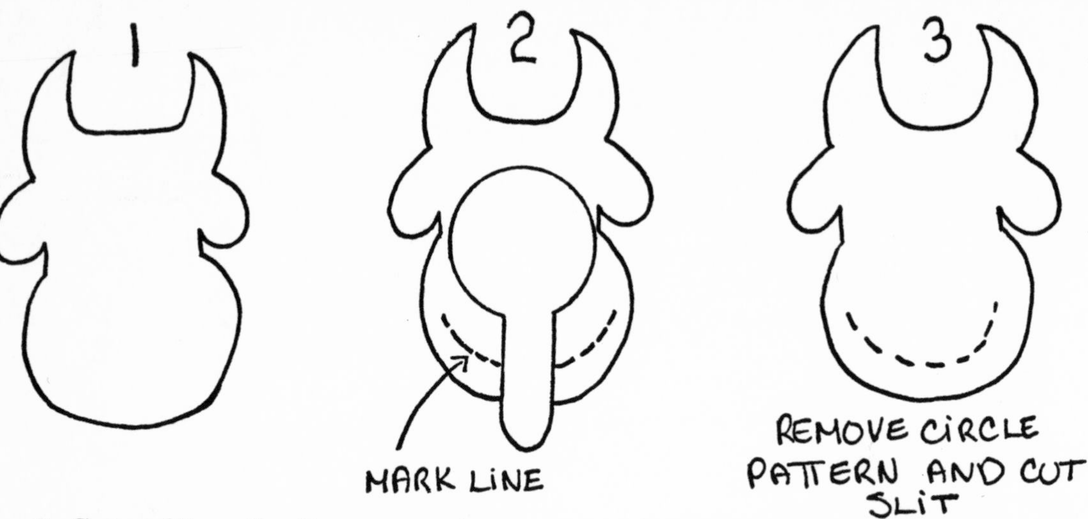

6. Cut a slit on the line you made.
7. Put the circle pattern on the backside of Bessy's head and slip the tongue into the slit that you cut. Mark the center of the circle and push the paper fastener from the front through the head and circle:

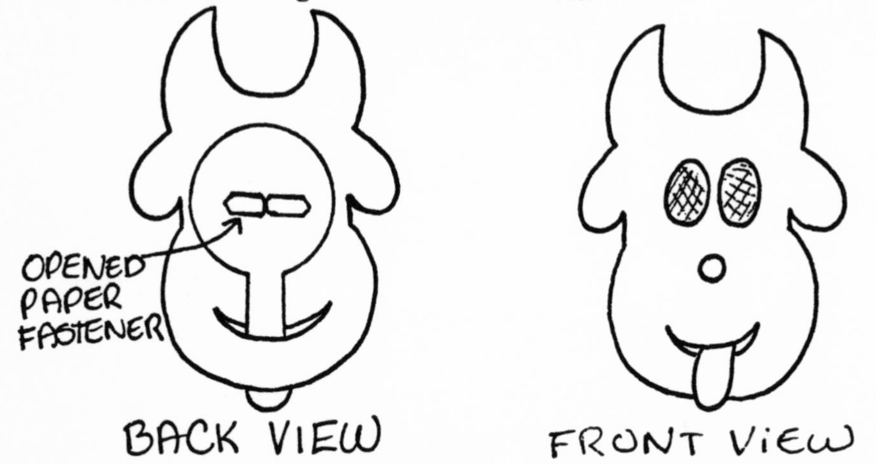

8. Push the tongue all the way to the left. Draw in "awake" eyes. Move the tongue to the right, draw in "asleep" eyes.
9. Make a handle for turning the circle:

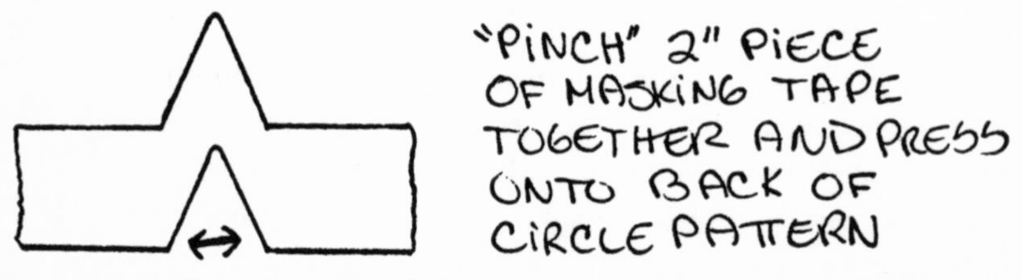

10. Use Bessy to tell some make-believe cow stories, or to talk about life on the farm.

18-2 "POKEY" THE PIG

Theme Animals

Skills Conceptual development—animals
Shape recognition
Eye-hand coordination
Small-muscle control

Ages 4–7

Pig Facts

The pig is an animal that first lived in many parts of Europe. In China, scientists have discovered remains of huge pigs that lived more than a million years ago. Pigs use the long, thick nose (snout) to dig into the ground and to push objects from one place to another. The male pig is called a boar and female is a sow. Pigs are very greedy eaters. They eat great amounts of corn and other crops, or almost anything they can find in the garbage. Their flesh is a nourishing meat; their fat is used to make lard; their skin is used for gloves, belts, and pocketbooks; and the pig's hair is used to make paintbrushes and hairbrushes.

Materials for Each Child

- 9″ x 12″ white construction paper
- Felt-tipped pens or crayons
- Stapler
- Scissors

Teacher Directions

Show the children how to place the patterns so that they all fit. Demonstrate what stapling two-thirds around looks like. (Stop and show them the one-third-and-one-half-points too.) (*Alternative*: This project may be photocopied or traced onto a ditto.)

Steps for Students

1. Trace all the patterns on your paper. Note the different shapes.
2. On one of the large circles give Pokey two eyes and a mouth. Then color the rest of his face, pink, gray, light black, or brown (or a combination of colors).

3. On the oval make two nostrils.
4. Color the rectangle and small circle pink or one of the colors you used on the face.
5. Cut everything out. Cut the small circle in half. Save the scraps.
6. Staple the two large circles about two-thirds of the way around the edge.

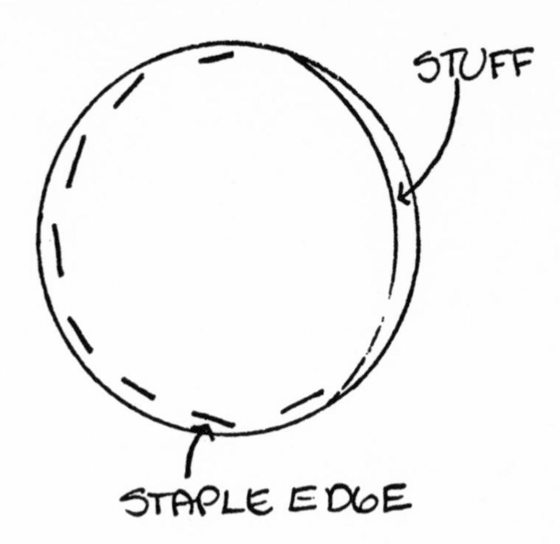

7. Stuff the scraps into the circle and continue to staple closed.
8. Glue the ends of the rectangle into a cylinder.
9. Lay the oval, nostrils down, on the table; put a line of glue around the edge. Slightly squeeze the cylinder into oval shape and set it on the glue. When it is dry, make an oval line of glue on Pokey's face and set the nose in place.

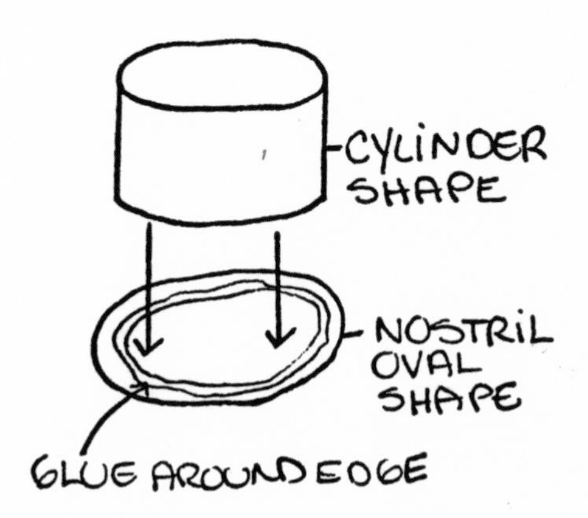

10. Bend the half-circles shown and glue to the back of Pokey's head:

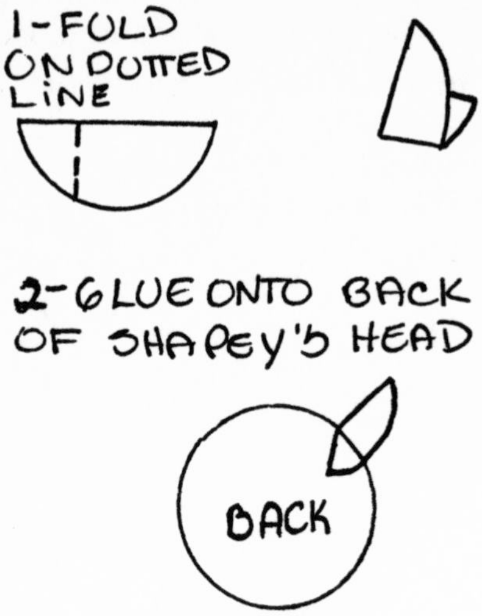

1-FOLD ON DOTTED LINE

2-GLUE ONTO BACK OF SHAPEY'S HEAD

BACK

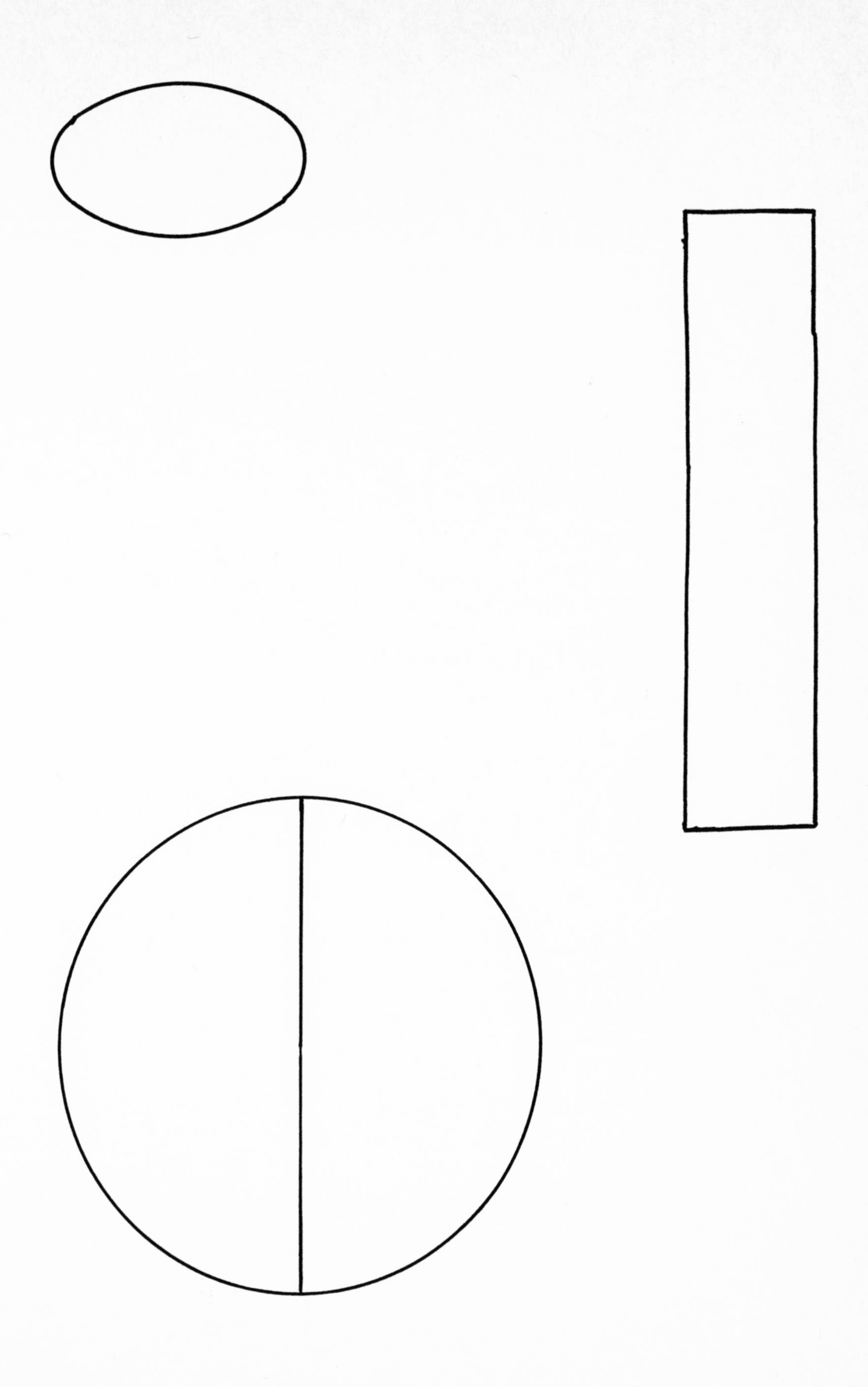

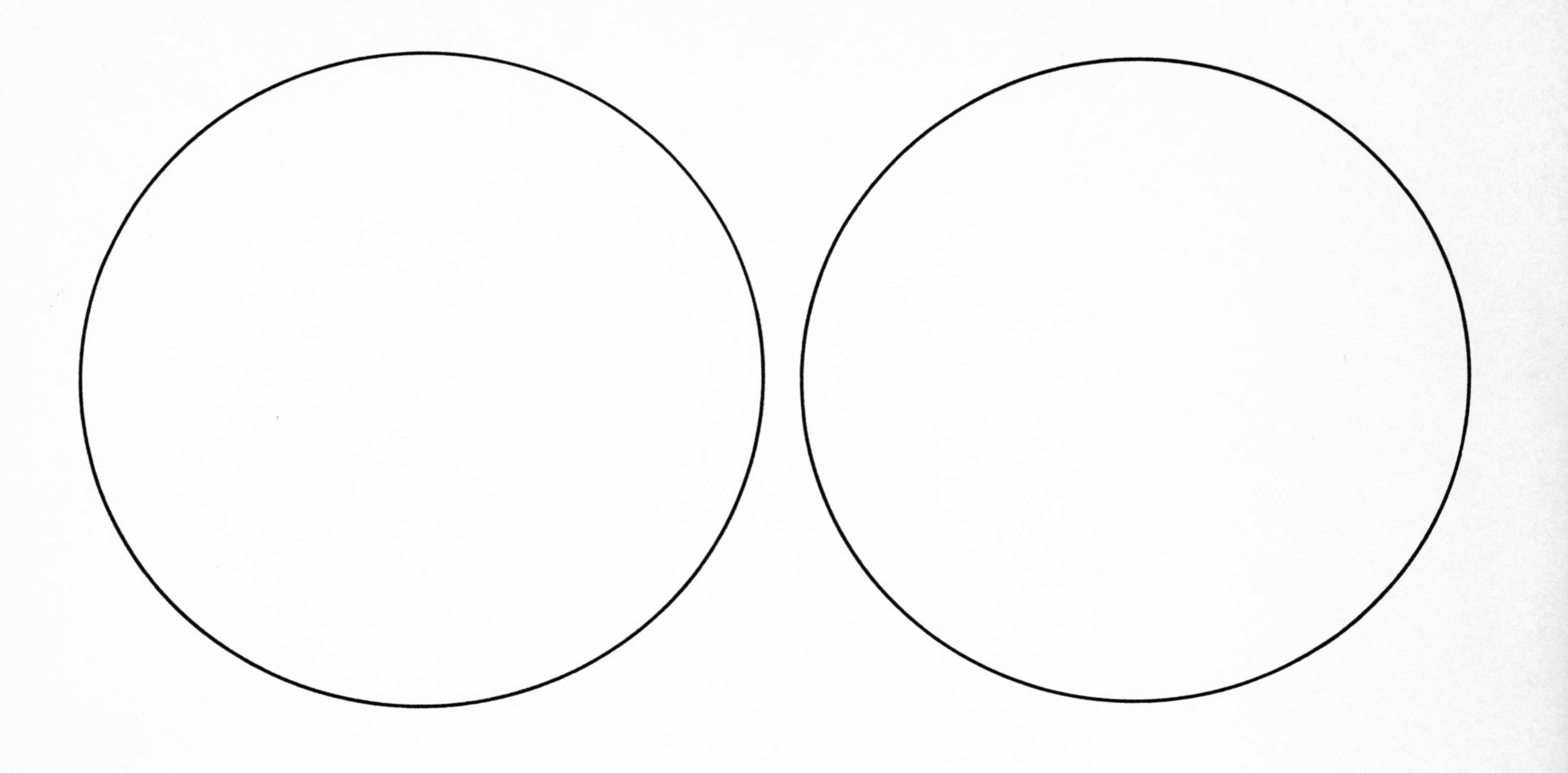

18-3 "BARNEY" THE BASSET HOUND

Theme Animals

Skills Conceptual development—animals
Shape recognition
Detail awareness
Eye-hand coordination

Ages 3–7

Basset Hound Facts

The basset hound is a short-legged hunting dog. It is used to hunt rabbits, foxes, pheasant, and raccoons. It also makes an excellent pet because it is very good-natured and gentle. The ears of the basset hound are very long, hanging below its shoulders. His face is long, wrinkled, and sad-looking, with drooping cheeks. Its tail is long and straight and is held almost straight up in the air.

Materials for Each Child

- 9″ x 12″ white construction paper
- Crayons or felt-tipped pens
- Stapler
- Scissors

Teacher Directions

Discuss the shapes that make up Barney the Basset Hound. Demonstrate placing the patterns so that they all fit.

Steps for Students

1. Trace the patterns on your construction paper.
2. The square is Barney's head. With your felt-tipped pens or crayons give Barney a nice face.

1

2

3. The wide rectangle is his legs and back. You can give four paws at the ends of the rectangle and some beagle spots.

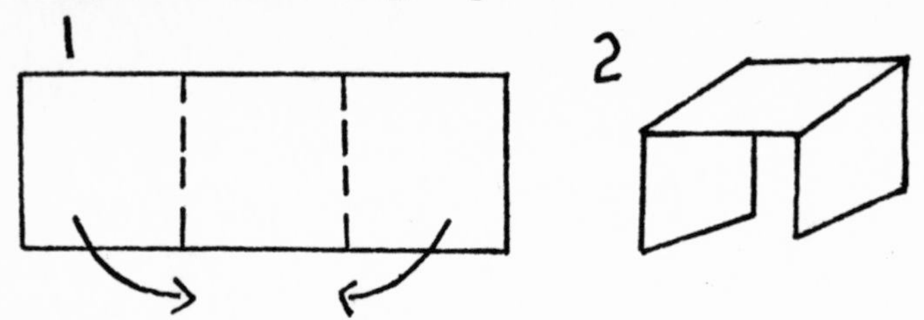

4. The ovals are Barney's ears. Give them some beagle spots.

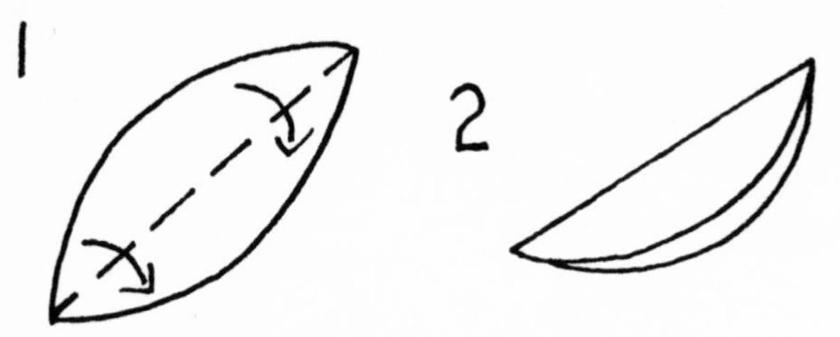

5. The end of Barney's tail is the triangle. Snip one side of the triangle to give a hairy look. Staple the triangle to the small rectangle.

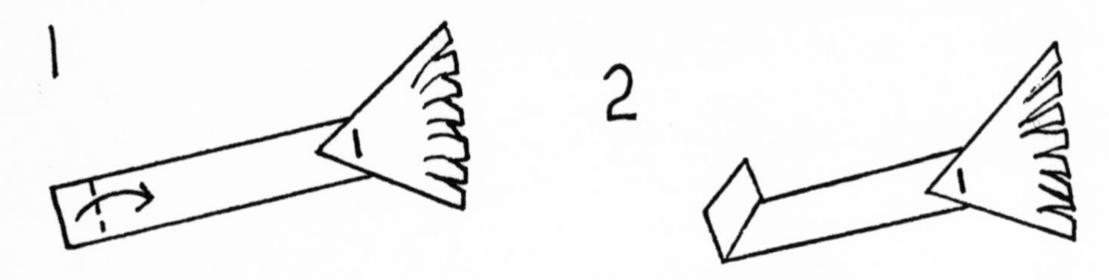

6. Fold all the pieces on the fold lines and staple as shown:

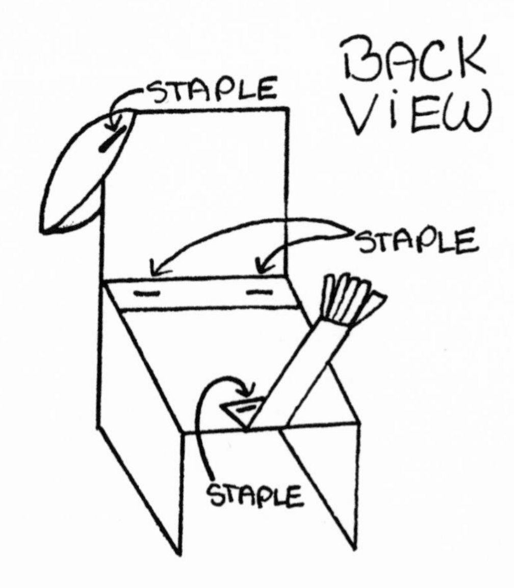

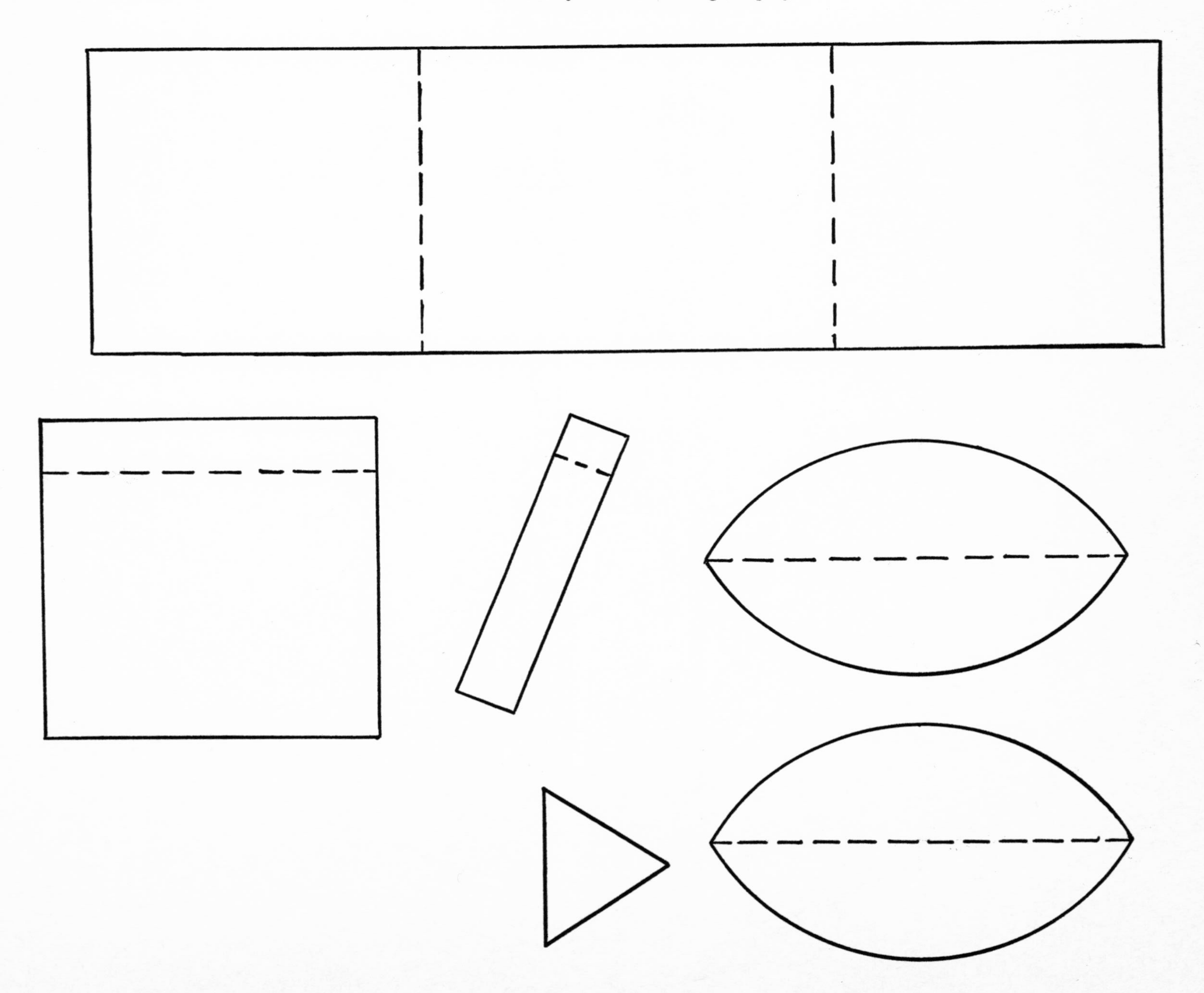

18-4 "SNEAKY" THE SNAKE

Theme Animals

Skills Conceptual development—animals
Shape recognition
Eye-hand coordination
Small-muscle control
Creative dramatics

Ages 3–7

Snake Facts

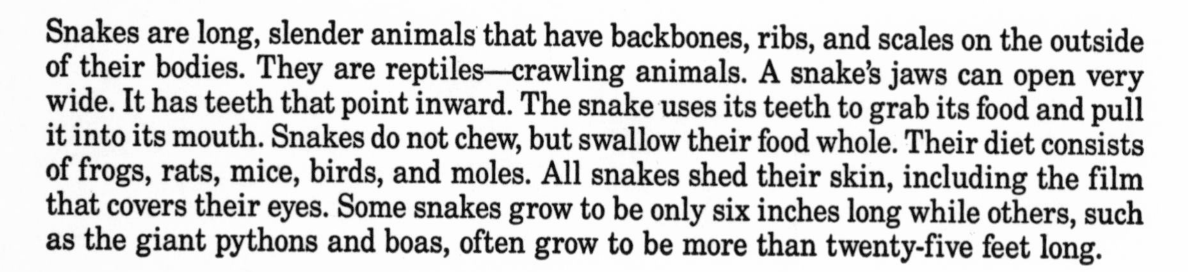

Snakes are long, slender animals that have backbones, ribs, and scales on the outside of their bodies. They are reptiles—crawling animals. A snake's jaws can open very wide. It has teeth that point inward. The snake uses its teeth to grab its food and pull it into its mouth. Snakes do not chew, but swallow their food whole. Their diet consists of frogs, rats, mice, birds, and moles. All snakes shed their skin, including the film that covers their eyes. Some snakes grow to be only six inches long while others, such as the giant pythons and boas, often grow to be more than twenty-five feet long.

Materials for Each Child

- 6″ x 9″ (½ of a 9″ x 12″) light-colored construction paper
- 6″ piece of yarn or string
- Felt-tipped pens or crayons
- Glue
- Scissors
- Hole puncher

Teacher Directions

Tell the children that Sneaky Snake is called "sneaky" because he tries to fool people into thinking that he's just a pretty colored circle when he's sleeping (lying curled up on a flat surface).

Since most snakes have beautiful markings, encourage the children to use bright colors and fancy designs. You may wish to demonstrate the cutting of the spiral. (*Alternative*: This project may be photocopied or traced onto a ditto.)

Steps for Students

1. Trace the circle pattern in the middle of your construction paper.
2. Trace Sneaky's top jaw in one corner and the bottom jaw in the other.
3. With your felt-tipped pens or crayons give Sneaky eyes, a colorful head, jaws, and tongue on both sides of these patterns.
4. Color the circle in an interesting pattern of spots, stripes, dots, and so on.
5. Cut out all the patterns.
6. Cut a spiral by starting at the edge of the circle and cut about a ½″ strip as you turn your circle around. Continue until you reach the center of the circle.
7. Glue the top and bottom jaws at their ends, on either side of the piece at the center of your circle:

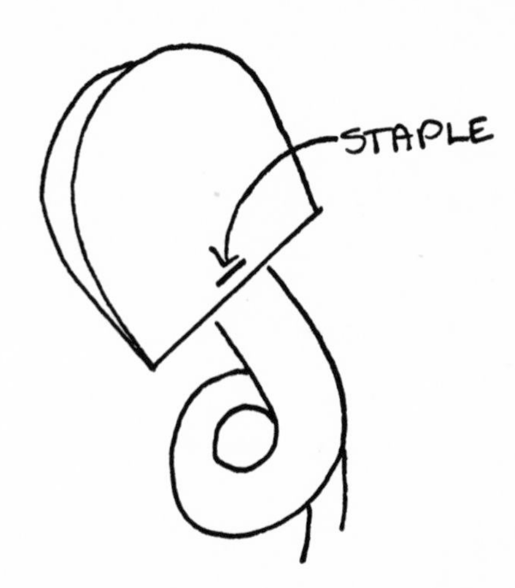

8. Punch a hole in Sneaky's head (top jaw) and string with yarn or string.
9. You can make Sneaky dance by twirling or winding up the string.
10. Make up a song to go with Sneaky Snake's dance.

18-5 CIRCUS BEAR

Theme Circus

Skills Conceptual development—animals
Creative dramatics
Eye-hand coordination
Small-muscle control

Ages 4–6

Bear Facts

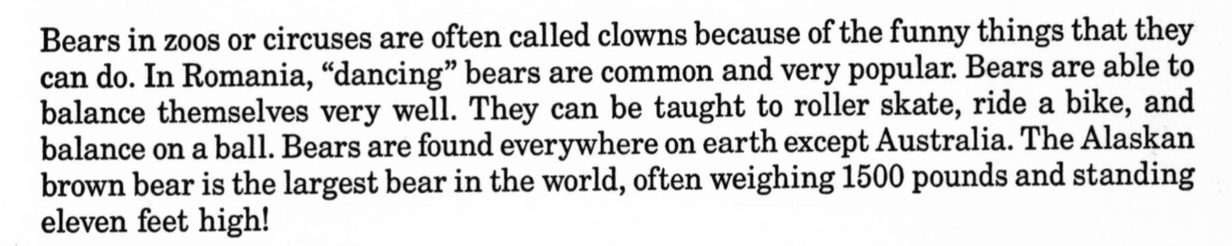

Bears in zoos or circuses are often called clowns because of the funny things that they can do. In Romania, "dancing" bears are common and very popular. Bears are able to balance themselves very well. They can be taught to roller skate, ride a bike, and balance on a ball. Bears are found everywhere on earth except Australia. The Alaskan brown bear is the largest bear in the world, often weighing 1500 pounds and standing eleven feet high!

Materials for Each Child

- 9″ x 12″ white construction paper or oaktag
- Paper fastener (brad)
- Felt-tipped pens or crayons
- Scissors

Teacher Directions

Show the children how tall an eleven-foot bear would be by standing on a chair and raising your arm. You may wish to mark the center of the circle and the spot on the bear's foot where the paper fastener would be inserted.

Steps for Students

1. Trace the bear and his ball on your paper.
2. With your felt-tipped pens or crayons, give your bear a nice face. Color his fur.
3. Color your ball. Use your imagination to make it look like a fancy circus ball.
4. Cut out the bear and the ball.

5. Insert the paper fastener through your bear's foot and into the center of the ball.
6. Turn the paper fastener around a few times to loosen it.
7. Roll your bear on a carpet or up your arm. Put on a show for your friends.

18-6 "JUMBO"

Theme Circus

Skills Conceptual development—animals
Eye-hand coordination
Small muscle control
Creative dramatics

Ages 6–8

Elephant Facts

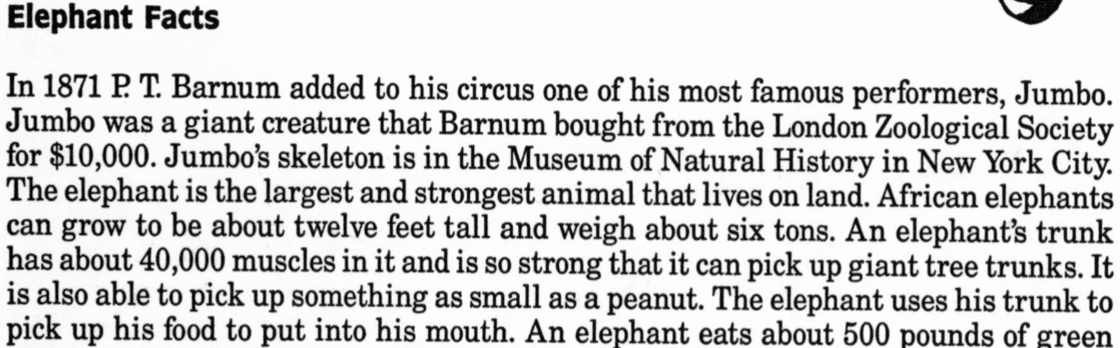

In 1871 P. T. Barnum added to his circus one of his most famous performers, Jumbo. Jumbo was a giant creature that Barnum bought from the London Zoological Society for $10,000. Jumbo's skeleton is in the Museum of Natural History in New York City. The elephant is the largest and strongest animal that lives on land. African elephants can grow to be about twelve feet tall and weigh about six tons. An elephant's trunk has about 40,000 muscles in it and is so strong that it can pick up giant tree trunks. It is also able to pick up something as small as a peanut. The elephant uses his trunk to pick up his food to put into his mouth. An elephant eats about 500 pounds of green plants and drinks about 50 gallons of water a day!

Materials for Each Child

- 9″ x 12″ white construction paper or oaktag
- Paper fastener (brad)
- Crayons or felt-tipped pens
- Glue
- Scissors

Teacher Directions

Demonstrate tracing the pattern on the fold. You may wish to insert the paper fastener through the trunk into Jumbo's head at the point where his eye would be.

Steps for Students

1. Fold your construction paper in half on the 12″ side.
2. Trace the elephant's body pattern on the fold of your paper—Jumbo's back will be on the fold.
3. Carefully cut Jumbo out. Do not cut on the fold.
4. Trace the tail, ears, and the trunk patterns on the leftover construction paper.

5. Cut them all out.
6. With your felt-tipped pens or crayons, color all of Jumbo's parts. Since he is a circus elephant, use your imagination to make him look exciting.
7. Glue Jumbo's tail inside the two pieces of Jumbo's body. Glue his ears on each side of his head. Insert his trunk between the two pieces of Jumbo's head. Push a paper fastener through one side of Jumbo's head (at the point where his eye would be), through the trunk, and out the other side:

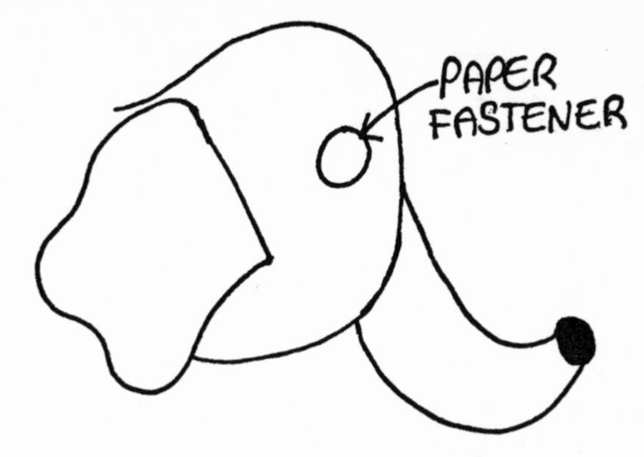

8. You can spread Jumbo's legs to make him stand.

Variation

Make a handle for the back of Jumbo's trunk:

Now, see what you can find for Jumbo to pick up. You may make some stand-up paper rings for him to pick up: